Guerrilla Marketing

GUERRILLA MARKETING

*Advertising and Marketing
Definitions, Ideas, Tactics,
Examples, and Campaigns to
Inspire Your Business Success*

JASON MYERS
JAY CONRAD LEVINSON
MERRILEE KIMBLE

NEW YORK

LONDON • NASHVILLE • MELBOURNE • VANCOUVER

GUERRILLA MARKETING

Advertising and Marketing Definitions, Ideas, Tactics, Examples, and Campaigns to Inspire Your Business Success, Volume 2

© 2022 Jason Myers, Jay Conrad Levinson, Merrilee Kimble

Published in New York, New York, by Morgan James Publishing. Morgan James is a trademark of Morgan James, LLC. www.MorganJamesPublishing.com

Proudly distributed by Ingram Publisher Services.

ISBN 9781631957468 paperback
ISBN 9781631957475 ebook
Library of Congress Control Number:
2021945598

Cover Design by:
Rachel Lopez
www.r2cdesign.com

Interior Design by:
Chris Treccani
www.3dogcreative.net

Morgan James is a proud partner of Habitat for Humanity Peninsula and Greater Williamsburg. Partners in building since 2006.

Get involved today! Visit MorganJamesPublishing.com/giving-back

We dedicate this book to the memory of Jay Conrad Levinson who began a global movement and has inspired us to continue his legacy of helping businesses grow and thrive.

CONTENTS

ACKNOWLEDGMENTS

We want to extend our appreciation to:

David Hancock and the Morgan James Publishing family. They share our gratitude for what Guerrilla Marketing has done to help businesses succeed for several decades. They also share our passion for how Guerrilla Marketing will continue to help businesses everywhere to understand what marketing really is and how it works for their success.

Cortney Donelson of vocem, LLC whose ease, skill, and dedication make book editing a delight.

All the successful Guerrilla marketers that have proven, over the last several decades, that intelligent Guerrilla Marketing is supported with knowledge, low-cost, unconventional, and creative tactics that convey and promote their compelling product(s), service(s), and ideas to drive limitless profits.

Lastly, and very importantly, we want to extend our appreciation for all the people whose dream it is to take their idea and create, grow, and eventually sell or hand-off their profitable business. To turn that dream into a successful business requires seizing proven techniques, such as Guerrilla Marketing, which uniquely set their business apart from the competition.

PREFACE

When Jay Conrad Levinson wrote *Guerrilla Marketing*, he stated his vision:

> *Guerrilla Marketing simplifies the complexities and explains how entre-preneurs can use marketing to generate maximum profits from minimum investments. Put another way, this book can help make a small business big. This book can help an individual entrepreneur make a lot of money as painlessly as possible. Often, the only factor that determines success or failure is the way in which a product or service is marketed. The information in these pages will arm you for success and alert you to the shortcomings that lead to failure.*

We're proud to have been selected to carry the torch forward with *Guerrilla Marketing* and to continue to level the playing field for entrepreneurs. *Guerrilla Marketing* shows entrepreneurs, businesses, and people with a burning idea they want to turn into a business all the ways they can be intelligent and successful marketers. In doing so, they lead their businesses to growth, impact, and prof-itability for the benefit of themselves and their families, employees, customers, community, as well as the world at large.

Welcome to Volume Two

We're thrilled you have selected to add Volume Two to your collection of the all-new series of *Guerrilla Marketing* books. This volume is packed with more tools, tips, and examples to grow your success.

Guerrilla Marketing is a 360-degree, consistent methodology that weaves through every aspect of your business. Each of your marketing tactics is woven together with others. Therefore, in each volume, we refer you to other related sections and tactics, within this book and other volumes, to help your business weave your marketing together for 360 degrees of powerful and consistent Guerrilla Marketing.

Guerrilla Marketing is intelligent marketing that utilizes knowledge, strategy, and a plan supported with a toolbox of tactics. With the all-new series of *Guerrilla Marketing* books, you have a toolbox of low-cost, unconventional, and creative tactics to choose from to convey and promote your compelling product(s) or service(s) and drive your competition mad.

WHAT MAKES THIS
VOLUME OF BOOKS UNIQUE?

Guerrilla marketers are unique, and they know it and promote it. Therefore, we had to ask ourselves: "How can we make this all-new series of books unique?" After all, Guerrilla Marketing, since the original *Guerrilla Marketing* book was introduced in 1984, has supported and empowered entrepreneurs, small and medium-sized businesses, solopreneurs, and people with ideas they want to turn into a business to:

- Start and/or build successful Guerrilla businesses
- Understand why and how marketing works, why Guerrilla Marketing is intelligent marketing, and your toolbox of options
- Weave the consistent methodology of Guerrilla Marketing through every aspect of their business
- Create profits for the benefit of themselves, their families, their employees, their community, and the world at large
- Tap into their Guerrilla Creativity to create highly profitable marketing
- Utilize Guerrilla Creative strategies to ensure that their Guerrilla Marketing tactics hit the target
- Create and execute their Guerrilla Marketing plan and Guerrilla Creative and Advertising strategy
- Utilize consistency in their marketing to build familiarity which, in turn, builds trust; and that trust creates sales, repeat purchases, and precious referrals from their customers
- Define the authentic attitudes of their business and use the power of authenticity in their marketing
- Identify their company attributes and consistently make their prospects and customers aware of them in their marketing and advertising
- Track their marketing to build on their successes and remove their unsuccessful efforts
- Make the truth fascinating
- Thrive with low-cost tactics
- Thrive with unconventional tactics
- Deliver their marketing tactics with creative, low-cost, and unconventional methods

- Upend their competition, big and small
- Sell their successful businesses and start all over again or perfect their favorite pastime as their full-time endeavor
- Win, on purpose

Where does it all begin? That's a simple answer: with a strong foundation of Guerrilla Marketing. In Volume 1, we reviewed the strong foundational elements of Guerrilla Marketing. We'll also provide a summary in this book, in Section I, called "The Strong Foundation of Guerrilla Marketing Success." It will be a great refresher for those who are currently using Guerrilla Marketing tactics in their business and a good overview for those who are new to Guerrilla Marketing.

For those who are new to Guerrilla Marketing (or those who want to learn more), we'll take it online with a FREE companion course (visit gMarketing. com/Club) to help you build your rock-solid Guerrilla Marketing foundation. In the companion course, we'll dive deeper with video tutorials, exercises, and the tools you'll need to build that crucial foundation from which your Guerrilla Marketing success will be born. Please know this: Businesses that fail have a poor foundation. If you build your castle on a poor foundation, don't be surprised when it collapses into rubble.

We'll spend the remaining sections of the book picking up where we left off in Volume 1 and sharing more of today's Guerrilla Marketing tactics, tools, and tips (many of which are free). These Guerrilla Marketing tactics, tools, and tips are options that every business needs to succeed and generate profits. You'll find a toolbox of information and resources to choose from to build a strong Guerrilla business and drive your competition mad.

In our free companion course, you'll also find a growing list of tools and resources to help you going forward. In addition, you'll find many examples at gMarketing.com/Club to give you a head start.

In Volume 2, we have numerous new Guerrilla Marketing tools, tactics, and tips to give you even more options to choose from. We are thrilled to continue Jay Conrad Levison's vision, and we're thrilled for the profits you'll generate in the pages that follow.

INTRODUCTION

Whether you realize it or not, you're marketing with every interaction you and everyone in your business have, inside and outside of your business. Therefore, be intentional about it and reap the rewards.

Guerrilla Marketing is intelligent marketing that utilizes knowledge, strategy, and a plan that is supported with a toolbox of low-cost, unconventional, and creative tactics to choose from to convey and promote a compelling product or service. Guerrilla Marketing makes the truth fascinating. Guerrilla Marketing turns knowledge, time, energy, imagination, and information into profits.

Guerrilla Marketing was introduced to the world in a self-titled book in 1984, by Jay Conrad Levinson, as an unconventional system of marketing that relies on knowledge, time, energy, and imagination rather than a big marketing budget.

We are continuing Jay Conrad Levison's unconventional system of marketing. By revealing not only what marketing is but why it works, we give small and medium-sized businesses (SMBs) the opportunity to think and grow big. When you understand the power of your SMB and what you can do with Guerrilla Marketing, it not only levels the playing field with your competition but also tilts the playing field to your advantage.

The pillars of Guerrilla Marketing are as strong today as they were decades ago when it was introduced to the world. The tactics, tools, and tips are continually evolving, and our desire is to keep you at the forefront of Guerrilla Marketing.

Whether you're an entrepreneur, an SMB, or a solopreneur, we understand that your business (or your idea that you want to turn into a business) is your dream, and you will never settle. What do you plan to do with your precious opportunity? Will you succeed beyond your wildest expectations? Will you give in to doubt and fold?

Guerrilla Marketing exists to give you a toolbox of tactics, tools, and tips to choose from to succeed beyond your wildest expectations. Your marketing options are growing faster than ever, and we are committed to keeping your toolbox full with this new volume in our new series of *Guerrilla Marketing* books. If you haven't already done so, we encourage you to pick up a copy of Volume 1, which is packed with tactics, examples, tools, and tips. If you've already done so, we want to extend our heartfelt gratitude.

To implement Guerrilla Marketing is to challenge yourself and/or your business to learn and implement intelligent marketing. You can stick to what you're doing now with your marketing. You can stick with what others are telling you to do with your marketing. Or you can challenge yourself to understand Guerrilla Marketing and implement it to your full advantage.

The simple question is: Will you act and succeed, or will you fold? We think you're ready to act and claim your success, so let's get to it.

Many business owners think marketing is a light switch that you turn on and off. Therefore, they conduct their marketing activities as if they are turning the switch on and off. As an SMB, you can perform excellent marketing as easily as you can perform poor marketing.

Fortunately, for those who wisely choose to understand and implement Guerrilla Marketing in their business, they understand that the light switch is always on, and the lights are always shining brightly. With the bright lights on, Guerrilla marketers are intentional with their marketing efforts, and precious profits are their rewards.

Many businesses fail to utilize Guerrilla Marketing to its fullest benefit. They do so by failing to execute the Guerrilla Marketing fundamentals, which guide your marketing and allow you to perform 360 degrees of intelligent, impactful, and consistent marketing that drives profits for your business. Instead of mastering the fundamentals, they jump right to the tactics and implement them like light switches—turning them on and off and flipping from one to another without a plan, strategy, consistency, repetition, or an understanding of who their prospects and customers are or who their business is and how it's seen in the marketplace.

Why? Many think it's not exciting or necessary to build a strong marketing foundation for their business. However, Guerrilla marketers understand that their strong marketing foundation is where their Guerrilla Marketing success is born.

Guerrilla Marketing isn't simply about implementing tactics that appeal to customers and prospects. It's a 360-degree, consistent methodology that weaves through every aspect of your business. A strong, successful Guerrilla business is built on a Guerrilla Marketing foundation that keeps you focused on, in part:

- Why marketing works

- Who your prospects and customers are, the problems you want to solve, and the way you want those problems solved
- Being clear as you tell your prospects and customers what you can do for them
- Caring about and knowing who your customers are, why they make additional purchases, and why they refer friends, family, and associates
- The input and opinions of your prospects, customers, employees, vendors, and community that can lead to long-term satisfaction, success, and profits
- Why ongoing relationships build your business
- What makes your business unique and fascinating and how to make sure everyone knows about it
- Why you're better than the competition and making sure everyone knows your advantages
- Why measuring your marketing and measuring your creativity turns into profits
- Understanding that you're marketing with every interaction, so you're intentional about it
- The power of consistency and repetition

As an entrepreneur, SMB, or a solopreneur, you need Guerrilla Marketing more than ever because the competition is smarter, more sophisticated, and even more aggressive than ever before. Fortunately, that is not a problem for successful Guerrilla marketers.

If your competition is a large business, you may find that they employ some Guerrilla Marketing tactics, but they don't have the advantages that you do as a smaller business. As a smaller business, you are nimble, engaged, and focused, which is the rich fertilizer that your Guerrilla Marketing needs to bloom.

More than ever before, consumers receive "vanilla" or "one-size-fits-all" service from large companies. That creates the perfect opportunity for you to utilize Guerrilla Marketing to make your business shine.

Guerrilla Marketing takes a quality product or service and sets it apart from the competition. How?

We'd venture a bold guess that fewer than ten percent of the new and existing small-business owners have a plan or strategy. Additionally, they have likely explored less than a dozen of the marketing tools and tactics available to them. Guerrilla marketers, on the other hand, recognize that the more they understand about how and why marketing works, combined with their plan, strategy, Guerrilla Creativity, and a toolbox of options, the better they will be able to take the right action that creates the right results.

Businesses that implement Guerrilla Marketing have a tremendous advantage over businesses that don't. The business that implements Guerrilla Marketing is ridiculously hard to replicate, and that makes their business unique.

That uniqueness makes their business more valuable. That increased value means that as the business grows, larger businesses are more likely to want to partner with or acquire the business. Without the unique advantages of that business, due to their successful Guerrilla Marketing efforts, the larger business wouldn't see their value. They would just replicate the business model and dominate the smaller business by competing with them.

If you're not where you want to be, it's a good indicator that there is more you can do. Guerrilla Marketing helps you to realize every facet of marketing— and the more you know, the more you can achieve.

In the wise words of Jay Conrad Levinson in the book *Guerrilla Marketing*:

> *Guerrilla Marketing is always intentional. It pays close attention to all the details of contact with the outside world, ignoring nothing, and realizing the stunning importance of those tiny but supercharged details.*

Guerrilla Marketing is about getting all of the details right so that when you deploy an attention-getting Guerrilla Marketing tactic, it works. Why does that make sense?

As an answer, let's look at an example If you drive by a business and see a street team or group of picketers, you're likely to look. Then you notice they are holding clever signs that promote the business and ask you to honk because you love this business. If you find it clever, amusing, or intriguing, your reaction will likely be to inquire via word of mouth (e.g., ask a friend) or look the business up (e.g., search engines, social media), whatever you prefer.

Street teams and friendly picketers are versatile (handing out samples, directing people to their location, working a booth at an event, etc.), and they can garner attention and pique the interest of your prospects and customers. However, it's what happens next that determines if that piqued interest will be turned into profits. Now is the time when your attention to the details (great reviews, a clear and compelling description of the business and what makes it unique, easy-to-access hours, and contact information) will make that attention turn prospects into customers.

If the business gets people's attention but then it's hard to find in an online search or its marketing is disconnected, its prospects:

- Aren't sure about the business and become skeptical
- See that its social media looks different than its website, which makes them more skeptical
- Can't understand the copy because the fonts are hard to read, and they find the graphics unappealing
- Find its hours and contact information are inconvenient, incomplete, or missing

That's a business that views marketing as a series of disconnected gimmicks, or it's a business that thinks marketing is a light switch they turn on and off. That business takes action, but it doesn't understand how to set itself apart with good Guerrilla Marketing.

Energy alone is not enough. Energy must be directed by intelligence. Successful Guerrilla businesses are intelligently designed and operated from the outside in (from the customers' point of view, needs, desires, and expectations), not the inside out. They are designed with forward and backward thinking. Equally, those businesses use intelligent marketing, which is Guerrilla Marketing.

Successful Guerrilla Marketing means prospects experience a business that's:

- Easy to find in an online search and whose social is consistent with its website
- Convenient to reach, in the way the prospects want to reach it
- Clear and appealing while it quickly explains a relatable problem and is compelling with how it solves it
- Unique and has several competitive advantages

The Guerrilla business has appealing and consistent marketing while being easy and convenient to do business with. Because the business has carefully and consistently executed its marketing, it builds familiarity with its prospects, and that familiarity allows the business's quality product(s) or service(s) to shine. Guerrilla Marketing emphasizes the truth that consistency builds familiarity; familiarity builds trust, and trust creates sales, repeat purchases, and precious referrals, which is the fuel for long-term success.

Often, the only factor that determines the success or failure of a business is the way they market their product(s) or service(s). Businesses who are successful Guerrillas get it right because they know the secrets of intelligent Guerrilla Marketing.

Guerrilla Marketing is a 360-degree consistent methodology that weaves through every aspect of your business. If you want to succeed with Guerrilla Marketing, and we know you do and can, let's get started with building a strong marketing foundation from which your Guerrilla Marketing success will be born.

To implement Guerrilla Marketing, it's time to challenge yourself and/or your business to implement intelligent marketing and use it to your full advantage. You'll begin in "Section I" by building your strong marketing foundation by focusing your energy and underscoring your understanding of:

- Research and Knowing
- Guerrilla Creativity
- Unique Selling Proposition (USP)
- Guerrilla Marketing Ten-Word Profit Challenge
- Guerrilla Marketing Plan Challenge
- Guerrilla Creative and Advertising Strategy Challenge
- A Guerrilla Marketing Calendar

To understand the role and importance of each of these building blocks for your strong marketing foundation, we'll first provide an overview in this book.

For those of you who are new to Guerrilla Marketing (or those who want to learn more), we encourage you to next take it online for your FREE companion course (visit gMarketing.com/Club). In the companion course, we'll dive deeper with video tutorials, exercises, and the tools you'll need to build that crucial foundation for your Guerrilla Marketing success.

With your rock-solid marketing foundation established, it's time for options. The tools, tips, and tactics that begin with "Section II" are the fuel you need to create success and profits for your business. We're excited to see you unleash your Guerrilla Creativity and guide your business to success beyond your wildest expectations.

SECTION I

The Strong Foundation of Guerrilla Marketing Success

Overview

Guerrilla Marketing is intelligent marketing that's built on knowledge and a rock-solid Guerrilla Marketing foundation. In Volume 1, we addressed those elements in detail. We encourage you, to maximize your success, to invest the time to establish your strong foundation with Volume 1.

In summary:

Research and Knowing

Effective Guerrilla Marketing starts with market research and defining your target market or prospects. Your market research time is the important time that you spend *on* your business, instead of *in* your business.

Think about marketing as a continuous and ever-growing game of darts. Your marketing is the dart, and your prospects (and customers) are the dartboard. However, both the darts and dartboard evolve and change over time.

In Volume 1 we provided the tools and resources that you need to learn about and keep up with your ever-changing prospects and customers. See Volume 1, Section 1.1, "Research and Knowing," for more information.

Guerrilla Creativity

The ability to tap into and stoke your Guerrilla Creativity isn't by chance. The more you know about marketing, and the more you know about your customers and prospects, the more creative your ideas will be.

In Volume 1, we addressed how to generate and measure your Guerrilla Creativity. See Volume 1, Section 1.2, "Guerrilla Creativity," for more information.

Unique Selling Proposition (USP)

A USP is a unique selling proposition. Your USP represents one of your greatest marketing opportunities. Most businesses neither promote nor have identified their USP. Your USP is your proprietary competitive advantage that is stated clearly and succinctly.

In Volume 1, we provided the four traits an effective USP needs. What is unique about your business is what makes it interesting and memorable, so promote it. Guerrilla marketers don't let their USP remain a secret. See Volume 1, Section 1.3, "Unique Selling Proposition (USP)," for more information.

Guerrilla Marketing Ten-Word Profit Challenge

The Guerrilla Marketing ten-word profit challenge is designed to help your business drive profits. In ten words, you'll express your core concept, make a memorable statement that will build familiarity, and compel your prospects to want to learn more.

In Volume 1, we provided exercises to help you determine the ten words that can help your marketing compel your prospects to notice your business and for your customers to want to make repeat purchases and provide precious referrals of their friends, family, and associates. See Volume 1, Section 1.4, "Guerrilla Marketing Ten-Word Profit Challenge," for more information.

Guerrilla Marketing Plan Challenge

Guerrilla Marketing is first and foremost focused on a core idea. All of your marketing must be an extension of that core idea: advertising, direct mailing, USP, sales presentations, packaging, online presence, uniforms, store design, innovation, etc.

Fortunately, Guerrilla Marketing is a 360-degree, consistent methodology that weaves through every aspect of your business. To succeed, it isn't enough to have a better idea; you need to have a focused plan and strategy.

In Volume 1, we provided a simple formula to help you develop a Guerrilla Marketing plan that you can commit to. That plan, which changes over time, will help you remain focused as you consistently market and advertise your business. See Volume 1, Section 1.5, "Guerrilla Marketing Plan Challenge," for more information.

Guerrilla Creative and Advertising Strategy Challenge

If you don't know it already, advertising and marketing are different. You're marketing with every bit of interaction you have with your business—with employees, prospects, customers, and the outside world.

Advertising, on the other hand, is a part of marketing your product(s) and/or service(s). Advertising is effective when it's done in combination with your consistent marketing.

In Volume 1, we provided clarity about your creative strategy and what you're offering (i.e., the benefits of your product or service) to your prospects and customers so you can develop a clear call to action that tells them exactly what you want them to do. See Volume 1, Section 1.6, "Guerrilla Creative and Advertising Strategy Challenge," for more information.

Guerrilla Marketing Calendar

A Guerrilla Marketing calendar enables you to take your successes and move them forward into the next year. By taking the time to document your efforts and grade their success, you focus your efforts and track your progress.

In Volume 1, we addressed the importance of tracking your results. By taking the time to analyze your results, you'll quickly be doing more of what works and less of what doesn't. See Volume 1, Section 1.7, "Guerrilla Marketing Calendar," for more information.

Your Strong Foundation

With a rock-solid Guerrilla Marketing foundation in place, you're then ready to proceed with ideas, examples, and tactics of Guerrilla Marketing. Guerrilla Marketing ideas, examples, and tactics are amazingly effective when they are utilized properly and in combination. Utilize and test as many as fit with your target audience research, customer knowledge, Guerrilla Marketing plan, and Guerrilla Creative and Advertising strategy.

With your Guerrilla Marketing calendar, you'll track your tactics and follow-up to remove what's not working. You'll then do more of what's working and add new tactics. The more you do well, the harder life is for your competition.

Many businesses, big and small, view marketing as a series of disconnected gimmicks. Different messages, different colors, different fonts, different target markets, and different tactics. Fortunately for you, you're not most businesses.

With Guerrilla Marketing, you'll benefit from the power of a combination of marketing initiatives that consistently market your business. Never forget that consistency builds familiarity; familiarity builds trust, and trust creates sales, repeat purchases, and precious referrals—and that is the path to profits.

The simple and powerful act of consistently marketing the right message to the right audience will rocket your success far above and beyond that of other businesses. While you're basking in the simplicity of your success with Guerrilla Marketing, you'll notice that other businesses (hopefully your competition) are struggling with their marketing.

Those other businesses may have success from time to time, but you'll notice they use disconnected gimmicks, and they turn their marketing on and off like a light switch. They also focus on price over value, sameness over uniqueness, and irrelevant benefits. Those businesses are constantly in pursuit of new customers because their existing customers do not make repeat purchases or recommend the business to their friends, family, co-workers, and social followers.

Our Guerrilla Marketing ideas, examples, and tactics are segmented into several categories:

- Guerrilla Maximedia Marketing
- Guerrilla Minimedia Marketing
- Guerrilla E-Media Marketing
- Guerrilla Info-Media Marketing
- Guerrilla Human-Media Marketing
- Guerrilla Non-Media Marketing
- Guerrilla Company Attributes
- Guerrilla Company Attitudes

These categories are classic to Guerrilla Marketing, but the toolbox of examples and tactics within them are ever-evolving and growing, and in each volume of this all-new *Guerrilla Marketing* series of books, we'll give you the latest tools and tactics to succeed right now. You'll find a broad array of tactics that will help you find the right combination for your business. Utilize them properly and test as many as fit with your target audience research, customer knowledge, Guerrilla Marketing plan, and Guerrilla Creative and Advertising strategy. Keep in mind that Guerrilla marketers don't jump straight into executing a mix of tactics without first creating a strong foundation.

Guerrilla Marketing should be thought of as a band, or even as an orchestra. The individual pieces of your marketing and advertising (i.e., the instruments)—when beautifully playing the same song in perfect harmony—contribute to an extraordinary piece of music that people enjoy hearing over and over. However, when one or more pieces are out of harmony (or playing a different song), it's the kind of music that people either never notice or, worse, they press dislike or skip or change the station.

Visit gMarketing.com/Club to access your free companion course and a simple Guerrilla Marketing calendar example.

As a reminder, in Volume 1, we addressed:

1.1 Research and Knowing

1.2 Guerrilla Creativity

1.3 Unique Selling Proposition (USP)

Now, we'll pick up where we left off. Without further ado, let's get started.

1.8 * CRUCIAL SKILLS FOR EFFECTIVELY USING GUERRILLA MARKETING

There's never been a better time to be a Guerrilla business, so it's important to know the crucial skills for effectively using Guerrilla Marketing. The skills have evolved from those that Jay Conrad Levinson had identified, and we've updated and expanded the current crucial skills to help your business succeed. As you build your business, you'll look for others that possess and/or complement these skills.

Creativity

Possibly the most crucial skill for successful Guerrilla Marketing is creativity. Guerrilla Marketing is effective for many businesses because of its focus on low-cost, strategic marketing concepts that creatively promote a compelling product or service.

From your Guerrilla Marketing plan to every tactic you employ, focused creativity wins sales and retains customers. Why is focused creativity critical?

When creativity is unfocused, people remember the cleverness or creativity of your marketing, but they are not compelled to take action or, even worse, they don't recall your business name. Unfocused creativity is akin to gimmick marketing, and it's a vampire that sucks attention away from your offer.

You can likely recall several television commercials that are funny or entertaining, but do you recall the advertiser? Equally, did you purchase their product or service because of the commercial? Guerrilla marketers avoid unfocused creativity and expensive missteps.

Your job is to employ focused creativity to compel your prospects to notice your business. Once they do, your call to action must then motivate them to take a desired action (e.g., download an ebook, make a purchase, etc.). Your existing customers also need to be motivated to make repeat purchases and precious referrals of their friends, family, and associates. See Volume 1, Section 1.2, "Guerrilla Creativity," for more information.

Nimble

The ability to change is part of the DNA of Guerrilla Marketing. Guerrillas start their business with a big goal, a Guerrilla Marketing plan, and only part of the resources they need to reach that goal. They know that change and the unexpected are a part of the journey to success.

When they get stuck or come across a challenge, they don't back off or try an easier route; they are nimble. They inventory what they need to learn and then determine what resources they need to take the next step. With increased knowledge and/or resources, they take that next step with confidence.

Sometimes, business and marketing opportunities come quickly. Being at the right place at the right time is only one part of the formula. Being prepared, nimble, focused, and ready to take advantage of those opportunities are the magic ingredients in the formula for success.

A Superb Listener

Listening to the customer starts with listening to yourself. It means suspending your ego and setting any stubbornness aside. Guerrilla marketers know that when you listen and ask the right questions, your customers and prospects will tell you what to do to make your business more profitable. Simply by listening to your prospects and customers, you will do the smart thing far more often than if you simply decide you know best and, therefore, go it alone.

An honest interest in people will be reflected in your ability to ask engaging questions that compel people to respond. In the process, you're proving to them that you care about them—and it's imperative that you listen very carefully to what they say to you. The more interested you are in people, the better a listener you are. A Guerrilla marketer is a superb listener. See Volume 3, Section 9.30, "A Superb Listener," for more information.

A Relationship Builder

Guerrillas place emphasis on creating relationships with other businesses and retaining existing customers instead of solely focusing on acquiring new ones.

Their listening skills and honest interest in people (see Volume 1, Section 9.6, "Honest Interest in People") boost their relationship-building skills.

Traditional marketers, at the end of the month, count money or sales. While those are important, Guerrilla marketers are different. Guerrillas are responsive to sales and profits, but they also count new relationships.

After all, it's easy to get caught up in market research, demographics, psychographics, consumer behavior (see Volume 1, Section 6.9, "Consumer Behavior"), and lose sight of the people—your prospects and customers. Fortunately, you know that people want relationships, and your relationship-building skills set you apart. Guerrillas do everything they can to establish and nurture a bond between themselves and each individual customer to create long-term profitable relationships. See Volume 3, Section 9.29, "Relationship Builder," for more information.

Resilience

Know this: Things are going to go what you might call "wrong." That's okay, and it's just a moment in time in your ever-evolving journey toward increased success. Maintaining that perspective helps a Guerrilla marketer in the face of things going "wrong" because they realize that nothing went "wrong;" something was just unexpected.

It's far easier to retain your resilience when you recognize the critical difference between "wrong" and "unexpected." When you think something went "wrong," it distracts and frustrates you and that is a waste of your time, creativity, imagination, and energy.

In 2020, it was easy to see the difference between businesses that thought something went "wrong" and resilient businesses that understood that something "unexpected" happened. Those resilient businesses were nimble, and they looked for opportunities in the needs of their prospects and customers. They knew they had the knowledge and skills to pivot, execute, and succeed. It's been said that necessity is the mother of invention, and by pivoting, you can find solutions.

Alternately, when you look at any industry, you'll typically see several successful businesses leading the way. Those successful leading businesses are different from one another. They have different names, logos, USPs, marketing, advertising, and so on. There are many ways to achieve success. There isn't *one* right way, making every other way "wrong." There will always be unexpected things that happen, and your resilience will show you the way to turn that unexpected event or circumstance into a successful opportunity. See Section 9.26, "Resilience," for more information.

Unconventional

A Guerrilla business owner seeks conventional goals, such as profits and joy, but achieves them using unconventional and creative means.

Guerrilla Marketing is a strategy in which low-cost unconventional means are utilized to convey or promote a product or an idea. Those unconventional means are fueled by knowledge, time, energy, and imagination, and they compel your prospects to notice your business. Once they do, your call to action must then motivate them to take a desired action (e.g., download an ebook, make a purchase, etc.). Your existing customers also need to be motivated to make repeat purchases and precious referrals of their friends, family, and associates.

Guerrilla marketers thrive on the nontraditional, and they do the unconventional if the conventional is nonsensical. They know the real name of the game is enjoying the journey to success, which is the best of all goals. See Volume 3, Section 9.27, "Unconventional," for more information.

Agile

Very large businesses may be bright and well-funded, but their marketers must maneuver through corporate politics, meetings, committees, and layers of decision-makers, many of whom are not skilled marketers, which makes great marketing challenging and the business clumsy and complacent.

The enemies of Guerrilla Marketing and business success are complacency, rigidity, and sluggishness. Guerrilla businesses of all sizes are nimble and agile. The lines of communication are wide open, and they frequently reassess and adapt, as needed, as they evolve toward continued success. According to *Business Insider*, Warren Buffet has been quoted as saying, "Guard against the 'ABC' risks of decay that all very large organizations face: arrogance, bureaucracy, and complacency." See Section 9.13, "Guerrilla Agile Mind," for more information.

Curious

Guerrilla marketers are curious by nature. They are excited about always having something new to learn. They are curious about how things work and how things can work *better*. They are also curious about their prospects and customers and their behavior, including their pain points and pleasure points (see Volume 1, Section 6.9, "Consumer Behavior").

A wise Guerrilla marketer pairs their curiosity with life-long learning. Curiosity can turn into negative action—chasing anything and everything new (often referred to as *shiny object syndrome*)—which can be a distraction. Therefore, it's important to balance your focus and your curiosity to gain optimal success. See Section 9.20, "Curiosity," for more information.

Commitment and Consistency

For Guerrilla marketers, commitment is the first secret of success in marketing and advertising. When you understand the meaning of commitment, it will pay off for you.

Have you wondered how Guerrilla Marketing is effective for so many businesses? The answer is simpler than you might think. Guerrillas learn by doing, imagining, experimenting, being realistic, keeping track, paying attention, improving, and committing to their successful experiments.

The difference between many successes and failures is a simple marketing plan and a commitment to continue to do what's working. Many businesses find what works, but they won't take the simple and powerful act of committing to it and consistently putting it to use. That lack of commitment means success is fleeting, and the business falls flat, possibly on the way to failing.

Guerrillas know the simple act of committing to an evolving plan and tracking the results allow them to consistently and repeatedly do what's working. What a simple way to let your success continue to rise.

It sounds easy, but that's not necessarily true. When we speak of the importance of commitment and consistency, it means you keep refining and repeating your success. That means using the same successful USP, logo, tagline, jingle, and everything else that's working with constant repetition. That repetition can be challenging for those that crave change. However, when you realize that change, for the sake of change, can undo everything that's working, it's easier to rely on your commitment.

When we speak of the importance of commitment and consistency, we find that people can mistakenly confuse consistency and complacency. Consistency should not be confused with complacency. Doing it "the way we've always done it" is not the way of Guerrilla Marketing. Doing it in a way that evolves and continually builds on what works, allows you to constantly grow your success, and that is the way Guerrilla Marketing works. See Section 1.9, "Guerrilla Marketing Consistency," for more information.

Patience

You begin your Guerrilla Marketing plan with solid market research. You evolve your Guerrilla Marketing plan based on your continued solid market research and thorough tracking of your marketing and advertising efforts. You put your marketing to work, and you stay with it, as it's showing results.

You're nimble and you do more of what's working and less of what's not. You make careful revisions along the way to make your efforts work better. Something that is not working you choose to lessen, and you make simple revisions to improve it, based on what you've learned from your efforts that are working. If it's still not working, it's time to eliminate it. You're continually evolving your powerful plan.

You watch your plan slowly (or quickly) take effect, rise, and falter. With continued tracking and market research, you make revisions. You do more of what's working and less of what's not. Your powerful plan is taking hold even more, and even if there are some stumbles, you continually grab on to the successes and soar.

Your plan is working; your register is ringing; your bank balance is swelling. And this is because you committed to your marketing plan, and you were patient.

At the outset, you won't have any way of knowing whether your plan is good or bad, except for low-cost testing, tracking, your own intuition, and the counsel of others, whose experience you trust. But once you believe in your plan, you've got to back your belief with patience and commitment.

What if you weren't patient enough during the time your plan was "slowly" taking hold? You might have changed the plan. Many entrepreneurs do and then they lose out.

Marketing plans often, at least temporarily, stumble. However, because you're nimble and focused, you stayed with your plan that's backed with your market research, tracking, and careful revisions—and it took hold. Your success was very much due to your understanding of the concept of patience and commitment. You didn't kill the plan—and kill your chances along with it.

Innovative

Guerrillas are constantly looking for ways to produce high-quality and compelling products or services with new ideas and creative thinking. They seek to let their innovations maximize their success, as they define it. They also seek to let their innovations fulfill their purpose, as they define it.

To be innovative, they rely on creativity, technology, automation, etc. Guerrillas also seek success-oriented and like-minded people to help by collaborating, delegating, and/or outsourcing.

Most importantly, at all times, Guerrilla marketers focus on the pain points and pleasure points (see Volume 1, Section 6.9, "Consumer Behavior") of their prospects and customers. They focus on improving their prospects' and customers' lives, which helps their products and services tell a story that sells (see Volume 1, Section 6.5, "Stories Sell"). See Volume 1, Section 8.11 "Innovation," for more information.

Quality

A crucial Guerrilla Marketing Attribute is quality. As we addressed, in Volume 1, Section 8.12, "Quality:" "You can use the skills and tactics of Guerrilla Marketing to sell products. However, the way you earn repeat purchases from your customer is by consistently delivering with the quality of your product, service, purchase process, delivery, and support level (before and after the sale)."

Guerrilla marketers are committed to providing the best quality in all aspects of their business, and it pays dividends. Consumers are willing to pay a premium for quality, and the superb ratings that quality products and services garner do much of the work in your marketing. Marketing is far easier when you're able to tell a compelling story that sells your product(s) or service(s), and the ratings and reviews motivate your prospects to take immediate action. At the same time, your existing customers are also motivated to make repeat purchases and provide precious referrals of their friends, family, and associates.

Profit/Outcome-Focused

Guerrilla entrepreneurs define success on their own terms. They not only buy into the standard notion of finances, but also the notion of balance—between work and leisure, work and family, work and humanity, and work and self. Guerrilla entrepreneurs have the enviable privilege of defining their own goals, and their creativity, focus, and commitment help them achieve those goals.

However, to accomplish most goals—regardless of how noble they are—your business must be profit-focused. For many businesses, being profit-focused is natural. For a noble-cause business, it can be a bit more challenging.

However, it's important to note that a business can't accomplish its noble goals without profit. A business that is first focused on noble goals should never be concerned with attracting too much profit. Too much profit simply means that you need to expand your noble goals. Your profitable success means you can accomplish so much more than you anticipated. At the end of the day, a business without profit or an outcome focus, unfortunately, doesn't accomplish its goals.

Balance (Work and Life)

When the journey is the goal, you can begin with work that satisfies you. That satisfying work is fueled by a work-life balance. Guerrillas spend time enjoying activities they love, ones other than work. By doing so, they gain a remarkable level of appreciation, gratitude, and freedom from work-related stress.

A balance between work and life makes you more creative and innovative. Therefore, you'll more easily find answers, opportunities, resources, and solutions. You'll also find it easier to build valuable relationships that help your business thrive, and it will show.

Joyful and Generous

Human kindness is part of the nature of Guerrilla Marketing. Warmth, caring, personal attention, and a genuine interest in people is also a part of the nature of Guerrilla Marketing. None of this costs money, just a bit of knowledge, time, energy, imagination, and patience. After all, not everyone you'll encounter is joyful and generous, so sometimes, you'll have to rely on your nature to work around their nature, without being adversely influenced.

Compelling

You can have the best product, the best service, and the best employees, but if you can't compel people to notice your business, you're lacking customers. Your business is compelling with quality products and services and Guerrilla Marketing, which helps you focus on things such as a well-crafted USP, authenticity, stories that sell, relationships, consistency, and so much more.

Your job is to compel your prospects to notice your business. Once they do, your call to action must then motivate them to take a desired action (e.g., download an ebook, make a purchase, etc.). Your existing customers also need to be motivated to make repeat purchases and precious referrals of their friends, family, and associates.

Focused on Success

You should know that if you're to succeed with Guerrilla Marketing, you: (1) start with a powerful plan that is based on solid market research and (2) commit to that plan, and (3) track your results. A plan is about succeeding on purpose— much like what sports teams do. They study the competition to find their weaknesses and strengths. They develop playbooks and plans to help them succeed on purpose. The scoreboard does their tracking, and it keeps them focused.

Success occurs with applied knowledge and when you simply do more of what's working and less of what's not. If you do that, you're off to the right start, and you're primed for and focused on success. See Volume 1, Section 9.10, "Focused" and Volume 3, Section 9.31, "Focused on Success," for more information.

Skilled Thinking

Successful Guerrilla marketers are not afraid to view thinking as a skill. It's a skill that can increase creativity, problem-solving, and innovation.

In Section 9.23, "Lateral Thinking," we'll address how you can learn to think differently to achieve successful results. Equally, Guerrilla marketers embrace skilled thinking, such as the 80/20 Rule. For Guerrilla businesses, the 80/20 Rule teaches simplicity, and it applies throughout your business; for example:

- 20 percent of your marketing generates 80 percent of your sales
- 20 percent of the time you spend working generates 80 percent of what you achieve at work
- 20 percent of a company's products usually account for 80 percent of its sales
- 20 percent of a company's employees contribute to 80 percent of the work that generates profits

Therefore, Guerrilla marketers seek to continually prune the 80 percent. They also delegate to people in their business to carry out the necessary workload so they can focus on the critical 20 percent that's difficult to delegate.

Conclusion

Why do these crucial skills matter? First, being an entrepreneur or the owner of an SMB is a dream. That dream is fully realized with greater ease and more profitability when you possess (naturally or with practice) these crucial skills that help you effectively use Guerrilla Marketing. Why? It's simple; you greatly reduce the amount of money that you need to invest into marketing your business, product(s), and/or service(s) when you possess these crucial skills.

If you don't currently possess all these skills, worry not. It simply means that you have an opportunity. You can build these skills, and we are here to provide the knowledge that will help you build them. Equally, you can look for these skills in the people that help your business. Be it through collaboration, outsourcing, or current employees, relying on other people that possess these skills can help you grow your business while you learn these skills yourself. Remember, Guerrilla marketers begin with a goal in mind and a portion of the resources needed, and they learn the rest and find the right resources along the way.

1.9 * GUERRILLA MARKETING CONSISTENCY

One of the simplest ways to make your Guerrilla Marketing successful costs you nothing. But it does take discipline and focus to commit to:

- Consistently marketing successful messages that compel your prospects and customers
- Consistently marketing a call to action that motivates your prospects and customers to take a desired action (e.g., download an ebook, make a purchase, etc.)

That might sound simple or even obvious, and it is, but many businesses don't do it. As we just addressed in Section 1.8, commitment and consistency are "Crucial Skills for Effectively Using Guerrilla Marketing."

In Volume 1, Section 9.11, "Consistency," we addressed the importance of consistency in Guerrilla Company Attitudes (see Section IX). It's also important to address *why* consistency is a part of the strong foundation of Guerrilla Marketing success.

Why is consistency so valuable and powerful? With Guerrilla Marketing, consistency builds familiarity; familiarity builds trust, and trust creates sales, repeat purchases, and precious referrals, which is the fuel for long-term success.

How do you ensure your marketing is consistent? It's amazingly simple: Guerrilla marketers make plans, and they let those plans guide their decisions. Therefore, they utilize:

- A consistent USP
- Consistent Guerrilla Company Attributes (see Section VIII and Volume 1, Sections 8.1, "Brand;" 8.2, "Name;" 8.3, "Identity;" 8.4, "Logo;" 8.5, "Memes and Jingles;" 8.6, "Tagline;" 8.7, "Color Palette, Typeface, and Fonts," and 8.8, "Intelligent Positioning")
- Consistent Guerrilla Company Attitudes (see Section IX)

Fortunately for Guerrilla marketers, they know that most businesses never make a plan, or they make a plan and:

- It's not aligned to their company attributes
- It's not aligned to their company attitudes
- They file the plan away and ignore it

Guerrilla marketers don't make those mistakes. They know that plans are how you keep your marketing consistent and how you win on purpose. Your simple Guerrilla Marketing plan will help you stay focused and consistent, and that means you're making intelligent marketing choices.

You'll quickly find that your plan will make it obvious when you're veering off course or being tempted to engage in gimmick, spray-and-pray, and other disconnected marketing that wastes your money. It's far easier than you might realize to make inconsistent choices that lead to inconsistent marketing. A simple plan will put the no-cost advantages of consistency to work for your business.

What does a football coach do? They do their research and then create a plan. During the game, they keep checking their plan, and they may recalibrate as the game progresses, but they know that executing their sound plan is the key to winning on purpose.

It's important to remember that having a plan doesn't mean that you never change it. That football coach, in every game, is continually recalibrating based on what's working. They track their effectiveness so they can do more of what's working and less of what's not working. Their plan and their ability to make changes help them win the game and be ready for the next one.

Without consistency, your business will view marketing as a series of disconnected gimmicks, or will be a business that thinks marketing is a light switch you
turn on and off. That business takes action, but it doesn't understand how to set
itself apart with good Guerrilla Marketing.

If we look back to the football coach reference, think of the football team
as a business. As a business, they consistently market their name, color palette,
logo, etc. If they chose gimmick marketing instead of consistent marketing, you
would go to the stadium to watch a game one week, and their colors would be
green and purple. Then, when you went the next week, they would have changed
their name, logo, and colors—now red and orange. As a fan, you wouldn't recognize the team.

It's the same for your business. Remember, many businesses, big and small,
view marketing as a series of disconnected gimmicks. Different messages, different colors, different fonts, different target markets, and different tactics. Fortunately for you, you're not most businesses.

Continual, dramatic changes and disconnected marketing gimmicks are the
enemies of consistency. Your friends, family, employees, and those that you're
paying to create your ads (who make money when you change your ads) will
tire of your ads far faster than your customers and prospects will tire of your ads.

You only get seconds, if you're lucky, of your customers' and prospects'
attention. Consistency works powerfully in your favor when you consider that
it makes your repetition turn those separate, fragmented seconds (i.e., separate
impressions) into consistent marketing. Consistent marketing compels your
prospects and customers to, first, become aware of your business (i.e., brand
awareness) and second, recognize your business and the product(s) and/or ser-
vice(s) associated with it (i.e., brand recognition). Once they do, your call to
action can then motivate them to take a desired action

The greatest compliment you'll receive about your marketing and advertising
are positive statements, such as:

- "I keep seeing your ad everywhere."
- "I know your ads by heart."
- "I love your ad with the . . ."
- "I've seen your ad so many times and I finally decided to . . ."
- "I remember your business from your catchy jingle."

When others encourage you to change your advertising because of what they
describe as "ad fatigue," remember that with Guerrilla Marketing, consistency

builds familiarity; familiarity builds trust, and trust creates sales, repeat purchases, and precious referrals, which is the fuel for long-term success.

Guerrilla marketers value and tend to the tiny, supercharged details, such as consistency, repetition, familiarity, trust, sales, repeat purchases, and precious referrals—all of which generate big profits. That's not to say that you should never change your advertising or marketing. Guerrilla marketers simply choose to make subtle changes to build on their success (instead of wasting money trying to reinvent it).

The enemies of Guerrilla Marketing and business success are complacency, rigidity, and sluggishness. When we speak of the importance of consistency, people can mistakenly confuse consistency and complacency. Consistency should not be confused with complacency. "Doing it the way we've always done it" is not the way of Guerrilla Marketing. "Doing it in a way that evolves and builds on what you've already done to continually grow your success" is the way of Guerrilla Marketing.

When you make significant changes to your advertising and marketing, instead of subtle changes, you reset your recognition and familiarity to zero and must start all over again with your prospects. Therefore, if your advertising and marketing are working, but you're compelled to make a change, make subtle changes, such as one or two things at a time.

At the same time, utilize your Guerrilla Marketing plan to ensure you're being powerfully consistent with your choices and decisions. Once you've created and launched your Guerrilla Marketing plan, you'll easily see the full picture of your marketing efforts and how one decision relates to the next.

Think of your plan as the hub on a bicycle tire and your marketing decisions as the spokes. To function well, each spoke is connected to and aligned with the hub. If the spokes are disconnected from the hub, the wheel is unstable.

With your Guerrilla Marketing plan, you'll also keep track of which of your marketing tactics are hitting your target and which are missing those targets. Merely knowing and taking needed action can double the effectiveness of your marketing budget. Sound daunting? It's not. Sound exciting? It is!

1.10 * GUERRILLA MARKETING REPETITION

We just addressed, in Section 1.9, "Guerrilla Marketing Consistency," the importance of consistency. The rocket fuel to power your consistency is repetition. Repetition and consistency build familiarity among your prospects and customers. Familiarity, in turn, builds trust, which creates sales, repeat purchases, and precious referrals, which are the fuel for the long-term success of your business.

There are many theories about how much repetition it takes to create a purchase. In practical terms, it takes as much repetition as it takes. Your goal is for your marketing to be so compelling that your prospects and customers are motivated to take immediate action, thereby reducing the repetition needed and reducing your marketing investment.

If you want people to purchase your product(s) or service(s), you're going to need to consistently repeat yourself and your marketing. The first goal of repetition is to get your prospects to notice your business name (i.e., brand awareness). Your goal then becomes to get them to recognize your business *and* recall the product(s) or service(s) associated with it (i.e., brand recognition). Your goal then turns to get them to care enough and be motivated by your call to action to take that desired action (e.g., download an ebook, make a purchase, etc.).

Once your prospects have enough trust in your business, are compelled to act, and buy your service(s) or product(s), your work is still not done. Repetition also helps to motivate your existing customers to make repeat purchases and provide your business the precious gift of referring their friends, family, and associates to your business. Repeat purchases and referrals are the fuel for the long-term success of your business.

The Guerrilla marketer understands how consistency and repetition make marketing messages powerful. When your prospects or customers see your marketing and advertising, their effectiveness is amplified when they also see the same marketing (look, feel, and messaging) in your:

- Direct mailer sitting on their counters
- Magazine ad lying on their coffee tables
- Radio advertisement they heard on the way home
- Commercial on their television screens
- Online search results on their phones
- Online advertising on their computers

- Email marketing in their inboxes
- Social media they are viewing
- Website that they will visit or have already seen
- Physical business location (e.g., signage, décor, uniforms, etc.) that they will visit or have already seen

A coordinated and targeted campaign allows your Guerrilla Marketing efforts to be amplified as they work together to consistently repeat your marketing message(s). Remember, repetition of compelling marketing messages encourages your prospects to notice your business.

Imagine if all the marketing efforts that we just listed were not consistent and didn't repeat the same marketing message. Your business wouldn't establish familiarity and trust. Instead, each marketing effort would be lost in the sea of all the other marketing messages that your prospects and customers are inundated with every day, and your prospects won't notice your business.

When your marketing efforts are working together, they are the rocket fuel needed to increase the overall effectiveness of your marketing. Your consistency and repetition are building familiarity. That familiarity is, in turn, building trust. Trust, combined with a motivating call to action, creates sales, repeat purchases, and precious referrals. That's a powerful advantage that comes without additional cost, and it's the fuel for long-term success.

Your coordinated and targeted campaign is amplified when you simply use consistency and repetition. When your well-crafted campaign is working, do more of it. With repetition, you're letting your success continue to grow. Think of repetition as a snowball rolling down a hill and getting bigger and bigger as it goes. Allow your marketing to make a bigger and bigger impact on your success.

Guerrilla marketers understand that they achieve an immensely powerful and simple advantage by choosing repetition. Let other businesses, such as your competition, waste their marketing investments by competing with themselves, using disconnected marketing and advertising efforts.

SECTION II

Guerrilla Maximedia Marketing

GUERRILLA MAXIMEDIA MARKETING

As Jay Conrad Levison stated in *Guerrilla Marketing*:

> *Guerrillas must use the mass media with precision, carefully measure the results, and make the media part of an overall marketing plan. When they use the media, Guerrillas must rely on know-how, intuition and business acumen. Maximedia Marketing is about two things: (1) selling and (2) creating a powerful desire to buy. Also, Maximedia Marketing enhances the success of Minimedia Marketing—response rates to simple circulars jump when radio advertising blazes the way for them, and telemarketing results improve when TV spots pre-sell the market.*

Guerrilla Maximedia Marketing is what many people think of when they talk about "traditional advertising." Guerrilla Maximedia Marketing is at its most powerful when your Guerrilla Marketing is in full congruence. Your Guerrilla Maximedia Marketing endeavors bring your business to light in front of large audiences. Additionally, your Guerrilla Maximedia Marketing and your Guerrilla E-Media Marketing (Section IV) are typically the largest advertising investments that your business will make.

Therefore, taking the time to skillfully create your Guerrilla Creative and Advertising strategy is a must. Effective Guerrilla Maximedia Marketing is creative, clear, focused, compelling, and consistent. Your Guerrilla Creative and Advertising strategy will keep you on the path to profitable advertising. As with every marketing investment you make, understanding how advertising works equips you to make wise investments that will help you sleep well at night while your business profits grow.

We'll help you maximize the low- and no-cost ways to make your Guerrilla Maximedia Marketing investments create maximum profits for your business. Those precious profits are the fuel that makes your business engine run so you can hire talented people, acquire loyal customers, improve your community, and make your dreams a reality. Let's dive in and see how you can put Guerrilla Maximedia Marketing tactics to work for your business. In Volume 1, we addressed:

2.1   Direct Mail
2.2   Newspaper Advertising
2.3   Radio Advertising

Now, we'll pick up where we left off. Without further ado, let's get started.

2.9 * RADIO PRESENCE/INFLUENCE

If you've determined that radio advertising is an effective way to reach your prospects and customers, your challenge is to find a way for your marketing and advertising to break through the crowd of advertisers. There are several ways to break through and get the attention of your prospects and customers:

- Influence/Endorsements: your business can benefit from paid endorsements by influential on-air personalities. You can hire radio DJs to be the voice in your scripted radio advertising, and/or they can make direct (scripted or unscripted) endorsements of your product. Those endorsements are, ideally, given as an authentically satisfied customer, who's sharing their exceptional experience with their listeners. Keep in mind that these endorsements can be partially or fully paid by bartering (i.e., providing products or services in exchange for paid endorsements instead of money. See Section 2.10, "Bartering"). See Section 2.15, "Endorsements," for more information

- Paid/Sponsored Programming: radio stations need to fill every hour of the day, and they can be welcoming to your engaging and expertly produced radio program. You can work with local stations, and/or you can work with media networks that specialize in placing high-quality talk radio programs. Be sure to learn and stay up-to-date with the Federal Communications Commission (FCC) rules that govern this opportunity

- Events: your physical business can be an asset to radio stations that are eager to meet their listeners' needs. Your business can host DJ appearances or participate in contests, scavenger hunts, giveaways, etc. Many radio listeners are excited to meet their favorite DJ(s), and your business

earns favor and implied endorsement by serving as the location that
gives them that memorable opportunity

- Interviews and Call-ins: by participating with radio stations (on-air and
online), you can compellingly share your expertise. Radio stations are
not interested in giving away advertising for free, so it's an effective strategy to contribute your expertise in a compelling manner that will motivate them to ask you "where do you work?" or "how can people reach
you?" In the process, you will compel your prospects and customers to
notice your business and motivate them with your call to action (i.e., the
clear messaging of the specific action you want them to take)

The keys to successfully breaking through the crowd of advertisers on radio
is knowledge, creativity, and action. When you know what compels and motivates your customers and prospects, and you know that radio is a good opportunity, it's time to act.

It's easy for a business to purchase radio advertising. A few clicks on the right
websites (see gMarketing.com/Club for links) will put your advertising on the
air with ease. However, it's a Guerrilla marketer that chooses to build a mutually
profitable relationship with the on-air talent and radio stations with whom they
advertise.

After all, you know, based on your research, that your prospects and customers like certain radio stations. Why not utilize a platform they like to compel
them to notice your business? Your ability to do so is enhanced when you utilize
on-air personalities that influence your prospects and customers.

Once your prospects and customers are compelled to notice your business,
your well-crafted call to action can motivate them to take a desired action (e.g.,
download an ebook, make a purchase, etc.). At the same time, your existing customers can be motivated to make repeat purchases and provide precious referrals
of their friends, family, and associates.

It takes an investment in knowledge, time, energy, and imagination to make
your radio advertising investment work harder for your business. However, when
you work with the stations that you're advertising with to create win-win relationships, it produces great results for both. The relationships you build with the
radio stations will unleash the benefits of collaboration.

Does that get harder as your business grows and you advertise with more stations? Not necessarily—if you choose to rely on your Guerrilla Marketing plan
and repeat your successes. With the power of repetition, you won't be tempted

to continually re-invent messaging and doing something new each time, if it's not necessary.

You evolve your Guerrilla Marketing plan based on your continued solid market research and the thorough tracking of your marketing and advertising efforts. You put your marketing to work, and you stay with it, as it's showing results.

You make simple revisions along the way to increase your success and track the results. If the results are successful, you have evolved your Guerrilla Marketing plan. Along the way, your plan helps you avoid temptations that can easily derail your existing success. By doing so, your business is harnessing the power of repetition (see Section 1.10, "Guerrilla Marketing Repetition") and consistency (see Section 1.9, "Guerrilla Marketing Consistency").

Staying focused on repeating and building on the successes that your business has achieved is how you help your business grow and achieve long-term success. The creative use of radio influence, appearances, and endorsements can help you along your way.

2.10 * BARTERING

Regardless of what stage your business is in, bartering is a low cost and effective means to increase your Guerrilla Maximedia Marketing success. The advantages of bartering are numerous.

When you barter by offering your expertise in exchange for appearances, your advertising partners receive valuable content that appeals to their audience. You receive valuable advertising, marketing and/or media exposure that increases your success.

On the other hand, when you barter with your product(s) or service(s), you'll value them at full price. That allows you to convert your typical mark-up value into marketing and advertising dollars that work for your business. For example, if you sell a technology product for $100, you'll barter/negotiate for $100 worth of advertising, marketing, or media value. If the cost of your $100 product is $25, your $75 mark-up is working for your business. Your bartering partner has a mark-up as well, so it's a win-win for both businesses.

Additionally, when you barter with your expertise, quality product(s), or service(s), you're adding value for the media partner with whom you're negotiating. Your valuable contribution helps their business success.

Becoming an "exclusive provider of . . .," "the official . . . provider," or their ". . . expert," builds appreciation for your expertise and/or high-quality product(s) or service(s). At the same time, it gives your business a valuable implied endorsement (see Section 2.15, "Endorsements," for more information) from your media partner.

Bartering with a media partner is made more valuable when you take the time to form a great relationship. By building a relationship, each business wants to creatively promote the other to help each succeed. Both businesses benefit from promoting the "exclusive" or "official provider" relationship. At the same time, both businesses benefit by sharing stories of how your product(s) or service(s) have helped their business and how their partnership has helped your business.

For example, the Food Network relies on the expertise of talented chefs for many of their shows (e.g., *Chopped* and *Diners, Drive-Ins and Dives*). In exchange for the chefs' appearance on these shows, the chefs' businesses or restaurants are promoted during their appearances on the programs. After the shows, the chefs have the ability to promote their appearances. For example, a restaurant can display "as seen on Food Network" signage at their restaurant and share photos and videos on their website and social media—all of which, along with the chef's appearance on the show, create an implied endorsement.

Bartering is a low-cost method of achieving high-quality media mentions that increase your reach and sales, product and/or service endorsements, new business opportunities, and valuable feedback. Guerrilla marketers maximize the opportunity by building valuable, profitable, strong, and mutually beneficial relationships (see Volume 3, Section 9.29, "Relationship Builder").

2.11 * AGENCIES

Marketing, advertising, and media agencies are prolific. Determining when it's time to delegate, designate, and engage professional agency services can be easier said than done. Equally, once you've decided to engage the help of an agency, where do you begin?

Types of Agencies

The services an agency provides can vary widely. From full-service to niche services, it's important to understand their expertise and match that expertise with your needs. Common agencies include:

- **Social Media Agencies:** they focus on building social media to increase engagement, lead generation, and sales
- **Digital Media Agencies:** they focus on all aspects of digital marketing and advertising including search engine optimization (SEO), social media, paid digital advertising, and more
- **Public Relations Agencies:** they increase the awareness of your business, product(s), or service(s) with news outlets, social outlets, community and professional organizations, community events, etc.
- **Branding Agencies:** they work with businesses that want to focus on opportunities to increase the awareness or reputation of their brand without necessarily seeking a response to a promotion
- **Direct Response or Promotional Agencies:** they seek to create immediate responses (e.g., engagement and list-building) and/or to increase sales with promotions
- **Media Agencies:** they are experts in buying media and can reduce the cost of your media investments and add unexpected media value with their negotiation skills

What Is the Purpose of Utilizing Agencies?

The purpose of utilizing a marketing, advertising, and media agency is to build on and improve your marketing and advertising results and to evolve your Guerrilla Marketing plan. An effective agency will collaborate with your business to evolve your Guerrilla Marketing plan, with solid market research and thorough tracking of your marketing and advertising efforts.

An agency that wants to ignore and discard your current successes, is displaying a red flag, that you don't want to ignore. A Guerrilla marketer repeats and builds on their success, they never ignore their successes.

The Time to Engage Agencies

Most business owners fall strongly to one end or the other of the "like" vs. "dislike" scale of enjoying the creation and implementation of the marketing for their business.

If you fall to the "dislike" end of the scale, it's a great idea to utilize marketing, advertising, and media agencies. However, regardless of how much you dislike leading the charge of the creation and implementation of your marketing, it's important to take the time to understand why marketing works. You've made a great choice by choosing these volumes of the all-new series of *Guerrilla Marketing* books to help guide you. The time you're taking to understand what marketing is, why it works, and the options you have will help you guide your marketing success.

If you fall to the "like" end of the scale, it's a bit more challenging to determine when it's time to engage marketing, advertising, and media agencies. There are many questions you'll likely ask, but the most important one is "Can you get more accomplished?" Consider that:

- Your time is valuable, and getting more of your time back by engaging an agency can pay dividends in other aspects of your business, such as focusing your time on the development of new products and services
- If your market research shows that your prospects are likely to respond to marketing or advertising tactics that you're not engaged in (because you don't have the know-how or you don't have time), an agency can provide expertise to expand your efforts
- If you have an employee or employees leading the charge on your marketing and advertising, an agency can provide additional skilled resources that can expand your success. Equally, they may be able to do so at a lower cost, which allows you to invest more in your marketing and advertising
- If your sales have plateaued or are declining, the right agency can offer increased skills, resources, and media discounts that can boost your sales and profits to reignite the growth of your business
- According to Fundera, "Almost half of small businesses spend less than two hours per week on marketing efforts." Are you spending a small percentage of your time on marketing your business?

Where to Begin

According to Fundera, "47% of small business owners run marketing entirely on their own." When you've determined that your business will benefit from an agency, where do you begin?

For starters, agencies promote their success, but it's your success that matters. Guerrilla marketers choose agencies that are a fit for their business goals and needs. You can begin with:

- Ratings and Reviews
- Recommendations: ask businesses, whose marketing you admire, for the agencies they are using. If you can't ask the business, search for the information online
- Location: if you're marketing and advertising in a defined geographic area, choosing a successful agency within that area is beneficial

Once you've selected some agencies to interview and consider, there are important factors to contemplate, such as:

- Do they truly understand what it means to be a Guerrilla marketer?
- Do they speak your marketing language? An agency that is more focused on speaking above you, rather than to you, isn't demonstrating an interest in you or your business success
- Personality. The success of your marketing is impacted by your ability to communicate and interact with the agency. Incompatible, non-flexible, or way too flexible personalities are obstacles that you don't need
- Can they represent your business? Do they share your passion for relationship building? If so, they'll multiply your ability to find creative win-win relationships with other businesses and media partners
- Do they understand the power of what makes your business unique? It's easy for them to lump your business into a sector of clients and assume you're just like the rest. An agency that shares your passion for your USP will be an expansion of what you can accomplish on your own
- Ask for a proposal so you can see samples of their ideas for your business
- Think about the long-term growth of your business. Changing agencies is not always easy. An agency that has the ability to scale and grow with your business is a great advantage
- Expertise. Does their expertise match your needs? An agency with expertise in one area may not have any expertise in another

- Fees and obligations. It's important to understand the fees they charge, the approval process for those fees (in advance of incurring fees), and the portion of your media investment that may go to the agency and not toward media. It's also important to understand your obligations and how you will separate from the agency if needed
- Your access to your assets. Your successful marketing is an immensely valuable asset for your business. Be careful to ensure that you retain all rights to that asset (e.g., creative assets, such as radio and television commercials, online advertisements, etc.)
- Tracking, measuring, and analysis. Robust information gives you the chance to make continual improvements. Data doesn't lie, but it can be easily manipulated. You'll want an agency with accurate, easy-to-use, and meaningful data and tools that are always available to you, and require them to review it with you on a regular basis
- Inspect what you expect. Many businesses are vigorous with their monitoring and involvement with their agencies at the beginning, and then they take their hands off the steering wheel. You're utilizing an agency to improve your performance; if that is not happening after a reasonable period of time, your expectations are not being met, and it's time to make a change. See Section 8.37, "Inspect What You Expect," for more information.

When you make the decision to utilize an agency, it's because you want to take what you've done (e.g., your existing marketing, your product, your service, etc.) and make it better—in collaboration—with their expertise. Viewing an agency as a collaboration partner is important because you both possess expertise that works better together to help your business succeed.

An agency cannot replace you and your passion for your business, product(s), service(s), customers, etc. Never reach the point where you're not involved and collaborating on your marketing because doing so can have dire consequences. Think of your collaboration as a wonderful pie; you're the crust and they are the filling. One, without the other, is simply not a pie.

Marketing is not an activity you can put on autopilot and step away from. You are the expert about your business, product(s), and/or service(s). You and your employees are in direct contact with your prospects and customers, and the agency is not. Your marketing needs your passion, expertise, and your prospect and customer knowledge because, rarely, can it be duplicated by anyone else.

Equally, remember that an agency typically has multiple employees and a tiered management style. Therefore, the communications within and management of the agency affect your results. A successful agency must be able to easily convey and carry out your advertising and marketing plans throughout their organization.

When you choose to put your marketing in the hands of another, remember that you're making an investment that directly impacts your success. That investment needs expertise and passion, and it needs to be monitored, managed, tracked, and adjusted. Forget assumptions; this is the time to actively inspect what you expect (see Section 8.37, "Inspect What You Expect"). It's never the time to set it and forget it.

2.12 * MEASUREMENT AND ANALYSIS

Measurement and analysis is a challenging and opportunity-rich aspect of Guerrilla Maximedia Marketing success. In Volume 1, Section 2.8, "Advertising Keys to Success," we addressed the core components of tracking and measuring. We'll consider more in this section, which will help you to identify what's working. When your business knows what's working, you can do more of it and turbo-charge your success. Equally, your business can identify what's not working so you can do less of it while you adjust it, either improving its success or, ultimately, stop doing it altogether.

The more advertising you're investing in, measuring your results grows in importance. Many business owners engage in tools to help them track their advertising (e.g., unique coupon codes, call-tracking phone numbers, unique URLs, unique offers, QR codes, etc.). It's the successful Guerrilla marketers that take the time to turn tracking data into measurements of their marketing. Why? Simply put, it's just not easy to do, and there are only so many hours in the day.

When you're advertising in multiple channels (e.g., online, television, radio, podcasts, etc.), measurement tools will help you see the patterns and impact of your advertising. One of the greatest advertising challenges for any business is to know what's working and what's not, and, just as importantly, how all of your advertising is working together. Finding the answers is not always easy, but the right answers are quite profitable.

When you combine measurement tools with your Customer Relationship Management (CRM) system, you can see when and where your sales are happening so you can find patterns that will help you make profitable improvements to your marketing. For example, by measuring your advertising and media with the right tools, you may find that a significant portion of your sales occur when your television commercials are airing.

You may also find patterns, such as radio advertising increases purchases at your physical business/retail locations and television increases your online sales. That information gives you valuable insight to help you improve your advertising by refining your messages and promotions. For example, assuming the same pattern, your television commercial promotions may be more effective with "free shipping" (since viewers are responding with online purchases), and your radio advertising may be more effective with in-store only or delivery promotions.

Your measurement can also help you determine how much of your budget to dedicate to each media format and what time of day is the most effective for each media format.

Fortunately, there are several measurement tools available to help you refine and improve your Guerrilla Maximedia Marketing success. There are media mention tools that can help you measure the quantity and places where your business name is mentioned. There are also tools whose focus is online mentions and tools that gather broader data, such as radio and television.

As examples, these tools can help with measurement and attribution:

- Nielsen Marketing Effectiveness Tools (multichannel along with non-marketing factors measurement and attribution)
- iSpot.tv (television measurement and attribution)
- TVEyes (television and radio measurement)
- Claritas (multichannel measurement and attribution)
- Cision (media monitoring and attribution)
- News Exposure (multichannel monitoring and data analysis)

Whether you're doing a lot of advertising or a little bit of advertising, the goal is to increase your business profits. You're making an investment when you advertise. When you make a financial investment, you measure your returns. Your advertising is made profitable when you measure it and optimize it.

Begin with free tools like Google alerts to help you track online mentions of your business, industry, product(s), and/or service(s). As your advertising investment grows, so should your investment in measurement and analysis tools to determine your results, which allow your business to repeat what's working and improve your success. Invest your time, as well, to determine and implement needed improvements. Measuring and analyzing your results is an ongoing process.

In Volume 3, Section 2.16, "Testing," and Section 2.17, "Attribution," we'll dive deeper into the options available to your business to improve your marketing success.

2.13 * ReSPONSe

Compelling your prospects and customers to respond to your advertising is the obvious key to engagement, building relationships, and creating sales and profits. Unfortunately, many businesses get in their own way and limit their potential responses.

There are multiple components that impact response rates. Let's look at the components that Guerrilla marketers proactively manage to maximize their responses.

Compelling

There are many factors that determine if your message is compelling, such as:

- Is your message relevant?
- Are you speaking the buying language of your customers and prospects?
- Are you expressing what makes your business, product(s), or service(s) unique?
- Are you taking your prospects and customers on a journey from where they are (e.g., speaking to their pain points) to where they want to be (e.g., speaking to their pleasure points)?

If your business is talking about pain points and pleasure points that your prospects and customers cannot relate to, your message is not compelling. If your business isn't clearly sharing how your product(s) or service(s) is uniquely the best solution, your advertising is benefiting your competition as much or more than your business.

Ease of Response

Removing all obstacles is important to maximize your responses. You may have a compelling message that your prospects and customers attempt to respond to, but they can't easily find the offer, product(s), or service(s), and your window of opportunity quickly closes. They get distracted and move on to something else or they may find your competition instead. Guerrilla marketers seek to be obstacle-free.

- Is your website able to handle increases in traffic?
- Have you tested your links to ensure they are working?
- Are your employees well-versed in your advertising efforts and promotions? Equally, are they well-trained to deliver on your promotions
- Are you using QR codes and/or coupon codes to ensure that your responding prospects and customers can easily access your product(s), service(s), and promotions? Have those codes been carefully tested and set up correctly to deliver a seamless experience?

Ease of Sharing

If your prospects and customers love to share a great product, service, or a wonderful shopping deal, Guerrilla marketers make it easy for them to do so. By utilizing social media sharing tools, your business gains valuable insight about what compels your prospects and customers—when you take the time to analyze the results. See Section 5.18, "Sharing Tools," for more information.

Tracking and Measuring

Guerrilla marketers continually improve their success with the simple act of doing more of what works and less of what doesn't. That sounds simple, but it means investing in tracking and measuring. It also means taking those results, assessing them, and successfully making changes.

Using simple tracking tools, such as unique promotions, hashtags, QR codes, coupon codes, URLs, and phone numbers are helpful. With that valuable tracking information, Guerrilla marketers take the time to measure and analyze their results. Be sure to refer to the prior Section 2.12, "Measurement and Analysis," to learn more.

Guerrilla marketers know that the more they understand what their prospects and customers respond to, the easier it is to increase their responses and engagement. Engaged prospects and customers help you build a business with long-term success.

2.14 * CREATIVITY AND PRACTICALITY

Effective Guerrilla Maximedia Marketing is creative, clear, focused, compelling, and consistent, and it results in purchases by your prospects, repeat purchases by your customers, and precious referrals, which is the fuel for long-term success. Guerrilla Maximedia Marketing requires finding the right balance between being creative and being practical, which pays off in profits for your business.

As we shared in the "Overview" at the beginning of the book and in detail in Volume 1, Section 1.2, "Guerrilla Creativity," the measurement of your creativity is determined by your profits. The more profitable your marketing is, the more creative it is.

There are several mistakes that can be made in pursuit of creativity. A Guerrilla marketer is careful to consider the common pitfalls and mistakes that marketers make.

Entertainment

Your job as a Guerrilla marketer is to increase your sales and profits. It's not your job to simply entertain your prospects and customers (unless you're in the entertainment/performance industry). Marketing that entertains people who don't feel compelled to make purchases is not producing the results you seek.

Humor

It can be effective to reach your prospects and customers by using humor. However, it's important to understand that humor is subjective, and what entertains one prospect can offend or repel another prospect. Humor also has a short lifespan, so you'll need to refresh it constantly. Additionally, effective humor must convey your USP and speak the buying language of your prospects and customers (including their pain points and pleasure points). Humor must also compel and motivate your prospects and customers to make purchases.

Minimalism

Many advertisers and marketers want to pique the interest of their prospects and customers and then, *ta-da*, reveal their business name, product, or service for a quick moment. When there are multiple commas in your advertising and marketing budget, you can choose to take that gamble and back it with significant (and expensive) repetition and see if it produces results.

Guerrilla marketers, on the other hand, seek to make every advertising and marketing investment work overtime for them. Therefore, Guerrilla marketers avoid minimalism and find creative ways to have their business, product(s), or service(s) promoted for the maximum time in their advertising and marketing. Therefore, they avoid *mistakes* like:

- Putting their business name, logo, QR code, and/or calls to action at the bottom of their online advertising. For example, Yahoo Mail has millions of active users who are served with vertical banner ads. Countless advertisers, every day, put their name and call to action at the bottom of their ads, which is out of view unless the user chooses to scroll down during the very short duration when the ad appears.
- Not speaking their business name and call to action in video-based advertising (online, television, etc.), which means that their prospects and customers who are not looking at the screen never notice their advertising. Equally, not showing their business name and call to action until the last second means that everyone who was not looking at their screens at that second, also never noticed their advertising.

Your prospects and customers are busy and distracted, and you must compete for their attention. You're doing well if you can get a fraction of a second of their attention, so don't waste that moment. Make sure they see your logo and see and hear your business name.

You can creatively weave your business name and logo throughout your advertising with signage in the background, uniforms and apparel showcasing your logo, a hashtag with your business name in the corner, a tagline, a meme, and a jingle. Don't hesitate to always keep your name/logo (and/or QR code) visible in your advertising. After all, have you ever noticed that many of the shows you view on your television or another device always keep their name/logo constantly visible?

It's important to recognize that your prospects likely have a variety of buying habits. Some of them know very quickly if they want your product. Others may take a lot longer to convince and compel. Consistency and repetition in your advertising, along with creating the right balance between creativity and practicality, will help you maximize the profits that your marketing investments generate.

2.15 ∗ endorsements

Guerrilla marketers set their Guerrilla Maximedia Marketing investments apart by maximizing endorsements. When you take the time and put in the effort to secure endorsements, you can break through the clutter of competing (direct and indirect) advertising that your business is up against.

Effective endorsements can be presented in a variety of forms and can be implied or direct.

Aspirational People in Your Advertising
A savvy Guerrilla Marketer knows who their prospects and customers are. By featuring people in their advertising that reflect who their prospects and customers are, want to be, or want to be seen as, they are receiving an effective endorsement. This persuasive endorsement mostly takes place in the subconscious minds of your prospects and customers (see Volume 1, Sections 6.9, "Consumer Behavior," and 8.32, "Subliminal Marketing," for more information). Guerrilla marketers tend to the tiny, supercharged details that can generate big profits.

Influential Personalities
Influential personalities can be niche, local, regional, or national in their reach. The more your prospects and customers admire them, the more value their implied or direct endorsement will have when it comes to selling your product(s) or service(s). Most people think of celebrities, which can be effective, but there are other options to consider, such as:
- News broadcasters (e.g., TV, radio, podcasts, etc.)
- Sports figures (current or retired)
- Social media influencers with targeted large or niche followings
- Writers/authors (e.g., books, publications, blogs, etc.)

- Broadcast personalities (e.g., radio DJs, podcasters, experts, etc.)

See Volume 1, Section 4.6, "Influencer Marketing," to better understand how to be effective.

Ratings and Reviews

Guerrilla marketers go the extra mile to earn the praise of their customers and promoting that praise is a fantastic and inexpensive way to attract prospects to your business and compel your customers to make repeat purchases. Direct endorsements from your customers in ratings and reviews are a powerful and compelling factor that motivates your prospects to become customers.

When it comes to ratings, the more positive reviews you have, the better, but it's not a rule. You can market your fifty five-star reviews instead of marketing an overall 4.3 rating. Your substantial number of five-star reviews can be more influential.

For example, while most television shows rely on promoting reviews from critics, to promote the show *Clarice*, CBS ran television advertisements that featured a few rave reviews from Twitter. Comments and reviews can be influential in smaller numbers when they are promoted effectively.

Positive reviews from sources other than your customers can also be effective. Industry, news, or media sources that provide positive reviews are effective, implied endorsements. By promoting those positive reviews to your customers, you'll motivate them to make repeat purchases and provide precious referrals of their friends, family, and associates to your business.

Guerrilla marketers are wise to pay extra attention to their competitors' reviews, either positive or less than positive. Why? Those reviews can provide free and valuable information about your competitors' product(s) and service(s). That valuable information also gives you the opportunity to identify improvements for your product(s) and service(s). Equally, that valuable information can help you identify new product(s) and service(s) that will appeal to your customers and prospects.

Interviews and Appearances

Interviews (as the interviewer or the interviewee) with influential people (e.g., DJs, news broadcasters, TV personalities, bloggers, podcasters, etc.) can create implied endorsements. The interviews leverage their followers, fans, and audience, thereby expanding yours. From local to national interviews, the opportunity to share your USP is your opportunity to compel your prospects to become customers and excite your customers so they make repeat purchases.

Utilization

A Guerrilla marketer is always on the watch for opportunities to combine their advertising with the use of their product(s) or service(s) to have a fully integrated marketing opportunity. For example, AT&T was the initial "message your vote" partner for *American Idol*. And coaches and players throughout NFL broadcasts are shown using Microsoft Surface tablets and Bose headsets.

Media Sponsorships

Guerrilla marketers look for opportunities to sponsor shows and segments (e.g., radio, television, etc.) to create implied endorsements. Those media sponsorships can include airing your custom-created advertising that connects your business to the show, and they can include promotional messages recorded by the show's stars.

For example, radio DJs can directly endorse your product(s) or service(s) (sometimes referred to as "DJ Chatter"). Your business can provide a script for the DJ, or you can work with them to speak from their own point of view and experience while promoting particular points you provide. Typically, the more they speak freely, the more effective their endorsement is at compelling their audience to take action and engage with your business, product(s), or service(s). See Section 2.9, "Radio Presence/Influence," for more information.

PBS is a great example of a television media outlet that works with its sponsors to promote its brands. Liberty Mutual has sponsored *Antiques Roadshow* (which often references insurance value in their appraised values) for fifteen years at the time of the writing of this book. They air custom-created advertising that connects their insurance products to the show and its viewers. Liberty Mutual is spotlighted and participates online as well as during the recorded *Antiques Roadshow* events. Their sponsorship gives them the ability to promote their insurance by connecting and interacting with prospects and customers while they're enjoying their favorite television show, one that Liberty Mutual's sponsorship helps to keep on the air.

Media sponsorships are effective at attracting the interest of your prospects when you customize your message and advertising to connect with the show and, thereby, its viewers and your prospects. Refer to Section 2.10, "Bartering," for additional opportunities to increase the success of your media sponsorships.

Keys to Success

To effectively utilize endorsements, you must know your prospects and customers and what entertains, compels, and motivates them. That knowledge helps you identify which endorsements would be influential and will positively promote your product(s) or service(s).

If you're unsure, it's wise to test your ideas before making an investment in promoting your endorsements. You can simply test your ideas with your customers by sending or posting a quote or story from different personalities or, alternately, you can share your ratings and reviews.

Guerrilla marketers monitor who/what their customers and prospects respond to the most. Taking the time to carefully review those responses will ensure that you're receiving the right responses. People are often more motivated to respond negatively than positively, so don't make the mistake of assuming that the quantity of responses implies a potentially effective endorsement.

If you decide to choose a personality, make sure that personality is influential in the media (i.e., TV, radio, newspaper, podcast, social media, etc.) that you've selected. For example, the endorsement of a social media influencer may have very little impact in your television advertising. Equally, a positive review from an industry expert may have little influence over a larger audience, which includes your customers and prospects.

Your investment in endorsements can include bartering with your expertise, product(s), or service(s). Refer to Section 2.10, "Bartering," for more information about successful bartering.

Lastly, Guerrilla marketers know that consistency builds familiarity; familiarity builds trust, and trust creates sales, repeat purchases, and precious referrals. Endorsements can take time to build and become memorable, persuasive, and effective. Being consistent with compelling messages is the key to connecting with your prospects.

SECTION III

Guerrilla Minimedia Marketing

GUERRILLA MINIMEDIA MARKETING

Your Guerrilla Minimedia Marketing lets your talent, Guerrilla Creativity, and style shine. You can color outside of the lines and be extraordinarily unconventional with your Guerrilla Minimedia Marketing. However, to be effective, your efforts must be built on a strong foundation and be consistent with all of your marketing.

When you align your Guerrilla Minimedia Marketing with your Guerrilla Marketing plan, USP, Guerrilla Creative and Advertising strategy, Guerrilla ten words, and Guerrilla Company Attributes and Attitudes, you're engaging in intelligent and effective marketing.

As a Guerrilla marketer, you know that your marketing efforts work together, just like each instrument in a band that, when playing the same song in perfect harmony, creates extraordinary music. Your goal is simple: Clearly and consistently communicate your compelling marketing messages (e.g., your competitive advantages, and USP, etc.) as you address the pain points of your prospects and customers to generate profits.

Resist the temptation to communicate many different and/or disconnected marketing messages. When you communicate too much, you're communicating nothing at all. Your prospects and customers have a limited attention span, which means you must make every word in your marketing message(s) compelling. Each marketing message should compel your prospects and customers to engage with your business and make a purchase or learn more.

Additionally, resist the temptation to communicate marketing messages that are interesting to you but irrelevant for your prospects or customers. Your goal is to be compelling, engaging, and motivating.

In Volume 1, we addressed:

3.1   Interior Design and Signage
3.2   Exterior Signage
3.3   Vehicle Wraps
3.4   Business Cards
3.5   Digital Templates and Stationery
3.6   Personalization
3.7   Telephone Marketing
3.8   Easy Contact
3.9   A Vanity Phone Number

Now, we'll pick up where we left off. Without further ado, let's get started.

3.22 * PROMOTIONAL ITEM ADVERTISING

Making a compelling impression that lasts and is sharable is a great marketing investment. Guerrilla marketers put their Guerrilla Creativity to use as they develop promotional items that serve as advertising for their business.

Where do you begin? Guerrilla marketers know that effective advertising and marketing always begins with their knowledge of their customers and prospects. Here are some examples of businesses with promotional items that advertise their business.

- Apple logo decals/clings included with their products
- Ron Jon Surf Shop branded automobile stickers/clings/decals
- Salt Life branded automobile stickers/clings/decals
- Automobile dealers that provide branded license plate frames
- A manufacturer that provides desirable branded clothing (e.g., a golf equipment manufacturer that provides an exclusive golf shirt)
- Retailers and businesses that provide branded and re-usable bags (see Section 3.29, "Shopping Bags," for more information)

- A business that provides branded computer camera privacy covers to their targeted and appreciated customers (who now see that business logo in front of them on their computer screens every day)

How do you create a promotional item that your customers want to display (and therefore advertise your business)? Guerrilla marketers begin by understanding the lifestyle of their customers. Once they do, they can identify opportunities to seamlessly provide a promotional item that their customers value, want to share, and will utilize to advertise your business.

For example, Salt Life and Ron Jon Surf Shop are lifestyle businesses. They sell products that appeal to and are aligned with the consumers' lifestyle of being near and in water. Stickers and clings are an effective way for their customers to celebrate and share their love of their lifestyle, while they are advertising for the business.

Additionally, customers connect with businesses they feel uniquely understand their needs and provide effective and high-quality solutions (e.g., automobiles, technology, etc.) to their problems. That connection creates customers who want to display and share (and therefore advertise) promotional items for the business.

To get your momentum going, your business can begin by giving away your promotional item. As the promotional item is displayed and demand increases, your business can begin selling them instead of giving them away. However, don't lose focus on your goal, which is advertising your business.

To advertise your business, effective promotional items must simply and clearly advertise your consistent business name and/or logo. You'll be effective if your name and/or logo are consistent and therefore recognizable.

It's important to note that effective promotional item advertising can also be on a smaller scale, such as:

- Installers and service professionals that place promotional stickers on equipment and provide magnets (e.g., heating, air conditioning, plumbing, etc.)
- Branded key chains that keep the dealer's name top-of-mind when the automobile is ready to be serviced.

While these promotional items don't garner the same advertising exposure as others, they provide valuable advertising at exactly the right time. Guerrilla marketers make their efforts successful by going beyond a simple, "For service, call . . ." Guerrilla marketers utilize promotional items that can convey their USP (e.g., stickers, magnets, etc.) to compel their customers to want to contact them first. To make it easy for that contact to happen, they utilize a QR code, unique URL, direct phone number, etc.

It's worth repeating that to be effective, your promotional items must simply and clearly advertise your consistent business name and/or logo and, if possible, a call to action. Ideally, your promotional items (from a service sticker to a car decal) will last for years, and the resulting benefit for your business is multiplied with your clarity and consistency.

For example, if your business name cannot be easily read/distinguished, that's years of lost advertising opportunities. Equally, if you change your business name and/or your logo, you've lost the advertising opportunity. Instead of reaping the success from your advertising building recognition, over time, of your consistent logo and business name on your promotional items, you're instead choosing disconnected images and names that get lost in a sea of advertising. That's an advertising investment that does little or nothing for your business's success.

3.23 * PROMOTIONAL ITEM MARKETING

Like many businesses, you want to give your customers and prospects a promotional item to express your gratitude, to keep your business top-of-mind, and to build your relationships. Whether it's at events, tradeshows, or one-on-one sales opportunities, promotional items can effectively market your business. How do you make your promotional item(s) stand out?

Guerrilla marketers utilize promotional items that are high-quality, unique, problem-solving, related to their business, and easily recognized as being from your business (i.e., brand recognition). They know the goal is for their promotional item to be frequently used and a consistent happy reminder of their business.

A promotional item, as simple as a pen can accomplish your goals by being unique, functional, problem-solving, and identifiable with your business. By making the pen your customers' and prospects' "go-to" (favorite) pen, you're part of the way there. By making it unmistakably from your business, you're making even more progress. By making it do something that no other pen, among the vast number of pens they have, can do, you're continuing to make progress.

When they contact you to make a purchase or a repeat purchase, and they mention how much they love that pen, now you've accomplished your goal. You'll happily include more pens with their order so they can share them with their friends and associates.

The list of promotional items is endless. The success of your promotional item marketing lies in finding items that your prospects and customers consider to be high-quality, unique, problem-solving, memorable, and worth talking about. At the same time, your promotional items need to relate to and be easily recognized as being from your business (i.e., brand recognition) and aligned with your Guerrilla Company Attributes (see Section VIII) and Guerrilla Company Attitudes (see Section IX).

When you accomplish success, you're utilizing quality items (a lack of quality can do far more harm than good), and your prospects and customers are clamoring for, raving about, and sharing your promotional items, which extends your marketing reach (without extending your budget) with powerful endorsements from your prospects and customers. For example, these promotional items have created wide-scale sharing and news coverage:

- Dairy Queen has marketed a "Sweeter Vest" that is cleverly designed with a pocket to hold their product
- Pizza Hut has marketed "Pie Tops," which are high-top sneakers with a button that orders pizza
- Red Lobster has marketed an insulated fanny pack to keep their signature biscuits warm

Both your successful promotional items for advertising (see Section 3.22, "Promotional Item Advertising") and your promotional items for marketing are great opportunities for your Guerrilla knowledge and Creativity to shine. When that opportunity is fully maximized, those items become so popular and desirable that they can also be utilized to stimulate sales (e.g., a gift with purchase). They can also, effortlessly, be products (e.g., the products referenced in the bullet points) that your business sells to help build your brand (see Volume 1, Section 8.1, "Brand").

3.24 * DRONE MARKETING

Drones can provide unexpected advertising and marketing opportunities. If your customers and prospects are innovative and technology-friendly, drone advertising can be an unconventional and creative way to break through the sea of advertising and marketing to promote your business, product(s), and service(s). Here are some examples of what your business can do with drones.

Advertising

Drones can be hired for numerous advertising initiatives to help your business stand out from the crowd. From banner advertising (indoor or outdoor) to programmed light shows that promote your business, there are a growing number of opportunities.

Content

From products to locations, drones are a great way to create dramatic and engaging video content to utilize in your marketing. You can use drones to film your product(s) (e.g., real estate), events (e.g., sports, entertainment, weddings, or parties), business location, and/or behind the scenes access (e.g., filming of a commercial, filming of a fashion photoshoot, etc.). Drone footage provides dramatic and compelling content that motivates your prospects and customers. For example, seeing pictures of your vacation rental, B&B, or hotel is interesting. Seeing a drone video of people enjoying your hotel at the pool, bar, golf course, and the beach is compelling, and it brings them into the experience and motivates them to make a reservation.

Service

By utilizing drones, businesses can show maintenance and service issues their customers may not otherwise see. Drones can also provide extraordinary video footage of issues prior to any service. When your business successfully completes the repairs and/or maintenance, for both residential and commercial service businesses, drones can provide video footage for you to share with your satisfied customers.

If drone marketing is a fit for your prospects and customers, it's a great opportunity to grab their attention and create a memorable experience that turns into profits for your business. To be effective, your drone advertising, for example, must contain a unique call to action that motivates your prospects and customers to make a trackable desired action (e.g., a download, make a purchase, etc.). That unique and trackable offer must then be measured to determine the performance and success of your drone advertising.

3.25 * MAPPING

If you have a business with a physical location, mapping services are an inexpensive way for Guerrilla marketers to succeed by tending to the tiny, supercharged details that can generate big profits. When you invest the time to complete your profiles and utilize convenient services for enhanced functionality, your prospects and customers can interact with your business with ease.

Google Maps

A profitable free tool is at your fingertips with Google Maps. When you fully utilize Google My Business, your Google Maps profile is robust with photos, business hours, promotions, ratings/reviews, and links for appointment setting, reservations, estimate requests, gift cards, online classes, and more. Refer to Volume 1, Section 4.22, "Google My Business," for details.

With your Google Business Profile fully built out, you can then begin advertising. Do keep in mind that placing ads prior to fully building out your (free) Google Business Profile is far less effective. Guerrilla marketers leave those unnecessary mistakes to their competition.

Utilizing local campaigns with Google Ads can allow your ads to be displayed at the right time, such as:

- **Auto-suggest:** your ad will be displayed in Google Maps when users search for a business like yours, in the area
- **Navigational:** your ad will be displayed while relevant users are navigating close to your business
- **Similar places:** your ad will appear when users are searching for a similar business nearby

Online Searches and Mapping

When your prospects and customers are searching for your business or a business like yours, it's time for your business to shine. It sounds easy—and it is—but keep in mind that you'll want to invest your energy and customer knowledge.

There are numerous ways they will search; some will turn to mapping services other than Google Maps, such as:

- Waze
- Apple Maps
- MapQuest
- Bing Maps

However, your prospects and customers may also turn to other search options, including:

- Social media, such as Facebook, Snapchat, Nextdoor, LinkedIn, etc.
- Travel and leisure sites, such as Foursquare City Guides and Trip Advisor, which allow users to select the places and businesses they want to visit and create a map
- Industry-specific apps and websites, such as OpenTable, Spafinder, and Rover that feature only participating businesses
- Search engines, such as Bing, Yahoo, etc.
- Directories, such as Yelp and Yellow Pages. Refer to Volume 1, Section 4.23, "Directory and Search Engine Listings," for more information about the many opportunities that are available for listing your business

Conclusion

Regardless of how your customers map and/or search for your business or businesses like yours, your goal is to, first, be found and to, second, be compelling, engaging, and motivating. By being motivating, your customers and prospects stop searching and head to your business.

Guerrilla marketers begin with fully utilizing their free profiles and listings. Once your business is fully maximizing those low-cost opportunities, as an ongoing and engaging activity, it's time to look at marketing and advertising opportunities to boost your business.

For example, Google offers search ads, and they offer promoted pins on Google Maps. According to Google, over one billion people use Google Maps each month. If search results for your business yield multiple results, a promoted pin can help your business stand out. With Google's performance tracking, your marketing investment is easily monitored to ensure that it's working for your business.

Your business can also participate in industry-specific apps and websites. Your prospects and customers may consider an industry-specific app and/or website to be their "go-to" option to find where they want to go or what they want to do. For example, restaurants can participate in systems, such as OpenTable and Resy, and food trucks can participate with Roaming Hunger. Tapping into the "go-to" apps and websites for your industry can be a worthy marketing investment to reach your prospects and customers at the important moment when they are ready to make a purchase.

3.26 * RECEIPT MARKETING

Guerrilla marketers value receipt marketing because it gives them multiple valuable opportunities. Whether your customer's purchase is made online or at your location, every receipt your business provides is an opportunity to build relationships and incentivize repeat purchases. Along with your gratitude for their purchase, your business can offer or promote:

- Coupons
- Event and sale promotions
- Surveys
- Membership clubs
- Loyalty programs
- Referral programs
- Online features, such as appointment setting, delivery, and/or curbside pick-up, etc.
- Gift cards and/or gift ideas
- Exclusive products or services
- Ratings and reviews
- Instructions and/or warranty information
- Your app

It's important to give careful consideration to any promotional offer to avoid harmful conflicts with their current purchase. The last thing you want to do is have a customer dissatisfied because your receipt marketing offers a promotion or sale they think should apply to the purchase they just made.

Making an offer that is clearly focused on a future purchase provides a welcome and compelling opportunity for your customers. Consider offers, such as:

- Complimentary products, based on what they purchased
- Early access to a future sale
- Discounts for online purchases for those that purchased at your store
- Reminders of your value, quantity discounts, and loyalty program

To enhance the response rate of your messages and offers, make it easy for your customers to connect by utilizing QR codes. Also, make an offer that is short in duration to keep your offer top-of-mind. Whether you're using e-receipts or printed receipts, don't miss out on the valuable opportunities that your receipts provide.

For printed receipts at your business location, you can simply preprint the back or attach a card or small promotional flyer, or you can use a receipt envelope to deliver your message. However, the most ideal way to deliver your message is to utilize an integrated point-of-sale system. Integrated point-of-sale systems, like those offered by Clover, Square, and Shopify, enable your business to utilize point-of-sale technology that is rich with features.

With the right integrated point-of-sale system, you'll have the ability to make dynamic offers, based on your customers' purchases. Perhaps you want to promote a product or service that's complementary to their purchase. You can also seamlessly track your responses, which is a necessity to learn what's working so you can do more of it. The more you know about your customers, the more effective you'll be with personalization, which is the fuel for long-term success. See Volume 1, Section 3.6, "Personalization," for more information about the power that personalization offers your business.

Your integrated point-of-sale system will also allow your business to send receipts to your customers' email addresses, just as online businesses do. Emailed receipts are a more powerful way to reach and connect with your customers. Many customers prefer the environmental benefits of skipping paper receipts and enjoy the convenience of emailed receipts. Guerrilla marketers understand the importance of meeting and exceeding their customers' technology preferences (see Volume 1, Section 9.3, "Technology Friendly").

When you're emailing receipts, it's a good practice to use a concise subject line and make it printer-friendly. Additionally, it's a good practice to let your customers know the email address that you'll be sending it from, to help them locate the receipt, should it end up in a tab or folder, instead of their inbox. Your ease of delivery opens the door for customer satisfaction and the precious gift of repeat purchases by your customers.

3.27 * RETAIL LOCATION SELECTION

Choosing a retail location is a daunting task for any business. The tiniest issues can dramatically impact your success at a location. Fortunately, Guerrilla marketers don't just look at what is, they look at what can be. They know a few good secrets to help guide them.

Matching Locations With Your Business

Fortunately, long gone are the days of "one-size-fits-all retail" location options. Businesses have numerous choices when it comes to selecting retail locations, such as:

- Store-in-store (such as the many businesses located inside Walmart)
- Vending machines
- Food halls or courts
- Pop-ups
- Kiosks
- Self-serve locker systems (for pick-up and/or drop-off services)
- On-wheels/mobile

Your Guerrilla Creativity will help you realize that those options are not either/or. Instead, your business can utilize a continually evolving mix of options to find what is optimal for your prospects and customers and for your business's success. For example, the bakery company Sprinkle's has a cupcake ATM at many of its locations. They also have the advantage of having locations in high-traffic areas (e.g., malls) that are cupcake ATMs only. Those ATMs provide a far less expensive way (vs. staffing a location around the clock) to make it easy for their customers to make a purchase anytime they choose. See Guerrilla Marketing Case Study 5 to learn more about Sprinkles.

Additionally, a dry cleaner can enhance its convenience by offering self-serve lockers at its location. It can also expand its business by offering self-serve locations in various other convenient locations (e.g., condominiums, apartment complexes, offices, grocery stores, etc.).

Also, consider that many existing retailers and office buildings are looking for ways to better utilize their existing locations. Therefore, they may be open and welcoming to your Guerrilla Creativity.

Perhaps a pop-up or a store within their store can be a mutually beneficial option. Equally, a daily pop-up restaurant with convenient lunch options, in an office building, can be an asset for the tenants.

Even if what you're thinking is not being done today, it doesn't mean that you can't convince them of what tomorrow could be. Imagine the first time someone suggested opening a coffee shop inside a bookstore. That winning idea may not have been initially welcomed with open arms.

Be Where Your Customers Are When They Are Most Likely to Purchase Your Product(s) or Service(s)

Many businesses think only of having a retail location where their customers live or work. Guerrilla marketers certainly understand that advantage, but they also know that where they live or work may not be where (and when) they are most likely to purchase their product(s) or service(s).

Your customers and prospects might be most motivated to make purchases at odd hours. Perhaps it's only when they're visiting someone else (e.g., family, friends, etc.), only when they're traveling, or only when they're at a particular venue.

Find Neighbors to Boost Your Business

When you have determined an area that is well-suited for your prospects and customers, it's time to turn your attention to your potential neighbors. Your customers and prospects may be more motivated to make purchases from your business simply based on your proximity to neighboring businesses. Equally, they may be unmotivated based on your neighboring businesses.

Compatible and complementary businesses that share your prospects', customers', and business's hours, can effortlessly boost your sales and profits. For example, a juice bar or health food store can benefit from being conveniently located near exercise and recreation stores or venues. Equally, a clothing or accessory store can benefit from being located next to a barber, salon, or spa.

Be aware that sometimes your ideal location may not be an option. Consider that many large retailers will sign exclusive leases that prohibit competing businesses within the shopping center. For example, a grocery store will often prohibit bakeries, flower shops, and/or wine or liquor stores. Therefore, those businesses must apply a bit more creativity to find optimal locations and/or collaborate with other businesses to accomplish their goals.

Consider Your Advertising Potential

Your retail location, ideally, is an advertisement that compels your prospects and customers to eagerly "step right in." Guerrilla marketers look for how they can make their business locations, regardless of their size, the most noticed business in the area. Will you be able to hand out samples, utilize the outside of your location, have dedicated parking with signs promoting your store, etc.?

The more options you have, the more your creativity will attract your prospects and customers. Even in a shopping center that requires every business to have the same size, shape, and designed sign, a Guerrilla marketer's creativity can make them stand out from the rest (see Volume 1, Section 3.1, "Interior Design and Signage," and 3.2, "Exterior Signage," for more).

Conclusion

Choosing a successful retail location requires Guerrilla Creativity, lateral thinking (see Section 9.23, "Lateral Thinking"), imagination, flexibility, and a great deal of current and ongoing research and knowledge about your prospects and customers. The tiniest issues can dramatically impact your success at a location, so Guerrilla marketers continually pay attention to the details. Just as your customers' needs and desires change and evolve, your business location(s) must be nimble and prepared to adapt to meet your customers where they are (see Section 6.16, "Meet Prospects and Customers Where They Are"). Also see Section 7.23, "Expanded Distribution," for more ideas.

3.28 * PRODUCT LABELS

Product labeling is often your greatest, and sometimes only, opportunity to compel your prospects to make a purchase and your customers to make repeat purchases. Your product labels may be embedded in the product (e.g., etched, engraved, embroidered, printed, etc.), affixed (e.g., with adhesive, custom packaged, and printed or sewn-in), or hanging from your product (e.g., hangtags).

While your product labels are conveying needed information, they are also the voice of your business, especially for consumer packaged goods (CPG). If your prospects discover your product(s) on the retail shelf, your labels are the only marketing and advertising they see for your business.

Therefore, product labels set a quality tone, and they convey the attitude of your business. Guerrilla marketers are intentional with their product labels. They know that effective labels are compelling and memorable as they convey the right call to action.

Your labels are conveying the personality and attitude of your business. Your prospects and customers see your labels and quickly form an impression (see Volume 1, Section 6.9, "Consumer Behavior").

For some, it's the first impression. For others, it's a reinforcing impression because prospects and customers are seeking your product based on prior purchases or your other marketing efforts. But for many, it's the last impression before they decide if they will or will not buy your product. Therefore, Guerrilla marketers are careful to consider what their labels say about their Guerrilla Company Attributes (see Section VIII) and Guerrilla Company Attitudes (see Section IX) related to:

- The environment
- Quality
- Creativity
- Exclusivity and uniqueness
- Value consciousness (e.g., a discount coupon)
- Splurge worthiness
- Innovation

This means you must pour your knowledge, market and customer research, and creativity into the marketing opportunity your labels offer. Perhaps your business could:

- Incorporate augmented reality, which allows your prospects and customers to utilize their smartphone or tablet camera and an app and focus on a designated image, turning it into an immersive and interactive product experience
- Print on both sides, especially when your label is affixed and clear packaging allows your double-sided labels to stand out
- Consider using innovative materials, such as metalized film, foiling, or innovative inks that make your product stand out
- Flaunt your positive ratings and positive reviews and use a QR code to take them to a specified URL that shows them more reviews, or state "more than 200 five-star reviews (see Section 6.18, "Five-Star")
- Tell your unique story and/or your cause by using a few compelling words and a QR code to take them to a specified URL, which tells them more (and makes it easy for them to join your mailing list or social media)
- Take them, when it comes to apparel, to a specified URL that shows images of the clothing and social media posts, to which they can also contribute

A couple of innovative label ideas can be found in the wine industry. Krug is a champagne producer. They feature both a QR code and an identification code on each bottle. Using their app or website, their customers enter the identification code from their bottle and are immersed in a curated experience. Their customers can learn about the composition of the champagne as well as enjoy curated music and food pairing suggestions. Their customers can also connect with Krug and enjoy even more unique experiences.

On the other hand, 19 Crimes is a wine producer. They are utilizing augmented reality to create an entertaining, memorable, sharable, and immersive experience. With an app (e.g., Living Wine Labels) and a smartphone or tablet camera (ideally while on wi-fi), their labels come to life.

The augmented reality experience tells historical stories while they invite their customers to become infamous insiders. Additionally, to be even more engaging, immersive, and profitable, they created nineteen different corks that are randomly distributed with the bottles. By doing so, they build a relationship with their customers. The different corks compel their customers to collect all nineteen, which means they creatively reinforce their name and motivating their customers to make additional purchases. When you consider that the measurement of Guerrilla Creativity is profits, their program has the makings to measure up.

These marketers have taken a necessity—a product label—and turned it into a memorable, engaging, and sharable relationship-building experience that makes their customers feel special. They take what could be an ordinary product label interaction that lasts about a second and turned it into a compelling experience that invites and motivates, not just to build long-term relationships, but also to create repeat purchases and a desire by their customers to provide precious referrals of their friends, family, and associates, which is the fuel for the long-term success of any business.

3.29 * SHOPPING BAGS

Many businesses see shopping bags as an expense, and they want to spend as little as possible. Guerrilla marketers, on the other hand, see shopping bags as a reinforcement of why your customers chose to purchase your product. When done well, that reinforcement turns into an endorsement, and your shopping bag becomes an advertising platform that your customers like to share.

Therefore, shopping bags are a great opportunity to put your Guerrilla Creativity to profitable use. Ask yourself a few important questions:

- What will make my shopping bag stand out and be noticed and compelling for my customers and prospects?
- Is my shopping bag reusable and desirable enough to be re-used (e.g., washable, a useful pocket, an appealing design, etc.)?
- Does my shopping bag reflect my Guerrilla Company Attributes (see Section VIII) and Guerrilla Company Attitudes (see Section IX)?
- Can my shopping bag have an appealing dual function?
- Can my shopping bag double as a gift bag? If you sell products that are often given as gifts, providing a shopping bag that is perfectly suited to be gifted and ready to wow is a must (e.g., Tiffany & Co.)
- How can I make my shopping bag so compelling that when my customers upcycle and second-hand sell my product, the product is worth more because they also have my shopping bag (e.g., luxury brand clothing and accessories)?

- Can my shopping bag work for my business? For example, QR codes can make it easy for your customers to reach customer service, leave a rating or review, or join your email list and/or rewards program—all of which help you create long-lasting relationships. Hashtags can also be used to encourage sharing of their purchase of your products

Luxury brands excel at creating desirable shopping bags that enhance the appeal and value of their products. If you're selling a luxury product, you must also excel at creating an experience with your shopping bag. Consumers purchase luxury items and most enjoy the experience of strolling with and sharing their coveted shopping bag, as much as they enjoy the product inside that shopping bag.

Regardless of what you're selling, providing an interesting, functional, and appealing shopping bag is a great way for your business to be recognized (i.e., brand awareness and brand recognition), shared, valued, and advertised. Guerrilla marketers look to the lifestyle, pain points, and pleasure points (see Volume 1, Section 6.9, "Consumer Behavior") of their customers to find creative ways to turn an expense into a marketing and advertising investment, which then turns into profits.

SECTION IV

Guerrilla E-Media Marketing

GUERRILLA E-MEDIA MARKETING

Guerrilla E-Media Marketing encompasses many online Guerrilla Marketing tactics, tools, and tips, including those used in social media marketing, paid online advertising, your website, email marketing, creating revenue streams, SEO, viral marketing, data privacy, cybersecurity, and so much more.

Guerrillas view online marketing as an opportunity to not only generate sales but also to build and nurture relationships. A Guerrilla marketer views a prospect or customer who walks into their retail store or physical location just as they view their online prospects and customers. Each prospect and customer is unique and desiring personalized service that inspires them to make new and repeat purchases and provide precious referrals.

With the right Guerrilla E-Media Marketing tactics, grounded in a strong foundation of Guerrilla Marketing (see Section I) and aligned with your Guerrilla Media (see Sections II, III, V, and VI) and Non-Media (see Section VII) efforts, Guerrilla Company Attitudes (see Section IX), and Guerrilla Company Attributes (see Section VIII), your business will be far ahead of the competition. That alignment builds valuable familiarity with your prospects and customers. And when you avoid inconsistencies, your business is sidestepping unnecessary and expensive disruptions and roadblocks in your marketing. In Volume 3, Section 4.57, "Marketing and Sales Funnels," we'll dive deeper into the best ways to see how your marketing compels your prospects and motivates them to become customers.

Your prospects and customers have expectations, and it's the job of your business to meet and exceed those expectations with every single interaction you have with them. Your Guerrilla E-Media Marketing efforts provide the opportunity to learn more about your prospects and customers and deliver personalized marketing that exceeds their expectations.

When it comes to Guerrilla Marketing, your goal isn't to do more things; your goal is to do more of the right things and do them very well. That means that when you find something that you think will be effective in reaching your prospects, you must evaluate your own skills to make sure that your marketing effort is done well. You may need to learn new skills, and you may need to reach out to find skilled and talented people to help you.

In Volume 1, we addressed:

4.1   Data Privacy and Cybersecurity

Now, we'll pick up where we left off. Without further ado, let's get started.

4.45 * VOICE SEARCH

Your prospects and customers, more than ever, are seeking to be hands-free (e.g., smart speaker devices, headsets/earbuds, Bluetooth devices, etc.). It's easier than ever to use voice search, instead of your fingers. Whether it's your phone, tablet, computer, or virtual assistant devices, by simply using your voice, you no longer need to touch your device to receive the information you're looking for.

According to Statista, revenues in the smart speaker industry are projected to top thirty-five billion by 2025, and they estimate that over 150 million US households have smart speakers. Additionally, it's forecasted that by 2025, 75 percent of US households will have at least one smart speaker.

The most widely known services/devices are:

- Amazon Alexa
- Google Assistant
- Apple Siri
- Microsoft Cortana

Whether you want search results or you're using voice commands to control devices (e.g., virtual assistant devices, smart speaker devices, televisions, cars, appliances, household systems, etc.), your voice can do the work for you.

Why fumble for your device when you can simply say:

- "Hey, Siri, get me a list of pizza shops nearby"
- "What is the weather forecast today?"
- "Add laundry detergent to my . . ."
- "Where is the nearest . . .?"

- "Turn off the lights"
- "Tune to . . ."
- "Set the oven to . . ."

Your business, product(s), or service(s) need to be found in those searches. Additionally, your business has a convenience advantage when your products can function and be controlled by the billions of various voice devices.

In Volume 1, Section 4.18, "Search Engine Optimization," we addressed the tactics required. Included in that is on-page SEO (see Volume 1, Section 4.19, "On-Page SEO"), which includes the importance of having robust information on your website. That robust information includes questions and answers.

When your business answers the questions people conduct online searches for, your website is practicing on-page SEO, and those efforts are boosting your ranking in the search engine results.

Similarly, you'll want to optimize and add to those questions and answers for voice searches. To do so, think about the most common questions people might have when performing a voice search, such as:

- Accurate and timely information about your business (e.g., hours, days, locations, ratings, etc.)
- Answers for a specific problem they have or instructions they need

As an example of your on-page SEO, the page title will be the question. The URL of the page will be the question. The content on the page will answer the question. The better your answer is, the more likely it is that it'll get picked up by the search engines and either used for a traditional search or a voice search.

A key to maximizing your SEO is to be featured in Google snippets. A Google snippet is the content that appears in search results that describes a page before the link to the page. According to Google: "We display featured snippets when our systems determine this format will help people more easily discover what they're seeking, both from the description about the page and when they click on the link to read the page itself. They're especially helpful for those on mobile or searching by voice."

Therefore, optimizing for those Google snippets, with clear and relevant questions and answers, is a great way to tilt the search algorithms in your favor.

Your business can also create custom skills for the convenience of your customers. For example, let's look at how your business can create a skill for Amazon Alexa, which returns voice results and can also provide a graphical representation for capable devices.

According to Amazon:

"A custom skill typically gets a question or other information from the user and then replies with an answer or some action, such as ordering a car or a pizza. Users can invoke your skill by using your invocation name in combination with sample utterances and phrases defined by Alexa:

- Alexa, Get high tide for Seattle from Tide Pooler
- Alexa, Ask Recipes how do I make an omelet?"

To understand voice search better, learning how to utilize the devices will give you a boost. To learn how to fully maximize the opportunity for your business, become familiar with the capabilities of the most widely known services/devices (e.g., Amazon Alexa, Google Assistant, Apple Siri, etc.).

When people are asking a voice question that's directly related to the answer that your business can provide, you have a wonderful opportunity to have your business noticed while promoting your solution, product(s), or service(s). When done well, you clearly stated call to action, will turn that inquiry into a sale.

4.46 * ENHANCED IMAGES AND DESCRIPTIONS

Guerrilla marketers tend to the tiny, supercharged details that can generate big profits. Enhanced images and descriptions are one of those tiny, supercharged details. Poor pictures, slow loading pictures, and inaccurate or inadequate descriptions create roadblocks and, ultimately, dissatisfaction and lost sales and/or lost repeat purchases.

Therefore, Guerrilla marketers utilize quality images and photos as well as compelling, robust, and accurate descriptions to convey the quality of their product(s) and/or service(s). Where do you begin? Let's start with images.

Images

It seems easy enough to take photos and/or videos of your product(s) or service(s) and add them to your website. However, there are a number of ways to ensure that they are quality pictures, such as:

- Titles: take the time to convert your image name (e.g., 006.jpg) to an accurate and appropriate title, such as a name that is descriptive of the product. For example, NavyRuffleApronKissTheCook2022.jpg
- Alt text and captions: these are easy ways to improve your SEO (see Volume 1, Section 4.18, "Search Engine Optimization," for more information) and your accessibility and readability for your prospects and customers that utilize the assistance. Your alt text and captions should be the word representation of the photo. When your words conjure the same image as what's seen in the photo, you've done your job
- Image quality: a picture is worth a thousand words. An accurate and engaging image is worth a lot of profit, which means utilizing realistic and quality images is critical. Web images are usually 72 dpi (i.e., dots per inch) resolution, and images used for print are typically 300 ppi (i.e., pixels per inch) or more. For videos posted online, it's best to use high definition, 1024x768 or better. When it comes to online images or video, you want the maximum quality and the smallest file size to ensure fast-loading images
- Crowdsourcing: businesses, including Target, are crowdsourcing and featuring their customers (and influencers) who submit their images to ensure the realism of their images. Equally, Amazon allows its customers to post images in their reviews. User-generated content such as this is powerful. Crowdsourcing your images can also come from social media, reviews of your product(s), images of your product being used, and even your product being unboxed. Those images provide a different perspective that your business can leverage because prospects and customers tend to trust other customers even more than your business

By utilizing quality images, titles, and descriptions, your images are working for your business as your website is indexed. Utilize this tiny, supercharged detail that provides an opportunity to help drive traffic to your website and create sales of your products and/or services.

Descriptions

Now, it's time to turn to the tiny, supercharged details of your descriptions. Traditionally, businesses utilized descriptions that simply conveyed the features and specifications of the product(s) or service(s). Guerrilla marketers do that as well, but they also choose to describe the qualitative and benefit-oriented information about their product(s) and/or service(s). For example:

- Who is the product for?
- What is the use and application of the product?
- What problems does it solve and/or what pain point does it solve?
- Any awards or honors
- What makes it exclusive—such as patents—and unique?
- Customer praise and accolades

When your prospects and customers are reading your descriptions, they are in a buying mode. This is your opportunity to persuade and compel them. Persuading and compelling your prospect and customer can be achieved by speaking their buying language. Connecting with their pain points and pleasure points is a great place to begin (see Volume 1, Section 6.9, "Consumer Behavior").

Very often, your rich descriptions are your last chance to convince your prospects and customers to buy your product(s) or service(s). It's especially important when you're selling products or services that can be purchased at competing businesses. When your prospects and customers are looking at your site and your competitors' site(s), your rich descriptions will shine. Your clear, concise, organized, and compelling descriptions are a tiny, supercharged detail that can generate big profits.

Conclusion

Enhanced images and descriptions may seem like an unnecessary concern. On the contrary, they are one of those tiny, supercharged details that Guerrilla marketers tend to while they generate big profits.

4.47 * MESSAGE BOTS

With the proliferation of artificial intelligence (AI) and its use in terms of customer service and lead generation, your business can deploy message bots on, for example:

- Your website
- Your email

- Platforms, such as Telegram and Facebook—which includes the Facebook messenger application—Instagram, and WhatsApp

Message bots can boost sales and satisfaction while reducing your costs. You can delegate a variety of services to message bots, such as:

- Around-the-clock and every-day-of-the-week interactions and services
- Basic customer service with challenge/issue submissions and responses
- Interactive FAQs, allowing your prospects and customers to ask questions and get answers
- Chatbots can be used when your prospects and customers initiate live chat. The chatbot can provide a welcome and begin the conversation with a few different questions/options. You click the one that is most like the information you need, and the bot can provide a first-level response. The chatbot can continue to respond in defined multiple-choice options, which can resolve the issue and/or provide needed product information to compel your prospects or customers to buy your product(s) and/or service(s). Chatbots can also reduce your cost of providing customer service while increasing satisfaction with the consistent quality of the information provided
- Robust logic flows to offer enhanced service. Chatbots are getting smarter and smarter—even bots without any level of artificial intelligence (AI) can offer very robust logic flows. Those robust logic flows provide the ability for questions and their answers to be put into different marketing and sales silos and tagged for email campaign follow-up messages and even sending text messages.

In Section 5.14, "Variety and Modality," we addressed the importance of appealing to the largest possible audience. Your customers and prospects are attracted to information in a variety of ways. Message bots can add to your appeal and help your business build and grow relationships with your prospects and customers. There are numerous options available to you.

To find the right solution, it's important to first know your needs. Are you looking for support with your website, social platforms (if so, which platforms), and/or email? With that in mind, start with the end in mind. For example:

- What's the objective?
- Do you want to make your FAQs more engaging?
- Do you need a customer service bot?
- Do you need a technical support bot?

- Do you need a sales/marketing bot?
- Do you need onboarding support and/or product tours?

Now that you know what you want to accomplish, you'll find a solution that meets your needs now and one that can grow with your business. These are just a few services that are beneficial to be aware of:

- **Intercom**: provides a conversational relationship platform with a variety of conversational support, engagement, and marketing solutions. Their tools can help your business provide live chat, auto-messages, product tours, self-serve tools, product and feature announcements, etc.
- **ManyChat:** helps your business promote products, book appointments, gather contact information, and build relationships through Facebook Messenger and Instagram. Their templates and drag-and-drop interface allow you to build your bot quickly. They also offer several popular integrations

Once you've found a message bot service that will fulfill your needs, it's time to turn your attention to your high-quality content. To create satisfying interactions that delight and build relationships with your prospects and customers, you must provide concise and high-quality information in your interactions. Therefore, you must think through the entire interaction. For example:

- List the most likely reasons that your prospects and customers will initiate a message or chat (e.g., instructions, product detail information, service questions, shipping information, business location information, returns and refunds, etc.)
- Now, list the easy and concise information they need to find their answers in as few back-and-forth interactions with the message bot as possible

Some message bots are utilizing AI and others are not. The non-AI message bots are script-based. They simply use programmatic questions and responses (i.e., scripts). Therefore, the responses from your prospects and customers will result in the same scripted responses from the bot.

With a script-based message bot, you'll deploy a script with a finite number of options and outcomes. Although you have the information on your website, if your business receives common questions, a script-based message bot can deliver the answers to the majority of your queries quickly and in a more personal and interactive way.

Your business can also pre-qualify sales queries to help your prospects and customers quickly find the best product(s) or solution(s) for their needs. That enhanced and convenient assistance can help boost sales and increase customer satisfaction as they find the right solutions to meet their needs.

If your customers and prospects are looking for quick responses, concise and consistent information, message bots can be a great way to create and build relationships with them. Guerrilla marketers know that consistently providing high-quality and compelling information builds trust, and trust creates sales, repeat purchases, and precious referrals, which is the fuel for long-term success.

In Volume 3, beginning with Section 4.65, "Artificial Intelligence (AI) Overview," we'll dive deeper into even more enhanced capabilities, which are at your fingertips. From marketing to advertising and business optimization (see Volume 3, Section 8.47, "AI Business Optimization"), your capabilities can be expanded and improved with AI.

4.48 * YOUTUBE CONNECTED TV

Video advertising on YouTube is as easy as creating a video ad right on your smartphone and using the creative insights and support available with YouTube. In Volume 1, Section 4.4, "Video Advertising," we addressed YouTube and their Find My Audience tool, which allows you to target your ad placement.

There are also a few important insights to be aware of when it comes to YouTube:

- Viewers say they're two times more likely to buy something they saw on YouTube
- Over 70 percent of viewers say that YouTube makes them more aware of new brands
- Viewers are four times more likely to use YouTube versus other platforms to find information about a brand, product, or service
- 70 percent of viewers in the US, Mexico, and Colombia say they bought a brand as a result of seeing it on YouTube

In this section, we'll focus on YouTube Connected TV (i.e., CTV). According to Google, "During 2021, nearly 83% of households will have at least one connected TV, used by at least one person every month."

In Volume 1, Section 2.5, "Television Advertising and Appearances," we addressed various types of television advertising opportunities, such as broadcast television (spot or national/network), cable television (spot or national/network), and Advanced Television.

Advanced TV, according to Cuebiq, is a term that includes:

- Connected TV (CTV), which is an internet-connected television, such as a smart TV
- Over-the-top (OTT) devices, such as Roku, Amazon Fire, Apple TV, smartphones, tablets, computers, and media players, including video game consoles
- Subscription video-on-demand services (SVoD), such as Amazon Prime and Netflix, and partially ad-supported services, such as Hulu, CBS All Access, and Amazon's IMDb TV
- Addressable TV via network providers (e.g., Comcast, Dish, Direct TV, etc.)

In December 2020, according to Google, over 120 million people in the US streamed YouTube or YouTube TV on their TV screens. Google's research also found that viewers prefer to experience YouTube on their TV because ". . . 26% of the time, multiple viewers ages 18 and over are watching YouTube together on the TV screen . . ." That preference gives your advertising valuable increased reach.

YouTube CTV offers Guerrilla marketers the opportunity to reach unique audiences that your television advertising may not be reaching. With YouTube's Reach Planner tool, you can customize your YouTube strategy.

By selecting your audience characteristics (e.g., interests, age, etc.), Reach Planner will make recommendations to help your business find the right combination of video ads based on your objectives and budget. Once you've entered your information, Reach Planner will display "a reach curve, frequency, and other key metrics for the audience you defined." You can make adjustments to maximize your reach and stay on budget.

The key to making smart YouTube CTV advertising investments profitable is knowing your prospects and customers. The more you know about your prospects and customers, the more highly targeted your YouTube CTV advertising investments will be. With emerging tools and features, YouTube viewers will find it easier than ever to engage with ads and respond to a call to action. That is opportunity knocking for Guerrilla marketers. Your advertising and profits will shine as ads become shoppable.

With the ease of creating effective advertisements that compel your prospects and customers to notice your business and the powerful tools to place and track your advertising, the advantages are clear. As it becomes easier and more convenient for your prospects and customers to immediately respond to your call to action, the opportunity for success is compelling.

4.49 * WHATSAPP

WhatsApp is, globally, one of the most popular mobile messaging apps. WhatsApp provides a low-cost messaging alternative to text messaging. According to Statista, WhatsApp had two billion users as of 2020.

WhatsApp users can send text, voice, image, and video messages and have voice or video calls. Users can also share documents, such as PDFs, spreadsheets, etc. (Note: There is a size limit.) From the perspective of a Guerrilla marketer, WhatsApp Business provides opportunities to connect with their customers and prospects to market their product(s) and service(s) and provide customer support.

WhatsApp is available in over 180 countries. WhatsApp Business is free to download and, according to the company, it was built with small businesses in mind. The business app allows you to:

- Create a business profile to share your address, description, email address, and website
- Create a catalog to market your product(s) and/or service(s)
- Interact with your prospects and customers
- Utilize efficient features, such as quick replies that allow you to reuse frequently used messages
- Utilize labels to quickly find contacts and chats
- Utilize automated messages for greetings and the times you're unavailable (i.e., letting them know when you will be available). This feature is a form of a messaging bot that we addressed in Section 4.47, "Message Bots"

- Utilize group chats with your customers and/or employees (Note: There is a limit to group chat sizes.)
- Beyond simple text messaging you have the powerful ability to label and organize your interactions

Promoting your WhatsApp number and utilizing the business features is a low-cost way to increase the appeal of your business. If you have an international business, WhatsApp is a particularly powerful option due to its useful features and low cost.

According to Statista, people ages twenty-six to thirty-five are the "largest WhatsApp users age group in the U.S.," and it's the leading mobile messenger app worldwide.

WhatsApp Business offers your business the opportunity to meet your prospects and customers where they are (see Section 6.16, "Meet Prospects and Customers Where They Are"), in the manner they choose to interact with your business, and in a way that builds credibility and convenience. When your business is utilizing the product/service catalog option to allow your prospects and customers to browse your offerings, and you're providing automatic responses, your business is quickly getting the right information into their hands.

A built-in QR code and short link generator enable easy sharing of your WhatsApp number to get the conversation started. Additionally, you can easily connect it to your Facebook and Instagram accounts so your prospects and customers can directly chat with your account from those profiles. When you visit gMarketing.com/Club, you'll find a link to the Guerrilla Marketing Facebook page where you can see this option in action.

4.50 * DIGITAL ACCOUNT-BASED MARKETING

When it comes to business-to-business (B2B) marketing, there are several approaches that Guerrilla marketers use to identify and make connections with their prospects. For example:

- Cold calling
- Cold email outreach (see Volume 1, Section 4.39, "Cold Email Outreach")

- Networking
- Attending events, conferences, and trade shows (see Volume 1, Section 3.19, "Events, Conferences, and Trade Shows")
- Digital account-based marketing

Digital account-based marketing is a B2B marketing strategy that allows your business to target an entire company or the people in a certain division or functional role in a company. Effective targeting can be accomplished in a variety of ways.

Demographics, Psychographics, Technographics, Firmographics

In Volume 1, Section 1.1, "Research and Knowing," we addressed demographics (e.g., age, income, sex, ethnicity, etc.) and psychographics (e.g., interests, activities, etc.), which relate to the employees of a business. For businesses, there are also technographics, which is the technology utilized by the business. This valuable information helps your business segment your B2B prospects to target those that are most likely to become your customers, based on the technology they are currently using. The technology information can help you exclude some prospects or simply rank your prospects based on their propensity to become your customers and/or to personalize your marketing.

Firmographics provide additional insight regarding your prospects. Hubspot breaks down firmographic data into industry type, organizational size, total sales and revenue, current location, ownership framework, and growth trends.

The more you know about your B2B target prospects, the easier it is to segment your data and then deliver personalized marketing. Your highly targeted marketing and advertising mean decreased investments and a greater return on investment (ROI). The more reliable data your business gains, the more your ROI increases.

Geofencing

For example, your business (we'll name it "Solution A") can target the headquarters of a business (we'll name it "Example A") and run well-crafted ads in a targeted radius of their headquarter location. When considering the radius, think about including the surrounding area where employees have lunch, socialize, run errands, and, perhaps, reside. When you then opt to run those ads at a high frequency, you increase your likelihood of compelling your prospects to notice your business.

Once they notice your business, it becomes familiar and top-of-mind. Now, you have an opportunity to build trust and motivate them to take a desired action.

By becoming familiar and top-of-mind, opportunities can happen organically. For example, during a meeting at "Example A" headquarters, they determine they need to find a platform that will solve a particular problem. A meeting participant asks, "Have you heard of 'Solution A'? I think they serve that particular need." Others in the meeting respond, saying they have heard of "Solution A" and that it's worth looking into.

By targeting, using your well-crafted ad, the headquarters of "Example A" in a specific radius, you've made an efficient advertising investment that results in an opportunity.

IP-Based Targeting

Alternately, your business can use tools that allow you to insert a piece of JavaScript into the code for your website. When people come to your website, it records their IP address. That is a great opportunity for B2B marketing because you can reverse lookup the DNS for that IP address for that business. Your business can now do IP-based targeting, and you can target any traffic coming from that IP address.

With IP-based targeting, you're marketing and advertising to people who are using that specific computer network in a specific location. Your business will be reaching the people at that location, along with others who are outside of that location but using a VPN (a virtual private network) with the same network. That can provide a greater reach for the same efficient advertising investment.

Retargeting

In Volume 1, Section 4.5, "Retargeting (or Remarketing) Advertising," we addressed the details of this cost-effective way to market and advertise to your prospects and customers. Utilizing retargeting allows your tracking cookies to help you determine interest and purchase intent, which enhances your digital account-based marketing.

Tools

The key to success with digital account-based marketing is a multi-pronged strategy. Fortunately, there are services to help. These are a few examples to become familiar with:

- **Leadfeeder**: turns anonymous traffic into high-quality leads by identifying the companies that are visiting your website, giving you the opportunity to close sales before your competitors do. Leadfeeder lets your business see the content your prospects are interested in to help your business personalize and customize your pitch. With numerous integrations, you'll easily connect with other productivity tools
- **Seamless**: offers a contact search engine to help your business filter, find, and reach decision-makers. With access to emails and direct dials, they take the work out of finding the right contacts. With their Chrome extension, you'll have the valuable information you need at your fingertips, and their integrations will streamline your activity
- **RocketReach**: provides advanced search options to help you find the right people to find their email addresses and direct dials. They can also help you fill in the holes with your existing database. Their Chrome extension discovers leads with actionable insights. Their outreach services allow you to use your own mailbox to send personalized and customized messages. You can also benefit from a variety of integrations
- **Terminus**: offers an extensive business database that can be layered with your CRM data to help your business identify more opportunities. They then allow your business to create fully automated campaigns across multiple channels to engage your prospects. Their connected data allows your marketing, sales, and customer support teams to work together. Add in their measurement capabilities, and you have data that is working for your business
- **Jabmo**: offers a platform to help your business select and prioritize prospective customers and engage them with multiple means of advertising and email marketing. Their platform helps your business create engaging personalized experiences for your prospects and keeps you informed of their engagement with reports and alerts. Your business will also be able to track your success by, in part, utilizing control groups
- **N.Rich**: provides your business the opportunity to segment your prospects "between firmographic account targeting or by account/cookie

intent data." That segmentation allows for your business to offer powerful, personalized, and customized marketing and advertising. With robust analytics and integrations, your business has powerful tools

When you combine a service with your CRM tool, you can utilize your automated marketing to begin marketing your compelling and customized messaging right away. With the right tools, you can identify the people in a certain division or functional role in a company and reach them with ads (retargeting, geo-based, and/or IP-based), emails, and phone calls (within the parameters of applicable regulations and laws).

Conclusion

These options give Guerrilla marketers the ability to make their well-crafted marketing shine. By placing the right messages in front of the right people, you have the opportunity to break through and get them to notice your business. Once they notice your business, it becomes familiar and top-of-mind. Now, you have an opportunity to build trust and motivate them to take a desired action. In Volume 3, Section 4.57, "Marketing and Sales Funnels," we'll dive deeper into the journey that your prospects experience (through your marketing), which compels and motivates them to become your customers.

Fortunately for Guerrilla marketers, there is a world of opportunity with digital account-based marketing. While one-on-one marketing is powerful, one-to-many marketing is also powerful because many businesses make decisions through groups.

4.51 * TEXT MESSAGE MARKETING

Guerrilla marketers know the power of text message marketing with their prospects and customers that have engaged with them. Of course, it's important to note that those prospects and customers need to explicitly opt in for your text message marketing.

Text messages are widely considered one of the most opened/read forms of communication. They far outperform email, voicemail, and most other forms of communication methods. In combination with your prospects and customers that have explicitly opted-in, you have a powerful opportunity with text message marketing.

Your ability to send concise and compelling texts is the key to having your call to action motivate them to take a desired action (e.g., download an ebook, make a purchase, etc.). Those compelling messages need to be sent with the right tools. Utilizing a platform is a must to send your messages from a special phone number and manage the opt-in and opt-out status. There are many platforms to consider, and here are some to be familiar with:

- **Call Loop:** allows you to automate your text message marketing and get people to opt in (for text and/or email) through text message. They also give your business the ability to "send mass texts, appointment reminders, send coupons, create SMS contests, and setup voice & SMS autoresponders to drive sales" along with voice broadcast capabilities, analytics, and powerful integrations

- **EZ Texting:** allows your business to unleash the power of text marketing with lead generation, contests, sweepstakes, coupons, vouchers, in-store or online promotional codes, alerts, notifications, scheduling, confirmations, customer service engagement and support, and much more

- **Text-Em-All:** is a mass texting and call platform allowing your business to quickly reach your prospects and customers in mass. Their platform is robust and offers many features to manage large lists, schedules, replies, and more. You're likely familiar with automated calling, and this is a platform that offers recorded message delivery capabilities along with the ability to connect to a live person, which can be useful for service reminders and notifications

Text message marketing can be effective for many businesses, and it can be used for a variety of functions, such as:

- Sales and promotions
- Exclusive offers
- Reservation and appointment reminders
- Shipment notifications
- Surveys

Always be sure that your prospects and customers have agreed to receive messages from your business and that they know how to easily opt out. Your business must be diligent about following the rules, regulations, and laws regarding text message marketing. Also, be aware that a text message can generate costs/fees for the user, so be careful to not overdo it and create dissatisfaction and opt-outs.

———————

4.52 * TWITTER

If your prospects and customers engage with Twitter, you have numerous marketing opportunities to reach and connect with them.

To begin with, Twitter can provide valuable insight and market research. Look at the Twitter followers of your competitors. Also create and follow Twitter lists and follow your customers and their lists. Twitter can help you follow trends, and you can search for tweets about your business, product(s), and service(s)

TweetDeck is a helpful tool offered by Twitter. It's an interface that allows you to:
- View multiple timelines to see and filter content that interests you
- Manage multiple Twitter accounts
- Tweet, like, and follow from multiple Twitter accounts
- Schedule tweets
- Build tweet collections to share with others
- Monitor retweets, likes, and mentions

The tools in TweetDeck make Twitter more effective for your marketing as your business drives engagement.

Additionally, there are other helpful tools to be aware of to maximize your effective marketing on Twitter.
- **FollowerWonk:** an analytics and discovery tool for Twitter
- **Agorapulse Twitter Report Card:** a free tool that provides a report card to help you set up a comparison, which lets you understand how you compare to the Twitter accounts that you choose. You'll be able to examine your audience quality, brand engagement, and content performance
- **Trendsmap:** allows your business to visualize the trending Twitter hashtags by local, regional, and global geography. It also offers top tweets, top users, and more. For example, their top tweets tool allows you to see the top posts in certain languages, verified accounts, and if

the tweet has media associated. Guerrilla marketers are wise to have this in their toolbox for market research, trend-chasing, and local awareness

Twitter recommends a few great ideas to help your business utilize its platform, such as being aware of current events so your tweets are sensitive to and aligned with shifting emotions and tones. They also recommend being genuine, thoughtful about your tone of voice, and considerate about adding value.

4.53 * PUSH NOTIFICATIONS

Push notifications are an opportunity to notify your customers with ease. VWO offers, "Push notifications are clickable pop-up messages that appear on your users' browsers irrespective of the device they're using or the browser they're on. They serve as a quick communication channel enabling companies to convey messages, offers, or other information to their customers. Subscribers can be anywhere on the browser and still receive these messages as long as they're online or have their browsers running on their devices."

With a small piece of code on your website, your business can motivate your prospects and customers to opt in for push notifications. Once they opt in, they're willing to receive messages from you, and that is a wonderful opportunity for a Guerrilla marketer.

You've probably seen push notifications on websites. A message pops up and says something like, "Would you like to receive exclusive . . ." The message gives you two options, such as "allow" or "maybe later." If you click "allow," then you're opting in and allowing their push notifications.

There are many tools and platforms to be aware of, such as:

- **Push Crew/VWO Engage:** a push notification platform for both desktop and mobile.
- **OneSignal:** a push notification platform for mobile, web, in-app, and more

You can target prospects, meaning you display the push notification opt-in by geography. Alternately, you can display the push-notification opt-in when they are entering or exiting your website.

Push notifications can be displayed to increase engagement and track key moments. For example,

- You can identify what page they are on when they allow push notifications
- You can identify cart abandonments and motivate purchases

An important aspect of push notifications to be aware of is regarding *when* your previous visitor has opted in. When they have opted in, your business can push messages to their browser when they are on other websites. This can be an effective way to compel and motivate your prospects and customers to come back. Your business can offer specials, reminders, a memorable quote, or anything to appreciate and engage them and entice them to visit your site again.

When you consider that push notifications are a part of your overall messaging and communication tactics, your business has a direct path to your prospects' and customers' browsers and the reporting to show engagement. Considering that other tactics, such as email, are increasingly congested and can have marginal open and engagement rates, push notifications offer your business a great opportunity. It is important to be aware that not everyone will opt in, and not every browser will allow the notifications to be pushed, so it is a tool but should not be considered as the only communication tool your business uses.

4.54 * REFERRAL SITES

Referral sites are aggregators and curators of valuable content. They focus their content and capabilities on the needs, pain points, and pleasure points (see Volume 1, Section 6.9, "Consumer Behavior") of their readers and subscribers. The following are examples of popular referral sites that you might already be familiar with:

- Bankrate
- NerdWallet
- ThePointsGuy

Referral sites curate compelling content, offers, and solutions for their prospects and customers. They create revenue and profits with a combination of advertising and referral/affiliate commissions.

In nearly every industry, referral sites exist. High-quality referral sites provide great value, and they can do a lot of the challenging and expensive marketing that is needed to drive qualified leads to your business.

By utilizing teams of contributors to create desirable content in combination with compelling and motivating advertising, referral sites engage their prospects. When their prospects are motivated to visit their sites (or use their apps), they find robust and high-quality information that is compelling and trust-building. Referral sites utilize their content and capabilities to build relationships with their prospects and customers.

At the time the prospects are motivated to "learn more" or make a purchase, they seamlessly hand the prospect (i.e., hot lead) off to your business. How that hand-off occurs will vary for many referral sites (i.e., some sites will fully manage and process the transaction, and others will vary). However, at the moment of the hand-off, accuracy and consistency is the key to continuing to either welcome them as a customer or continue building their trust and allow that trust to turn them into satisfied customers.

Your prospect is accustomed to the interface and the ease of using the referral site, and they trust the information they received. One inconsistency will create doubt and an unnecessary and potentially insurmountable roadblock.

Never forget that with Guerrilla Marketing, consistency builds familiarity; familiarity builds trust, and trust creates sales, repeat purchases, and precious referrals, which is the fuel for the long-term success of your business.

In addition to referral sites, it's also helpful to be familiar with these related marketing options that can produce sales for your business:

- Volume 1, Section 3.14, "Coupons and Coupon Sites"
- Volume 1, Section 3.15, "Cash Back/Point-Shopping Portal Sites"

4.55 * SOCIAL MEDIA MONITORING

Monitoring online chatter regarding your business, product(s), service(s), and competitors allows you to improve engagement while managing your reputation. Social media monitoring is also valuable to spot trends, problems, and opportunities.

There are great tools available to be aware of brand mentions or more robust solutions to enhance your workflow by scheduling posts, in advance, across multiple social media accounts along with monitoring comments, sentiment, and measuring performance. You can even use the tools to monitor your competition.

Being able to curate the comment feed can prevent issues from growing. For example, if you're investing in paid social media advertising and people are commenting on your ads, you want to be able to monitor those comments. Maybe they're making positive comments, or maybe they're being negative, trolling, or posting competing or unrelated offers and taking over the feed. On one hand, a comment or interaction is viewed well by the algorithms on the social platforms; however, negativity can ruin your results. Interacting by responding to positive and less than positive comments and deleting or hiding irrelevant or harmful comments is a wonderful social-proof boost for your business.

Google Alerts

Google Alerts is a great tool, at your fingertips, to keep you in the know, and it's free. In Volume 1, Section 8.26, "Awareness," we shared the multiple uses for Google Alerts to keep your business informed. You can get email alerts for any topic you choose (e.g., your business, products, services, competition, etc.) using Google Alerts. Google searches news, blogs, the web, videos, books, discussions, and finance information to source those alerts.

Hootsuite

For a robust tool for monitoring relevant conversations about your business, product(s), service(s), competition, industry, etc., Hootsuite is a tool to know. They also offer tools to ensure that any issues that need to be addressed can be assigned and shared within your team. According to Hootsuite, "You can monitor what people are saying based on keywords, hashtags, locations, and even specific users." As your needs grow, so do their tools and options for more robust monitoring to help your business grow.

Zoho Social

Social engagement tracking and notifications are offered along with your own social listening dashboard. They also offer a chat-style interface for your direct messages from your audience on Facebook and Twitter. According to Zoho Social, they also offer a contact directory so you can "Discover what your followers and people you follow are saying on social media. View and manage connections across all your social channels."

Later

This is an all-in-one social marketing platform to help you plan, analyze, and publish your content. Whether you're just getting started or are a pro, they offer the tools needed to schedule posts and find and share content while monitoring your traffic and conversions. Their reporting tools also offer unique suggestions to optimize your strategy.

AgoraPulse

Manage your social media with a unified inbox to organize all of your incoming messages, comments, and reviews. Your team can collaborate and schedule your content and social listings to help you identify trends and opportunities for your business and your competitors. With insightful analytics, you can identify what's working and what is not.

Conclusion

When you're utilizing a platform that connects to your social media accounts, you want to make sure you're using a reputable platform.

If your business relies on reviews and ratings, a review tracking tool is a must. Become familiar with tools such as:

- ReviewTrackers
- ReviewPush

Guerrilla marketers don't leave their social media success to chance. They utilize tools that help them measure and monitor their online reputation and give them insight into the tiny, supercharged details that can generate big profits.

4.56 * DISCOVERY ADS

Discovery ads offer you the opportunity to reach targeted prospects to compel them to notice your business and motivate them to take a desired action. In Volume 1, Section 4.3, "Display, Search, and Native Advertising," we addressed the related native advertising. In this section, we address Discovery ads with Google.

Discovery ads allow your business to utilize Google's insight and platforms to target your prospects and expand your reach to attract additional prospects. According to Google, "Thanks to Google's audience and customer intent signals, this campaign type helps you deliver highly visual, inspiring personalized ad experiences to people who are ready to discover and engage with your brand — all through a single Google Ads campaign."

Guerrilla marketers appreciate getting more done with less effort. With Discovery ads, a single ad campaign allows your business to reach your prospects as they interact across the different Google platforms. As Google simply states, "You enter the building blocks for your ads — like headlines, high-quality inspirational images, and logos — and we'll show your ads to highly interested customers using the cost-per-action (CPA) bid and budget that you set."

Connecting with your prospects while they are enjoying the content and are engaged, requires the right combination of elements, such as:

- Compelling, high-quality, and consistent images (see Section 4.46, "Enhanced Images and Descriptions")
- Compelling messages
- An effective call to action

That combination works for your business, and it makes your discovery ads effective while your prospects and customers are engaged in Google platforms, such as:

- A highly personalized Discovery feed
- YouTube
- Gmail

Reusing your current high-performing online advertising (e.g., remarketing) can get you pointed in the right direction. The right combination, along with the right tools to measure your performance, is a great formula for creating familiarity, which leads to sales. As Guerrilla marketers know, familiarity builds trust, and trust creates sales, repeat purchases, and precious referrals, which is the fuel for long-term success. In Volume 3, Section 4.57, "Marketing and Sales Funnels," we'll dive deeper into the journey that your prospects experience (through your marketing), which compels and motivates them to become your customers.

SECTION V

Guerrilla Info-Media Marketing

GUERRILLA INFO-MEDIA MARKETING

Guerrilla Info-Media Marketing encourages businesses to leverage the appeal of valuable information in their marketing. Whether it's the information you currently possess or the information that you learn along the way, information is a powerful marketing opportunity for any business.

People seek information every day, and the more interesting, appealing, fascinating, and relevant information a business provides, the more fulfilling it is for the people seeking that information. From the news to social media, blogs, podcasts, and videos, the right information in the right place gives a business the opportunity to deliver the story of their business, expertise, USP, and the benefits of their product(s) and/or service(s). Many businesses are discovered, not based on their latest promotion, but instead based on the information they provide.

Utilizing Guerrilla Info-Media Marketing tactics improves both offline and online marketing efforts. Online, a website that is packed with useful information is attractive and engaging to prospects and customers, and it's advantageous for SEO. Offline, information-filled catalogs, consultations, and demonstrations are engaging to prospects and customers.

When utilized in combination, the tactics of Guerrilla Info-Media Marketing work together to create authenticity, fascination, consistency, and trust. Those are the cornerstones of a successful and thriving business. Guerrilla marketers know that consistency builds familiarity; familiarity builds trust, and trust creates sales, repeat purchases, and precious referrals, which is the fuel for long-term success.

Guerrilla Info-Media Marketing is your opportunity to build important connections and relationships with your prospects, customers, vendors, suppliers, employees, community members, and media contacts—and to attract Fusion/Affiliate marketing partners (refer to Volume 1, Section 7.6, "Fusion/Affiliate Marketing and Collaboration"). All those connections and relationships fuel the growth of your business over the long term.

In Volume 1, we addressed:

5.1   Presentations, Speeches, Consultations, Demonstrations, and Seminars
5.2   Customer Data and Studies
5.3   By-Product
5.4   Blog and Newsletter Copy

Now, we'll pick up where we left off. Without further ado, let's get started.

5.12 ✱ MENUS AND OPTIONS

If your business has multiple options and you rely on menus or other ways to convey your product options, you have a great opportunity to set your business apart. Menus or lists of options can be standard and ordinary, or they can be unique, engaging, compelling, and worthy of sharing.

Whether your menu or list of options is online, affixed to the wall, or handed to your prospects and customers, it's never been easier to set your business apart. For example:

- Offer a QR code to take your prospects and customers online. Whether at your business or at other businesses, many people have become used to this option, and many prefer it. It gives them the ability to, for example, adjust the type size to what is most comfortable for them. Also, your business can easily ask them if they would like to connect to hear about your specials, events, new products and to join your loyalty program

- Embrace digital options that allow your business to include quick videos, ratings, reviews, social posts (photos and comments), additional appealing options to consider, etc.

- Your unique descriptions and visuals are your opportunities to bring your products to life. If, for example, your business is serving food, visuals appeal to people who taste with their eyes first (see Section 4.46, "Enhanced Images and Descriptions")

- Make it easy for your prospects and customers to quickly hone in on what appeals to them. Their ability to sort and filter to quickly find options that interest them can translate into increased satisfaction and additional purchases

- Your Guerrilla Company Attributes (see Section VIII) and Guerrilla Company Attitudes (see Section IX) should come to life for your prospects(s) and customer(s). Your business shines with consistency, personality, efficiency, quality, uniqueness, innovations, etc.

Guerrilla marketers reimagine the ordinary and create an unconventional and engaging experience that's easy and encourages sharing.

5.13 * REALITY TV

Appearing on reality TV shows on network television, streaming networks, and online outlets (e.g., TikTok, YouTube, your website, etc.) is an unconventional way to reach your prospects and customers. When done well, it's a great way to make a connection with your prospects and customers that goes beyond what advertising alone can achieve.

A key to your success is to ensure that you and/or your business are appearing in front of the right audience. Utilizing reality TV is only valuable if it helps you expand your marketing reach to the right audience. The right audience, regardless of its size, is one that is a significant match to your customers and prospects.

The show or content can be directly related to business, such as is the case with *Shark Tank or Unicorn Hunters*, or to your profession/industry, such as with *Project Runway* or a cooking show or competition (e.g., *MasterChef*, *Chopped*, etc.). Alternately, the show or content can be unrelated to your business (e.g., competitions and social interaction such as *The Amazing Race*) if it's a match to the interests of your prospects and customers.

By reaching your prospects and customers at an unexpected time and unconventional way, you have an increased opportunity to make a positive impression. That positive impression can be compelling, and it can motivate them to notice and interact with your business, product(s), and service(s).

Guerrilla marketers are keenly aware that not every reality TV option is a good option. Your goal is to positively promote your business and/or your skills and talent and turn that exposure into profits. Don't make the mistake of thinking that any attention is positive attention. For example, your appearance on *Worst Cooks in America* is not likely to boost your restaurant sales.

If you want to look at existing shows, Backstage.com is a resource for open casting calls and auditions for reality TV. When you think creatively, you quickly realize that your options are not limited to what is. You can also choose to create your own show and/or create unique and engaging online content that your prospects and customers want to view and subscribe to.

For example, if your business is unique and/or it simply piques people's curiosity, it may be well-suited for its own reality show. Engaging behind-the-scenes content from your business is valuable to share online. Consider that people currently enjoy watching shows that are built around businesses—from wedding dresses to house flipping, real estate, and pet grooming. People are curious and find it interesting and compelling to be behind the scenes of a small business, perhaps even yours.

Also, consider the examples of other businesses that have created programming that is tightly aligned to their brand and products. Red Bull has created engaging programming around adrenaline sports (see Volume 1, Guerrilla Marketing Case Study 4, "Red Bull," for more information). The Purina Pro Plan Incredible Dog Challenge showcases the amazing feats of a variety of dogs with a series of television programs. There are many opportunities for your creativity to shine while you engage your prospects and customers with content they want to view and subscribe to.

5.14 * VARIETY AND MODALITY

Your Guerrilla Info-Media Marketing is most effective with variety and modality, which allow it to appeal to the largest possible audience. Your customers and prospects are attracted to information in a variety of ways. According to Inspire Education, there are seven learning styles:
1. Visual (spatial)
2. Aural (auditory-musical)
3. Verbal (linguistic)

4. Physical (kinesthetic)
5. Logical (mathematical)
6. Social (interpersonal)
7. Solitary (intrapersonal)

For example, the ebook that you've created may have valuable information, but the format limits that appeal. The same information as an audiobook, podcast, or video can increase the appeal.

Additionally, how your business provides instructions for your product(s) or service(s) can affect your ratings and reviews. If you're providing instructions in video and your customer wants a quick and simple answer, they will be dissatisfied with going through videos to find their answer. At the same time, some of your customers will be satisfied with written instructions; others want a video; some need accessible options, and then there are those who want a combination of these options.

When it comes to how your business provides instructions for your product(s) or service(s), you can maximize your effectiveness by:

- Utilizing online filters, links, a table of contents, and/or multiple categories and descriptors will allow people to easily filter your information and find what they need
- Providing downloadable documentation that includes easy links to videos or podcasts
- Using different titles (try online, Portent Idea Generator) and images
- Making suggestions of other information that could be appealing and useful

When it comes to your marketing, it's rare that one size fits all for your prospects and customers. When you expand your options in the right way, you expand your appeal, and that compels your prospects to notice your business and your customers to make repeat purchases.

5.15 * CONNECTIONS

Once you have compelling and engaging information, products, and/or services to market, you want to find the largest possible audience to share it with.

Beyond sharing your information with your prospects and customers (via social media, your blog, a newsletter, webinars, print materials, etc.), you can expand your reach by making additional connections.

To get started, your business can utilize your existing contacts while also creating new contacts to promote your compelling news and content to:

- News outlets
- Industry associations
- Chamber of commerce members
- Community and social groups
- Forums (see Section 4.17, "Online Groups, Chat Rooms, and Forums") and broadcasting (see Section 5.17, "Video and Audio Broadcasting")
- Fusion/Affiliate marketing partners and collaborators

Guerrilla marketers know that working with others is an ideal way for businesses to grow while providing high-quality information, products, and services that delight their prospects and customers. Refer to Volume 1, Section 7.6, "Fusion/Affiliate Marketing and Collaboration," for more information regarding how online and physical location-based businesses can work together to help build and grow an audience for their desired products, services, content, and information.

You can also expand your reach by issuing press releases, which allow your content to make it to new outlets and audiences. Refer to Volume 1, Section 7.8, "Public Relations (PR)," for numerous low-cost ways to garner high-quality exposure and publicity for your business by building strong, collaborative relationships with leading and influential people from the media to authors, bloggers, podcasters, and more.

If you and/or your business utilize the power of LinkedIn, which has over 770 million active users, you can increase your connections with a few tactics. If you or your business is currently not utilizing LinkedIn, now is the time to jump in and put these tactics to work for your business. These tactics will help you and your business to establish and/or grow your valuable connections:

- Build a network that is focused on your goals (e.g., industry experts, peers, colleagues, prospects, customers, etc.)
- Ask a connection of yours to introduce you to a particular connection of theirs, with whom there is mutual interest and value. It's far more valuable to receive the benefit of an endorsement or implied endorsement that the introduction will provide

- When you're sending an invitation to connect, take the time to use the "personalize invite" tool. This is your time to mention where you may have met or to let them know that you appreciate the information they share, and you would like to know more
- Share valuable information on a daily basis. That valuable information could be a tip, tactic, or a particular tool that is valuable to you and that you believe will also be valuable for your audience
- Comment, like, and share other people's posts. Be sure that the post is aligned with your Guerrilla Company Attributes (see Section VIII) and Guerrilla Company Attitudes (see Section IX) so that it's building your valuable credibility

The more engaging, relevant, news-worthy, entertainment-worthy, and compelling your information, content, and expertise are, the more likely your business will be shared (also see Volume 1, Section 7.3, "Buzz and Shares"). Equally, you're growing your credibility, which opens the door to more connections, which is powerful when you keep your content aligned with your Guerrilla Company Attributes (see Section VIII) and Guerrilla Company Attitudes (see Section IX).

With your credibility and expertise established, when you or your business make an irresistible offer, you'll encourage sharing, which compels more people to connect for more information. The more people that want to share your information, the more profitable your investment of time will be.

Beyond your connections, in Section 5.17, "Video and Audio Broadcasting," and Section 8.42, "Leveraging Social Live Broadcasting," we'll provide more ideas to help your business find the largest possible audience to share your compelling and engaging information, products, and/or services with.

5.16 * SUBSCRIPTIONS

Offering your information, product(s), or service(s) as a subscription is a great way to generate profits while establishing and growing an engaged audience of customers. Subscription offers, online or at your physical location business, can be marketed in a variety of methods from one-on-one to one-on-many.

Regardless of whether the information, product(s), or service(s) you're marketing is consumer packaged goods (CPG), fitness, cooking, personal development, business development, or anything else, there are a few keys to help your success, such as utilizing:

- Compelling and high-quality information products and/or services
- Easy-to-use app and website
- Free trials and previews
- Proper pricing
- Appealing options
- Promotions (e.g., quantity discounts, two-for-one, discounts for annual pricing, etc.)
- Bonuses
- Ratings and reviews
- Chat options and/or private online groups to let your customers ask questions and easily receive support
- Easy cancellations (clarity, transparency, and ease of cancellation, removing obstacles)
- Quality guarantees

It sounds easy enough, but finding even the proper pricing can be a daunting task. Both pricing your subscription rate too high or too low can be turn-offs for your prospects. Your prospects may be unlikely to say the price is too high, so they will claim other issues. At the same time, if your prospects think the price is too low, they likely assume the quality is not sufficient.

Your business can consider offering a few payment options that can help broaden your appeal. For example:

- If you're offering monthly payment options, a quarterly or annual payment option with a discount can be appealing, and it often encourages your customers to remain longer than with a monthly payment option
- A premium one-time payment for unlimited and/or all-access can also bring big value and no-hassle appeal
- Pay what you can or think it's worth is a creative option that some businesses are utilizing. It can be especially effective as a trial when you're launching a new subscription to help you gauge what your prospects and customers are willing to pay

A note of caution, offering too many options can make it easy for your prospects to dismiss your subscription plans as too confusing or unnecessarily complicated.

Offering demonstrations, free trials (with a credit card or without a credit card at registration/account set-up), and free previews are great ways to gauge if your content and marketing are appealing. If your prospects are consuming the free trials and previews but not purchasing your subscription, you have a good indicator that your marketing is compelling and working, but your content or product is not. Alternately, if you find that your prospects are not choosing the free option and are instead subscribing, congratulations, you have both your marketing and content working well for the success of your business.

We'll dive deeper and provide more valuable ideas and options for your marketing content in Volume 3, Section 5.21, "Creating Sellable Content."

5.17 * VIDEO AND AUDIO BROADCASTING

As we noted in Section 5.15, "Connections," the more engaging, relevant, news-worthy, entertainment-worthy, and compelling your information and expertise is, the more likely it is to be shared. It's also more likely to compel your prospects to take action because it builds the credibility of your business. Therefore, you want to broadcast your information as widely as possible.

Many businesses believe they are broadcasting their video and audio content when they use one outlet. Realistically, they are likely only narrowcasting to a small group, as compared to the potential audience they could reach with broadcasting. When you explore all the opportunities there are for broadcasting, you can easily expand your reach without much more effort. When you increase your reach with regards to your target prospects and customers, you increase your sales opportunities.

Guerrilla marketers choose to re-use and repurpose their content to broadcast on multiple outlets to increase their reach. There are numerous options and platforms that are ready and waiting to help your business expand your reach. Your business can utilize a combination of options for broadcasting your information online, such as:

- Webinars (also see Volume 1, Section 4.25, "Webinars")
- Podcasts (also see Volume 1, Section 4.30, "Your Podcast")
- Clubhouse
- Live Video (e.g., Zoom, Jet Video, etc.)
- Social Media (e.g., TikTok, Instagram, YouTube, etc.)

For example, a business that is hosting a room in Clubhouse can (with disclosure to the participants) repurpose that content into a podcast to increase their reach.

In Section 8.42, "Leveraging Social Live Broadcasting," we'll expand on social media broadcasting and platforms that allow you to simulcast across multiple social platforms. The use of a simulcast platform can allow your business to expand its reach with ease.

Your business can also utilize your video content to repurpose into engaging native outstream advertising (also see Volume 1, Section 4.3, "Display, Search, and Native Advertising"). Native and social outstream ads are explained well by AdAge as: "Social outstream is video ads that autoplay on mute with headlines and formats that match the look and feel of social feeds on Facebook, Instagram, Twitter, etc. Native outstream is the same as social but made to match the look and feel of editorial feeds." AdAge found these ads perform well, and viewers often read engaging and relevant headlines—regardless of whether they unmute the video ads—because people are scrolling through their feed and, therefore, are in headline-reading mode.

Your business can also easily repurpose your audio-only content to extend its reach by using it as the voice-over on an engaging video roll. In a short video format, that engaging video roll can be as simple as a solid background with the words that are being spoken, creatively displayed.

Your audio and video content that has a useful, long life (e.g., recipes), which we refer to as evergreen content, will continue to work for your business for years to come. Your audio and video content containing information that is ephemeral can be engaging, but it can quickly become outdated. Therefore, the need for continual updates limits your ability to effectively re-use your information.

In Volume 3, Section 5.20, "Creating Personalized Content," we'll provide more ideas and options to enhance content for your video and audio broadcasting.

5.18 * SHARING TOOLS

According to Statista, the share of "U.S. Facebook users sharing content on a weekly basis" is 53 percent. Additionally, Reddit receives more than 1.5 billion visits each month with people who are eager to share.

Given that sharing is an effective way to make connections (see Section 5.15, "Connections"), broadcast information (see Section 5.17, "Video and Audio Broadcasting"), and build your audience and your business, it's crucial to make sharing easy for your prospects and customers. At the same time, you want to be able to monitor social sharing. Fortunately, it's easy for your business to monitor social shares, and that data provides valuable insight that can help your business build engagement and relationships with your prospects and customers.

The most common tool is the use of social sharing buttons (e.g., Facebook, Twitter, Instagram, etc.), which are available from numerous providers. Unfortunately, many businesses install social sharing buttons, but they don't utilize the tools that help them monitor and optimize the activity and effectiveness of their content.

Fortunately, Guerrilla marketers know there are numerous social interaction and content marketing tools to consider. Here are a few examples:

- **Google Analytics**: a great tool to set up and monitor social interactions. Social interactions can be monitored by the social network, the social action (e.g., like, tweet, share, bookmark), and the page where an action took place. With their Source/Medium report, Social Conversion report, and Multi-Channel Funnel report, your business can monitor interactions and find trends in the data

- **Shareaholic**: offers a suite of tools for your website to help you grow your audience through sharing. According to Shareaholic, they provide ". . . a comprehensive set of marketing tools to engage with your audience, get found across search and social, and grow your following. All for Free. Code-free Customization."

- **ContentStudio**: if your business is focused on content marketing, they offer numerous valuable tools to help your business curate and market content across multiple social platforms. Their collaboration, automation, and analytics tools will help your business deliver desirable content that engages your audiences and followers

Utilizing the right tools and platforms will help your business create high-quality, engaging content that people want to share. Collaboration, interaction, and automation tools will help your sharing grow with ease. In Volume 3, Section 5.19, "Creating Sharable Content," we'll provide more ideas and options to enhance sharing in your marketing.

SECTION VI

Guerrilla Human-Media Marketing

GUERRILLA HUMAN-MEDIA MARKETING

Guerrilla Marketing embraces the realism that you're marketing with every bit of contact your business has with people (internally and externally). Therefore, you utilize your marketing knowledge and insight, and in doing so, you're being intentional with your marketing.

Guerrilla Human-Media Marketing harnesses the power of marketing know-how, consumer and customer behavior, and the role that you and your employees play in your marketing. Marketing is a series of moving parts. When they work together, they move your business forward. When they don't work together, your business is stalled.

The moving parts of your marketing are not just your social posts, blog, website, advertisements, product(s), and/or service(s). The moving parts are also the human components, which are optimal when they're a consistent element of your marketing.

The ability to present oneself well, be engaging and appealing, and delight your prospects and customers, while remaining consistent with every other aspect of your marketing, are the goals of a Guerrilla marketer. If that task sounds daunting, remember that it's far better to do a few things very well than to do many things poorly, and a successful Guerrilla marketer tells instead of sells.

Therefore, it's wise to ensure that the moving parts of your Guerrilla Human-Media Marketing are working in beautiful harmony to maximize the results of all your marketing efforts. After all, the best advertisement can rarely overcome an interaction with a business that has employees with poor relationship and selling skills. Also, if you're marketing a story or solution that your prospects don't relate to, the register is not ringing.

Guerrilla marketers take the time and put energy and creativity into mastering the tactics of Guerrilla Human-Media Marketing. Getting all of the moving parts of your marketing working together is a simple and powerful tactic. It's just as easy for people to do marketing well as it is for them to do it poorly. Guerrilla marketers intentionally choose the tactics that work, and they execute them well to move their business forward and create profits.

In Volume 1, we addressed:

6.1   Your Employees and Representatives
6.2   Business Attire and Uniforms
6.3   Your Expertise and Credibility

Now, we'll pick up where we left off. Without further ado, let's get started.

6.16 * MEET PROSPECTS AND CUSTOMERS WHERE THEY ARE

Many people have an idea that they nurture and grow into a business. Unfortunately, they don't focus enough attention on the single most vital element of business success, which is their prospects and customers.

You can have the most brilliant idea. You can pair that brilliant idea with the best marketing and advertising. And it can fall flat and be unprofitable. Why?

Guerrilla marketers know that they must always meet their prospects and customers where they are. You may recall from Volume 1, Section 6.9 "Consumer Behavior," it's often referred to as speaking the "buying language" of your prospects and customers. Simply put, it's a matter of speaking the right compelling words with the right compelling offer, images, and sounds to connect with your prospects and customers. When you reach them where they are, they notice your business, which allows your business to become familiar.

A secret to Guerrilla Marketing is the importance of familiarity. After all, familiarity builds trust, and trust creates sales, repeat purchases, and precious referrals. That is the fuel for the long-term success of your business.

Therefore, when you meet prospects and customers where they are and become familiar to them, you have the opportunity to show them where your product(s) or service(s) can take them. Your familiarity and connection demonstrate that your marketing is starting to work for your business.

However, even with familiarity and a connection you can, typically, only take your prospects and customers to the limits of their imaginations, beliefs, and mindsets (see Section 6.17, "Consumer Mindset"). Meaning, if you take them to where they can imagine being, they quickly want to become your customer. If you take them beyond where and what they think is possible, you've lost the connection, the precious familiarity, and the sale.

For example, if you connect with your prospects' and customers' pain points (refer to Volume 1, Section 6.9, "Consumer Behavior") about their struggles and challenges with weight loss, you've met them where they are. If you then tell them the story of how they can lose one hundred pounds in thirty days for free, that's normally beyond the limits of their imagination, beliefs, and mindset.

If instead, you were to tell them the story of how you did it, and they can lose a compelling and "reasonably" large amount of weight in a "reasonable" and unique way, you're more likely to maintain your connection and familiarity. Now your familiarity builds trust, and they are motivated to respond to your call to action. With trust, your business creates sales, customer satisfaction and, repeat purchases. Now, if your business delivers a high-quality product or service, you've created fuel for the long-term success of your business, as your customers and prospects provide precious referrals of their friends, family, and associates.

It's important to remember that if you want long-term success for your business, your business needs to meet people where they are, and that doesn't end when you've completed a sale. Guerrilla marketers embrace the enormous opportunity that repeat purchases and precious referrals by their customers represent for their success. To attract those repeat purchases and referrals, your business must continually meet your customers where they are to achieve ongoing familiarity and trust.

We've all experienced businesses that met us where we were and took us on a fantastic journey. They delivered high-quality products and/or services, and we continued to make purchases. Eventually, though, the business lost its familiarity.

Perhaps they made numerous undesirable changes. They may have closed a retail location near you or changed their hours, become outdated, and/or failed to innovate and make needed changes. Perhaps their quality, style, or value decreased. Perhaps a competitor introduced a compelling innovation, superior quality, greater style, stronger value, or more convenient retail locations. Perhaps they let themselves slip away from all the important Guerrilla Marketing tactics that worked for their business.

Regardless of why, when familiarity is lost, and you're no longer meeting your prospects and customers where they are, they are no longer interested in making purchases. Additionally, they are no longer interested in providing referrals. Instead of promoting your business, now, when speaking of your business, they say "they used to . . . but now they . . ."

Therefore, Guerrilla marketers value the importance of always meeting their prospects and customers where they are to make them feel noticed, welcomed, and motivated to continue to be your customer.

6.17 * CONSUMER MINDSET

Mindset is defined by *Psychology Today* as ". . . a belief that orients the way we handle situations—the way we sort out what is going on and what we should do. Our mindsets help us spot opportunities, but they can also trap us in self-defeating cycles."

Beyond demographics and psychographics, understanding as much as possible about the consumer mindset will help you better understand the behavior of your prospects and customers. With that knowledge, a Guerrilla marketer is well-equipped for success.

In Volume 1, Section 6.9, "Consumer Behavior," we touched on some fundamentals to help you be a better Guerrilla marketer. Those fundamentals include:
- Apathy and Repetition
- Conscious Mind and Subconscious or Unconscious Mind
- Know, Like, and Trust
- Left Brain and Right Brain Tendencies
- Pain Points and Pleasure Points of Prospects and Customers
- Generations
- Cultural Influence

In the prior Section 6.16, "Meet Prospects and Customers Where They Are," we touched on the importance of making connections and becoming familiar. With that familiarity, you have the opportunity to show them where your product(s) or service(s) can take them. However, normally that is limited by their imagination and mindset.

In a world of endless information, the consumer mindset filters information by detecting cues and determining what they should do. The consumer mindset also serves to suggest what is possible and achievable and what is not.

Psychology Today offers additional insight into several different mindsets. For the sake of better understanding consumers, there are two important categories to be aware of:

- **Fixed mindset:** these consumers think their ability is innate. They think failures are mistakes, and it's unsettling, creating doubt and defensiveness. These consumers are more focused on being perfect because they want to prevent failures.
- **Growth mindset:** these consumers expect they can improve and, therefore, failures create motivation for them to bounce back and work harder to grow and improve. These consumers are less focused on failures because they believe they can find solutions and become better because of the experience.

Your prospects and customers, out of habit, can be fixed in their mindsets, or they can be motivated to change. Therefore, it's likely that you'll need to appeal to a mix of both mindsets. That means that your marketing must seamlessly appeal to and compel consumers with both mindsets.

Referring to the example in the prior Section 6.16, "Meet Prospects and Customers Where They Are," it's easy to understand the challenges of compelling consumers. The fixed mindset and growth mindset are very differently motivated.

Once you've met them where they are, the consumer with the fixed mindset is likely to be more responsive to a message that helps them feel relief from guilt and defeat. This consumer has a mindset that tells them they must avoid mistakes and failure. As a result, they are skeptical and that is a roadblock for your marketing. Guerrilla marketers focus on ways to remove that roadblock (i.e., fear of making a mistake), such as offering money-back guarantees, free trials, and testimonials they find believable.

On the other hand, once you meet your growth mindset consumers where they are, it's likely they will be more responsive to new ideas and new goals. Showing them a new or unconventional way to accomplish their goals is engaging. They're likely to also respond well to encouragement and the right motivation.

The more you understand about what motivates your prospects and customers, the more success you'll have compelling and motivating them. A recent survey by Accenture provided insight regarding shifting consumer mindsets because of the pandemic. In a study of 25,000 consumers across fourteen countries, Accenture found that many consumers are re-evaluating and shifting in areas, such as:

- "Forty-two percent say the pandemic made them realize they need to focus on others more than themselves."
- "A full 50% of consumers say that the pandemic caused them to rethink their personal purpose and re-evaluate what's important to them in life."

Of the 50 percent of consumers that ". . . say that the pandemic caused them to rethink their personal purpose and re-evaluate what's important to them in life"—which Accenture refers to as "Reimagined"—most in that group have interesting new mindsets. For example, "66% said they now expect brands to take more responsibility in motivating them to live by their values and to make them feel more relevant in the world."

Those findings show a significant mindset shift for some consumers that Guerrilla marketers are wise to understand and consider regarding the impact on their business. After all, when you understand the mindset of your prospects and customers, it will help you better understand their behavior, and therefore, you can market more effectively to compel and motivate them to become your customer.

In Volume 3, Section 1.13, "Consumer Decision Making," we'll address more valuable information to help your business better understand how to appeal to and motivate your prospects and customers.

6.18 * FIVE-STAR

Positive ratings and reviews are a Guerrilla marketer's dream and focused work come true. Five-star ratings will do a tremendous amount of the work when it comes to your marketing success. Your positive reviews are a competitive advantage, a compelling quality statement, and social proof for your prospects and customers.

When your business is offering a high-quality product(s) and/or service(s), your efforts to accumulate positive reviews are a profitable marketing investment. Fortunately, there are countless ways to build your ratings and reviews for your marketing success, such as:

- **Podium**: offers tools to help your business gather more reviews on multiple sites, instead of just your website. It also provides automated review invitations after a purchase. With customizable templates, an inbox for your reviews, notifications, reporting, and more, your business will be attracting more reviews, all while responding and tracking your success.

- **Birdeye**: helps your business easily collect new reviews on top sites, such as Facebook and Google. With a single dashboard, your business can monitor and respond to reviews. You'll also have customizable templates to garner more reviews and custom auto-response rules to aid your quick responses. With features like spam and slander detection and productivity tools, you'll easily manage and monitor your reviews.

- **Review Monitoring**: focuses on product reviews for consumer packaged goods (CPG) clients on Amazon and twenty-plus other major retail sites. When you're selling CPGs on third-party retail sites, your ratings, images and their descriptions (see Section 4.46, "Enhanced Images and Descriptions"), and labels (see Section 3.28, "Product Labels") are often your most important marketing opportunity.

Even if your overall rating is less than five stars, your business can still focus its marketing on an overall rating above 4.5 stars, assuming that your rating compares well to your competition's rating. Alternately, your business can focus its marketing on the number of five-star reviews that you've achieved. Statements such as "over 500 five-star reviews" are compelling in your marketing (as long as your overall rating is well above four stars).

If your product is new, and you don't have any or many reviews, you can stimulate sales and reviews with giveaways and sampling (see Volume 1, Section 7.10, "Giveaways and Sampling"). From small businesses to large businesses, sampling and giveaways have been an effective way to stimulate sales for countless decades.

6.19 * TOUCH POINTS

Guerrillas know that every touch point with prospects and customers is an opportunity. It's easy to get caught up in reports, to-do lists, and tasks and forget that none of that exists without your prospects and customers. They are the reason that your business exists and creating relationships with them is the key to your long-term success.

What you can learn with each touch point with your prospects and customers is limitless. Guerrilla marketers, to begin with, are looking for opportunities to:

- Build relationships and trust
- Thank them for being customers or, with prospects, for considering your business, product(s), or service(s)
- Learn how they found your business and why they decided to become your customer
- Learn about their consumer behavior and mindset
- Learn about their opinions
- Learn about their doubts and concerns before they turn into negative reviews or social media sharing
- Learn about their ideas that can turn into product innovations and additional product(s) or service(s)
- Capture referrals of their friends, family, and associates that might be interested in your product(s) or service(s)

Guerrilla marketers seek to increase their touch points by increasing their access. The more convenient ways your prospects and customers can connect, the better. Fortunately, beyond traditional contacts, such as in-person, online chats, phone, (including online click-to-call), and e-mail, there are numerous ways to increase your touch points, such as:

- Messenger options (e.g., Facebook Messenger, WhatsApp, etc.)
- Slack dedicated channel(s)
- Social media groups (private and public)
- Video (e.g., broadcast videos, personalized video messages, etc.)

Every touch point your business has with your customers and prospects is a priceless opportunity to build strong and long-lasting relationships. It's also an opportunity for your business to learn from your prospects and customers while your business continues to build familiarity and trust. As Guerrilla marketers know, familiarity and trust create repeat purchases and precious referrals from your customers.

6.20 * INFLUENCE

As a successful business owner, you have influence, which means . . . you are an influencer. Be it online or offline or both, you have valuable influence, and that's an easy opening to help you market your business.

However, with influence comes skepticism, criticism, doubt, and the questioning of your authenticity (see Section 9.16, "Authenticity"). Therefore, your attitudes (see Section IX, "Guerrilla Company Attitudes") and actions are always being evaluated to confirm your authenticity. Your prospects, customers, employees, community, etc. are continually evaluating your authenticity by evaluating your attitudes in areas, such as:

- Generosity (see Volume 1, Section 9.12, "Generosity")
- Inspiring (see Section 9.14, "Inspire")
- Responsiveness (see Volume 1, Section 9.5, "Responsive and Attentive")
- Focus (see Volume 1, Section 9.10, "Focused")
- Energy and action (see Volume 1, Section 9.9, "High Energy and Take Action")
- Mentoring (see Section 9.22, "Mentoring")

When you're intentional about your influence, you're a great listener with an honest interest in people. Therefore:

- You're thoughtful about like-minded fellow business owners, and you're eager to recommend and help promote their businesses
- You enjoy listening to, learning from, and helping your prospects and customers identify opportunities and find solutions, whether it's yours or it's a solution that others provide (from recommending your favorite dry cleaner, a great movie, a complex business solution, etc.)
- You're eager to learn from and share your influence and expertise with the community, business, and industry associations

- You provide great stories, expertise, and experience with media contacts, which gives them incredibly valuable content while they give you valued marketing and advertising exposure
- You're eager to help your employees, vendors, and suppliers grow and achieve their potential

In short, you believe, as John F Kennedy coined, "A rising tide lifts all boats." Therefore, you intentionally let your influence inspire and help others rise up along with yourself.

6.21 * HUMAN BILLBOARDS AND DIRECTIONALS

Human billboards have been around for countless decades, and there is a good reason: they work. Though the space may seem crowded now for human billboards and human directionals, it's not for Guerrilla marketers. Why?

Guerrilla marketers see the status quo and seek to replace it with knowledge, low-cost, unconventional, and creative tactics to convey and promote their compelling product(s), service(s), or ideas. When you go to gMarketing.com/Club, we'll share several examples that range from traditional to expensive to gimmicky. The examples are not highlighted for the purpose of replicating them but, instead, for the purpose of your business finding its own creativity and inspiration that will attract your prospects and customers.

The job of a Guerrilla marketer is to compel your prospects to notice your business. Once they do, your call to action must then motivate them to take a desired action (e.g., try a sample, make a purchase, etc.). Your existing customers also need to be motivated to make repeat purchases and precious referrals of their friends, family, and associates.

Your human billboard and human directional marketing is made effective when it's attention-getting and consistent with all of your marketing efforts. As an example, as we mentioned in the Introduction, if you drive by a business and see a street team or group of picketers, you're likely to look. Then you'll notice they are holding clever signs promoting the business and asking you to honk because you love this business. If it gets your attention and you find it clever, amusing, or intriguing, your reaction will likely be to look the business up (search engines, social media, or whatever you prefer). At that point, consistent marketing will determine the next step.

Street teams and friendly picketers are versatile (handing out samples, directing people to their location, being stationed at a booth at an event, etc.) and can garner attention and pique the interest of your prospects and customers. However, it's what happens next that determines if that piqued interest will be turned into profits.

Now is the time when your attention to the details (i.e., consistency, USP, repetition, great reviews, a clear and compelling description of the business, easy-to-access hours, and contact information) will or will not make that attention turn prospects into customers. It's really just that simple. Guerrilla marketers thrive because they tend to the tiny, supercharged details that can generate big profits.

If the business gets the attention of their prospects, but they then find it hard to locate the business in an online and/or social search or the marketing is disconnected, their prospects:

- Aren't sure about the business and become skeptical
- See that their social media looks different from their website, which makes them more skeptical
- Can't read their copy because the fonts are hard to read, or they find the graphics unappealing
- Find their hours and contact information are inconvenient, incomplete, or missing

That's a business that views marketing as a series of disconnected gimmicks, or it's a business that thinks marketing is a light switch they turn on and off. That business takes action, but it doesn't understand how to set itself apart with good Guerrilla Marketing.

Successful Guerrilla businesses are intelligently designed and operated from the outside in (i.e., from the customers' points of view, needs, desires, and expectations) and with consistency and repetition. Those businesses use intelligent marketing, which is Guerrilla Marketing.

Successful Guerrilla Marketing means that prospects, whose interest has been piqued by the street team or friendly picketers, then experience a business that's:

- Easy to find in an online search and whose social media is consistent with their website and/or retail locations and all other aspects of their marketing
- Well-rated and reviewed
- Convenient to reach and interact with, in the way the prospect wants to reach and interact with them
- Clear and appealing while they quickly explain a compelling and relatable problem that is solved in a way the prospects find motivating
- Unique and has several competitive advantages
- Innovative and/or has an appealing product(s) and service(s)
- Consistent and trustworthy
- Easy to do business with (e.g., in-store, online, delivery, curbside pick-up, etc.)

Your knowledge of what compels your prospects and customers, combined with your Guerrilla Creativity and your consistency, will make your human billboard and directional marketing not just noticeable, but also a sales producing and profitable marketing tactic. After all, when your human billboard and human directional marketing garners attention but not sales, it's not working. You're not in the attention-getting business, you're in the business of turning prospects into highly satisfied customers who are loyal to your business for years to come.

6.22 * BE STICKIE AND COMPELLING

Guerrilla marketers are keenly aware that for their long-term success, the importance of compelling their customers to make repeat purchases and precious referrals is critical. The question is, how do you make your business stickie and compelling to achieve those precious repeat purchases and referrals?

Be Unique

Your USP is what sets your business apart. Whether it's your patented product(s) or service(s) or the quality of your product(s), and service(s), what makes your business unique makes it interesting and memorable, so promote it.

Appeal to the Senses

As we addressed in Volume 1, Section 8.32, "Subliminal Marketing," senses influence purchase decisions. Your prospects and customers are motivated by what they see, touch, smell, taste, and hear. That sensory stimulation is compelling and memorable, and it motivates your prospects to make purchases and your customers to make repeat purchases. We'll expand on this topic in Volume 3, Section 8.46, "Appeal to the Senses."

Be Relevant

Beyond what makes your business unique is how your business is relevant, particularly in the mindset of your prospects and customers. Does your business name make them feel relevant? For example, does your business make your prospects and customers feel:

- Environmentally conscious?
- Leading edge and/or innovative?
- Important, influential, etc.?
- Exclusive?
- Inclusive and friendly?
- Trendy, popular, etc.?
- Value conscientious?
- Splurge worthy, successful, etc.?
- Charitable and/or cause-committed?
- Intelligent?
- Social media/word of mouth share worthy?
- Unique, because no other business that can . . .?

Loyalty, Reward, and Referral Programs

Loyalty, reward, and referral programs are a great way to attract prospects to your business and encourage your customers to make repeat purchases while stimulating precious referrals. Within your programs, you can offer sneak peeks, early order access for new products, exclusive products and services, etc. Redeemable points and rewards are also valuable for customers. Customers can earn compelling loyalty rewards, such as cash, free products, and/or charitable donations to a cause to which they are committed.

As much as feasible, Guerrilla marketers are wise to incorporate multiple stickie and compelling elements. As an example, think about a hyper-competitive industry/sector, such as selling coffee.

There could be five or more different coffee sellers within a block. One of them will be the busiest. Why? What makes that one coffee seller so stickie and compelling?

It's unlikely that one thing created their stickiness; it's more likely to be a combination of or all the above examples. Perhaps, it's their rewards program and how their store makes customers feel (e.g., relaxed and rewarded or awake and invigorated). Regardless, it's what makes that business unique and why their customers don't consider the four other coffee sellers within a block.

The more you learn about what appeals to your customers, the easier it is to make your business stickie and compelling.

SECTION VII

Guerrilla Non-Media Marketing

GUERRILLA NON-MEDIA MARKETING

Low-cost opportunities abound with Guerrilla Non-Media Marketing tactics. These low-cost Guerrilla Marketing tactics take your knowledge, time, energy, and creativity and turn them into profits.

When implemented correctly, Guerrilla Non-Media Marketing tactics will generate long-lasting opportunities to tell the story of your business, share your USP, and give your prospects compelling reasons to become your customers. Equally, they give your customers a compelling reason to make repeat and additional purchases and to refer their friends, family, and co-workers to your business.

Guerrilla Non-Media Marketing tactics are often far more memorable than other Guerrilla Media tactics. They provide your business with the opportunity to interact and connect with your prospects and customers. With that interaction, you have the ability to build long-lasting relationships with your customers, which investments in paid advertising may not achieve.

When you engage in Guerrilla Non-Media Marketing tactics, you'll showcase the expertise of yourself or your business while sharing the benefits and advantages of your product(s) or service(s). These tactics utilize your relationship-building skills to forge productive arrangements with employees, customers, complementary businesses, industry contacts, media contributors, and community members. These relationship-building skills may be utilized online or in-person or a combination of the two.

Many businesses never take the time to engage in these non-media tactics, and that's great news for Guerrilla marketers. Once you start realizing the kind of success and profits you can generate from these Guerrilla Non-Media Marketing tactics, you'll want to include more of them in your Guerrilla Marketing plan.

Invest a bit of your knowledge, time, energy, and creativity in these Guerrilla Non-Media Marketing tactics and see how you can turn them into satisfying and profitable relationships for your business.

In Volume 1, we addressed:

7.1   Organizing and Hosting Meetups
7.2   Benefits and Competitive Advantages
7.3   Buzz and Shares
7.4   Gift Cards
7.5   Memberships

Now, we'll pick up where we left off. Without further ado, let's get started.

7.15 * KNOW YOUR SURROUNDINGS

Imagine that you've enthusiastically attended a community event that attracted thousands of attendees. As the event is closing in the late afternoon, you turn your attention to local businesses that you would like to visit. Much to your surprise, many of those local businesses are closed (e.g., closed for that day or they don't open until later).

Thousands of dollars walked up to those businesses, but with closed doors, those dollars went to another business. It's hard to imagine, but many businesses don't maintain an awareness of their surroundings. It can be more common with physical business locations than online businesses. However, it's not exclusive. Many online businesses have had their sites crash (i.e., no sales and negative impressions) when they receive a surge of business.

It's a challenge to prepare for those unknown situations (e.g., a mention from an online influencer or something that goes viral). Let's focus on preparing for the known. An online business that knows, for example, that it's going to be marketed by an affiliate partner, appear on television, or be mentioned by an influencer, must over-prepare for the opportunity to ensure that their website is accurate and capable.

Equally, a physical business location must be tapped into the local community and adapt to be ready for opportunities. Your business's participation in clubs, Chamber of Commerce activities, neighborhood associations, and Nextdoor will be valuable. At the same time, you can keep your business aware with municipal, entertainment venue, convention center, and shopping center notifications.

Both physical business locations and online businesses can also use Google Alerts with targeted terms that surround your business. The online social listening tools that we covered in Section 4.55, "Social Media Monitoring," can also be used to become aware of industry, business, or location-specific mentions.

The more your business is "in the know," the more prepared you'll be when opportunity is knocking. Guerrilla marketers want to be sure their doors (virtual or physical) are wide open and their business is eager, welcoming, well-stocked, and staffed to embrace opportunities that build their success.

7.16 * LEAVE BEHINDS

Guerrilla marketers reap the rewards from unexpected marketing. Leave behinds are opportunities to make lasting impressions. An unexpected gift that is useful, creative, fun, and engaging helps your business build long-lasting relationships with your customers.

Your promotional items that we discussed in Section 3.22, "Promotional Item Advertising," and Section 3.23, "Promotional Item Marketing," are useful for compelling prospects to become customers, but they are also great leave behinds for your customers. In addition to those items, your business can consider offering:

- Samples
- A bonus (e.g., free dessert in a to-go bag)
- An extra item (e.g., the "baker's dozen," which is giving your customers thirteen items instead of just twelve)
- A credit to use for a future purchase
- "The next one is on us" offers (e.g., providing a favorite item for free on the next visit)
- An exclusive experience, such as a sneak-peak or behind the scenes access that is only for your customers (see Volume 3, Section 7.24, "Exclusive Experiences")

- Extra reward points in your loyalty program to say thank you, Happy Birthday, etc.
- A handwritten thank you note that's personalized

Effective leave behinds are a surprise, hassle-free, thoughtful, and memorable marketing opportunity. Being thoughtful means carefully considering what appeals to your customers. For example, if you give samples of your tea bags to a customer that only buys coffee, your leave behind is likely to fall flat. However, an unexpected thank you card that provides a free coffee on their next visit is thoughtful and memorable.

Leave behinds are your opportunities to extend your customers' experiences, beyond their purchase or transaction, to reinforce their positive impressions of your business. That experience leads to building long-lasting relationships that become repeat purchases and a shareable experience that creates precious referrals for your business.

7.17 * RETURNS AND EXCHANGES

Returns and exchanges are a necessary part of being in business. Fortunately, Guerrilla marketers know that this necessity is also an opportunity. Guerrilla marketers know these are the times for their low-cost, unconventional, and creative tactics to shine.

The common components that you can reimagine and be creative with are:
- Method of refund (e.g., full refund in the original form of payment or options, such as a store credit, a gift card, etc.)
- Time period (e.g., "30 days" or opt for a much longer time period)
- Reason for return (e.g., restrictions can apply or opt for no-hassle, no questions)
- Receipt (e.g., required or not)
- Condition of the item being returned (e.g., new and "as purchased" with original tags/packaging or allow for other conditions)
- Ease of shipping returns (e.g., customer must contact the business and interact to arrange for a return or a pre-paid shipping label is provided with the order)

- Ease of returning at a physical business location (e.g., a well-marked dedicated area or returns can be processed at the same time and place as new purchases)
- The time it takes to process a return (at a physical business location, satisfying speedy returns give your customers the extra time they can use to shop for new purchases)

Guerrilla marketers create (or refine) their return policies with the end in mind. Given that having as few returns as possible is the best goal, it's ideal to proactively prevent the vast majority before they happen. Therefore, you want to proactively stop the issues that cause returns. Consider:

- If your product or service is often gifted, make your gift cards an appealing option to reduce returns. For example, offer a $10 gift card to the buyer for each $50 card they purchase; offer unique and spectacularly packaged gift cards that are attractive and engaging, etc.)
- Online, enhanced pictures and descriptions (see Section 4.46, "Enhanced Images and Descriptions") can make all the difference. Photos that are unrealistic regarding quality, color, size, fit, etc. will only increase your returns.
- Consistency in your service and/or product quality, sizing, usability, etc. will give your customers an experience they trust. When your customers know they can rely on your business, you've made it easy to increase their number of repeat purchases.

Your ratings and reviews and those of your competitors will tell you exactly what your customers are satisfied and dissatisfied with when you take the time to listen and react. Fortunately, the better your products' or services' quality and marketing are, the lower your return rate is, and that allows for a Guerrilla marketer to be creative, unconventional, and even a bit outrageous with their return program.

However, when your business does have a customer that wants to return or exchange, make the most of the opportunity. For example:

- Market and merchandise your return area in your physical business location. Forget standing in long or unorganized lines. Instead, fill the area with appealing merchandise and turn a return into an exchange or a new purchase (e.g., T.J.Maxx, utilizes one organized and merchandised line for returns, exchanges, and new purchasers)

- Provide extended conveniences and benefits within a tiered loyalty program or within a subscription and/or membership program
- Don't require receipts for those who opt to receive their receipt via email as a great way to encourage your customers to provide their email addresses
- Be transparent and clearly communicate the hassle-free process (e.g., provide tracking with your pre-paid labels for returns that are shipped, provide the processing time, etc.)
- Make "no hassle" clear, but also talk to and listen to your customers as you create and build relationships. Ask if they would mind providing their feedback because you know returns inconvenience them, and you want shopping at your business to be convenient and delightful. By capturing the answers on a short questionnaire, you can understand the changes you need to make in your business to prevent returns, and you're creating a relationship while delighting your customers.

Many businesses dread returns and exchanges. Fortunately, Guerrillas know that a certain number of exchanges and returns are inevitable. Choosing to see them as opportunities, allows the unconventional marketing by your business to shine.

From your customers' point of view, your business can take the return and exchange experience and make it positive and memorable. It's a great time to put your lateral thinking skills (see Section 9.23, "Lateral Thinking") to work to help you reimagine the entire process, from the customer's point of view and with the end in mind.

7.18 * CUSTOMER LOYALTY

Guerrilla marketers understand, better than most businesses, the importance of customer loyalty. Loyal customers make repeat purchases and offer precious referrals, which is the fuel for the long-term success of your business. In fact, according to Bain & Company, companies that lead their industry in customer satisfaction rankings for three or more years ". . . grow revenues more than twice as fast as their industry peers," Any opportunity to grow your revenues more than twice as fast as your peers is an opportunity Guerrilla marketers don't let slip away from them.

Businesses whose customers don't make repeat purchases and referrals are in the constant and expensive pursuit of prospects. These businesses operate like a sieve—customers come into the top, and they go right out of the bottom. Guerrillas don't make that mistake. Instead, they know to focus on loyal customers and precious referrals.

In Volume 1, Section 6.11, "Satisfied and Delighted Customers," we shared numerous ideas to help your business succeed. By making your business irresistible, you are part of the way toward creating loyal customers. Now, it's time to turn your attention to making them feel appreciated so they want to remain engaged with and loyal to your business.

Guerrillas invest knowledge, time, energy, creativity, and imagination when creating their loyalty and reward programs that keep their customers delighted. According to Statista research, customers belong "to 14 loyalty programs on average but actively used half of those."

For your loyalty program to be engaging for customers, it must be unique and valuable (as determined by your customers) while being easy to understand and hassle-free. A loyalty program can be as simple as a business-sized punch card that, with repeat purchases, earns discounts or free product(s) and/or service(s).

However, for most businesses, a high-quality platform is needed for your loyalty program. Getting to know these options will help you find the right features to fit your business:

- **FiveStars**: helps your business combine customer loyalty with automated marketing. With the use of tags, you can pour your customer knowledge into their system, which allows for personalized, targeted, unique, and engaging offers
- **TapMango:** offers customizable loyalty programs with a quick set-up and a fully automated point-of-sale (POS) integration with all major systems. With an automated viral friend referral system, customizable promotions, and flexible reward structures, you can create an engaging loyalty program that also generates revenue
- **PreferredPatron**: has both reward levels and tiers to influence loyalty and purchases. With monetary, in-store, or downloadable rewards, your business can customize an engaging experience that motivates and delights your customers

- **Kangaroo**: has the option of rewarding customers by visit or by spend, and they offer a geolocation feature to target nearby customers. With branded digital gift cards, social media referral tools, and POS integration, you can create a measurable loyalty program that helps you build long-lasting relationships
- **Influitive**: offers an engagement platform that focuses on personalization (e.g., content, rewards, etc.) to increase the appeal of your business. They also utilize gamification with customizable incentives and rewards to engage and motivate your customers. Their measuring, tracking, and analytics keep your business focused on creating and keeping loyal customers

Once you've found the right platform to utilize, you'll quickly have a loyalty program that is easy for your business to administer and easy for your customers to engage with. When your loyalty program is also rich with rewards that motivate them, you're making your business irresistible, and they want to remain your loyal customer.

Now, it's time to turn your attention to unconventional and creative ideas to reward customer loyalty while building long-lasting relationships. Your loyalty program stands out when it's different from the rest. Therefore, Guerrillas look for ways to make their customers feel not just appreciated and rewarded, but also noticed, exclusive, and special. To get your creativity and ideas flowing, consider:

- Hosting customer appreciation events. For example, a B2B business can provide networking opportunities to help their customers grow their businesses and/or find valuable resources
- Treating your customers like the VIPs they are (see Section 7.21 "Customer Entertainment")
- Offering customer exclusives, such as sneak peeks, early sale access, early access to new products, behind-the-scenes access (photos, videos, etc.), exclusive products, etc. For example, successful luxury/exotic automobile manufacturers utilize exclusive products to delight their customers. They exclusively offer certain models and products to their existing customers (non-customers are unable to purchase them). That is a winning way to make your customers feel noticed, exclusive, special, delighted, and motivated to be loyal

The more personalized, unique, engaging, valuable, easy to understand, and hassle-free your loyalty program is, the more it's working for the long-term success of your business. A successful loyalty program, along with a successful referral program (see Volume 1, Section 8.25, "Referral Programs"), gives your business the necessary low-cost and profitable fuel for your long-term success.

7.19 * TALK OF THE TOWN

Guerrilla marketers thrive by being at the center of the positive talk of the town. Your town could be online or on a map. Regardless, Guerrilla Marketing is a 360-degree consistent methodology that weaves through every aspect of your business. Your intelligent, impactful, and consistent marketing drives attention to your business, which then turns into profits.

So, how do you become the positive talk of the town? It begins with understanding that your business is marketing with every interaction you have, so be intentional about it. You have many opportunities at your fingertips.

Public Relations (PR) Efforts

Guerrilla public relations is a low-cost method of garnering high-quality exposure and publicity for your business by building strong, collaborative relationships with leading and influential people. Guerrilla public relations helps establish the identity of your business (or yourself), promote your USP, and gives you authority that turns into profits. To learn more about what you can do, see Volume 1, Section 7.8, "Public Relations (PR)."

Be The Place Where People Go to Connect

Online, many social media companies began as small businesses with a vision of how people can connect. Whether your primary business focus is online or offline, at your physical business location(s), your business can be the place where people go to connect. From Facebook groups to Clubhouse, Reddit, Slack channels, and smaller-scale options, like WhatsApp group chats, you have numerous online tools at your fingertips that can allow your customers to interact and connect. You can also host video meetings in an Ask Me Anything format (AMA) to get valuable insight, drive engagement, and support.

At your physical business location(s), you can host Meetups, distribute community newsletters, be active on Nextdoor, offer conveniences (see Volume 1, Section 8.21, "Convenience") that attract people to your location. You can also organize or participate in charitable events, such as hosting donation drop-offs and perhaps contributing a set dollar amount or physical item for each donation. That opportunity is particularly powerful if your locations sell items that people want to donate (e.g., a toy store or children's clothing store).

Conclusion

The more you do to attract your prospects and customers and encourage them to connect and interact, the more you'll learn about them. At the same time, you're making your business memorable, stickie (see Section 6.22, "Be Stickie and Compelling"), and part of the positive talk of the town.

7.20 * BOXING

If your business is shipping and/or boxing (e.g., actual boxes, carry-out containers, dry cleaning bags, etc.), you're presenting your product(s) to your customers. Without much of an investment, you can make that presentation memorable.

Most companies ship in plain brown packaging and place the items in the box or container without consideration for presentation. While those companies are being ordinary, Guerrilla marketers seek to be unconventional and utilize creative tactics.

Guerrilla marketers seek to make their boxes and packaging a memorable experience that promotes their business name and USP. For example:
- Make your business stand out by utilizing printed boxes or containers (or more economic options, such as printed tape and/or stickers) to market your business
- Print messages on your boxes or containers that invite your customers to interact a bit longer—while your business creates an experience/emotion and builds a positive impression. Imagine a package arrives, and the printed message on the box is "You're my favorite customer," "Whew,

so happy to be at your doorstep," or "[insert your business name] loves you." The options are limitless with your creativity and customer knowledge

- Provide unexpected experiences, such as samples, recipes, a discount on their next purchase, an invitation to an exclusive event that is only for customers, a thank you note, etc.

- When appropriate, utilize the promotional items that you're using for advertising (see Section 3.22, "Promotional Item Advertising") and marketing (see Section 3.23, "Promotional Item Marketing") for an element of surprise

- Pay attention to the presentation inside the box or container. For example, the inside of the box or container is marketing space to promote your business and thank your customers. You can also customize the packing materials, such as with the air-packs, tissue, or packing paper, etc.

- Look at re-usable packaging and container options that will extend the experience with your business and make it more memorable

- Place your order materials (e.g., receipt, packing slip, instructions, return labels, warranty registration, catalog) in a "thank you" envelope, and make it easy for them to access videos or customer service if they prefer (see Section 5.14, "Variety and Modality")

- Ask for their five-star review. Use a QR code to make it easy for them to provide their ratings and reviews. By capturing their ratings and reviews at the time when they are delighted with your presentation, you can capture their best impression of your business

- Utilize a second QR code to make it easy and welcoming for them to connect with your business if they feel their experience is less than five stars so you can quickly correct any issues. Most customers are forgiving of issues if they are easily resolved

How can you make the experience unique and memorable for your business? Regardless of your budget, there are always unconventional and creative tactics to make your packaging and containers stand out to provide a memorable presentation. For example, a children's store, with some crayons, can make their packaging unique while providing an entertaining coloring opportunity for the children in their store. The result is customized and engaging artwork on their boxes or packaging that turns into significant social sharing, which the business harnesses while building relationships.

Once you have your packaging ready to shine, consider that getting your package to your customer in a timely manner is also a significant factor in determining their satisfaction. Whether your business is using a shipping service (e.g., FedEx, UPS, USPS, etc.) or a delivery service (e.g., UberEats, Door Dash, Instacart, etc.) it's necessary to:

- Avoid lengthy processing times
- Avoid add-on fees from your business, such as handling charges, which are roadblocks that create dissatisfaction
- Make sure your items are packaged to arrive intact

For example, you can tell when you've ordered food delivery from a Guerrilla business. Your items arrive in a creative bag (such as a reusable shopping bag), each item is labeled, the food containers are leak-proof, the condiments and utensils are in a separate bag, or there is a thank you note and/or a surprise that makes you look forward to your next order—all as you share a photo with your friends.

If packaging and shipping is not your expertise, there are great resources ready to help so you can remain focused on your marketing and other aspects of your business. If you're just beginning, there are resources to help with a few packages, such as Fed-Ex Office and The UPS Store. As your business grows, there are order fulfillment businesses you can integrate with. They store your products and automate your shipping for fast turn-around and robust shipping options to delight your customers. Additionally, if you're selling on Amazon, Fulfillment by Amazon can give your products the "Prime" delivery experience.

See Volume 1, Section 8.10, "How Your Business Delivers," for more ideas.

7.21 * CUSTOMER ENTERTAINMENT

Customer entertainment was once thought of as a tool for big-budget B2B entities. By entertaining their customers, B2B entities seek to build relationships, motivate additional purchases, and receive referrals. The big-budget B2B entities often utilize their big-budget advertising and marketing sponsorships to acquire those customer entertainment opportunities.

Guerrilla marketers share the value in those opportunities. However, they view customer entertainment on a different scale and as an even larger opportunity. After all, what is the purpose of customer entertainment? For Guerrilla marketers, customer entertainment is an opportunity to build relationships and create memorable and shareable experiences that keep their business top-of-mind with their customers, well beyond the purchase or service experience. By doing so, they're extending the effectiveness of their marketing investments.

Customer entertainment can take on many forms. If your budget allows for high-priced items, such as luxury box access at a venue, tickets to sporting or entertainment events, and/or access to something unique or exclusive, those are great ways to entertain your customers. However, if your budget is not there just yet, there are still opportunities for your business. Customer entertainment is not limited to big budgets and high-priced items.

Customer entertainment can be as simple as taking an ordinary experience and making it entertaining and memorable. For example, if appropriate, your business can provide coffee, beverages, food, wi-fi, power outlets, printers, a gift shop, television, and/or video entertainment at your physical location business. But a Guerrilla marketer does not stop there.

For example, an automobile service center can provide all the above, but it's not likely to be memorable. Therefore, they add in an entertaining virtual reality experience that showcases the latest car models, video game consoles, and/or a driving simulator for more entertainment. They also seek to make the experience personalized. Therefore, the service professional intentionally observes their customer drinking a hot beverage in the waiting area, and they see an opportunity.

When their automobile is ready, the customer discovers that the service professional has placed a thank you note and a hot beverage travel cup (with the business logo from their gift shop) in their automobile and/or a gift bag (with their logo) with the coffee or tea the customer was enjoying.

That business has entertained their customer while they waited for their service to be completed and extended the experience well beyond the time they spent having their automobile serviced. The customer, in turn, has shared their delight with the great service they experienced with their friends, family, and associates.

Additionally, each time the customer uses the travel cup, they are reminded of that delightful experience and the business is top-of-mind. At the same time, the customer is promoting the business with the visual (i.e., the business logo on the travel cup) and their praise for the business when a prospect inquires.

The Guerrilla business takes it a step further. With an adaptable CRM system, the service professional tags the customer's profile with the item they've provided (i.e., beverage travel cup and/or coffee or tea gift bag) so they can provide something different and appealing the next time.

The extra step is how Guerrilla marketers set their businesses apart and make their customers feel special, appreciated, and noticed. After providing an entertaining experience, that Guerrilla business, with a gift under $10, took an extra step to make the interaction with their customer sharable and memorable. At the same time, they extended the experience beyond that day, which keeps their business top-of-mind longer, thereby extending the effectiveness of their marketing investments.

Effective customer entertainment is an opportunity to build relationships and create delightful, memorable, and shareable experiences that keep your business top-of-mind well beyond the purchase or service experiences. By doing so, your marketing investments are effective, and they're working harder. An entertaining experience is sharable, and it motivates your customers to recommend your business to their friends, family, and associates. Those precious referrals supercharge your marketing investment and are the fuel for your long-term success.

For more ideas, refer to Section 3.28, "Product Labels," to learn more about how Krug and 19 Crimes utilized their labels to create entertaining experiences for their customers.

While using entertainment in your marketing can easily be effective, using entertainment in your advertising is a risk to be very carefully considered. Consider this:

- Dollar Shave Club marketed entertaining videos that attracted prospects and compelled them to become customers, which turned into sales and profits
- Pets.com entertained their prospects with a sock puppet, but it didn't translate into enough sales and profits and the business failed

You, likely, can think of a number of entertaining advertisements, but do you remember the entertainment or the advertiser? Equally, were you compelled and motivated to purchase their product or service? Never forget that your creativity is measured in profits (see Volume 1, Section 2.8, "Advertising Keys to Success," for more information).

7.22 * INCENTIVIZE

Guerrilla marketers appreciate the power of incentivizing a desired behavior. Incentives are effective for motivating employees, prospects, and customers. You can incentivize sales, referrals (see Volume 1, Section 8.25, "Referral Programs"), loyalty (see Section 7.18, "Customer Loyalty"), and more. Those incentives can take on numerous forms, such as:

Ethical Bribes

Ethical bribes mean your business is giving your prospects and customers an ethical incentive to take a particular and ethical action. For example, if you're selling through a third-party platform (e.g., Amazon, Walmart, etc.), then your business success is predicated upon positive reviews. To achieve those positive reviews and to, more importantly, create a direct connection with your customers, your business can offer an ethical bribe to incentivize those actions.

For instance: *Receive an exclusive product when you register and send us a link to your five-star review.* With this ethical bribe, a customer has purchased your product, and you're providing a thank-you incentive (i.e., a desirable and exclusive product) that encourages a five-star review. Your customers are excited to register and provide their information to receive a desirable and exclusive thank you gift. As a result, your business achieves more five-star reviews and has a direct connection with the customer, which gives your business the opportunity to encourage repeat purchases and encourages them to join your loyalty and referral programs.

Warranty programs (see Volume 1, Section 7.13, "Warranties, Guarantees, and Service Programs") are also ethical bribes that increase customer satisfaction while requiring registration. That registration provides your business with opportunities to create relationships with your customers. Those relationships provide opportunities for repeat purchases and precious referrals which, of course, is the fuel for long-term success.

Programs that provide their products and/or services to people for free, in exchange for reviews, are widely considered to lack ethics or transparency or both. Guerrilla Marketing always obeys the highest code of ethics and transparency. Guerrilla Marketing is also completely and totally honest.

Reward Programs

Reward programs are powerful incentives for your employees, prospects, and customers. Reward programs improve satisfaction while encouraging repeat sales, referrals, and loyalty (see Section 7.18 "Customer Loyalty") to/for your business, and they can be structured in a variety of ways, such as:

- Points that accumulate and earn products, services, experiences, gift cards, monetary discounts, etc.
- Cashback, such as a rebate or programs like Rakuten
- Bonuses for employees to meet defined goals

Whether your business wants to incentivize employees' sales or customer loyalty, reward programs can go a long way toward achieving your goals.

Compensation

Employees are, of course, motivated by compensation. That compensation is an incentive, which can be monetary, through benefits, and/or via recognition. Though recognition is rarely thought of as compensation, being dynamic with regular on-the-spot recognition is an incentive. An employee that knows they may be in the spotlight today for their great work, shows up to work with more focus, enthusiasm, and satisfaction.

A Guerrilla working environment rewards and spotlights individual and team performances. The goals of the business should be widely known, and every successful milestone should be celebrated along the way. Your compensation program should be carefully crafted to incentivize the right action. See Section 8.35, "Compensation," for more information.

There are several keys to success when it comes to incentives:

- Tiered approach (i.e., providing the greatest incentives to the greatest achievers)
- Ease of use

- Value (i.e., the more perceived value your incentives have, the more motivating they are)
- Easy feedback
- Monitoring

Carefully consider and monitor your incentives to help to ensure success. Weaknesses in your incentives can be quickly and easily exploited, without regard to the impact on your business. For example, if you create an incentive to reward sales/service people who get the most five-star reviews, your well-crafted incentive, which is intended to reward excellent service, can quickly turn negative (in an expensive way) if your employees create fake accounts/customers and fake reviews.

7.23 * EXPANDED DISTRIBUTION

In Section 3.27, "Retail Location Selection," we addressed many ways you can expand your business beyond your current location (e.g., store-in-store, vending machines, food hall or courts, pop-ups, kiosks, self-serve locker systems, on-wheels/mobile) while lessening your financial risk and offering convenience to your customers and prospects.

Conveniences such as curbside pick-up and delivery can also increase your reach, sales, and profits. However, there are several other ways that a Guerrilla business can expand its distribution to increase sales and profits.

Wholesale

Having your product discovered by retailers is a challenge. There are the traditional options, such as industry wholesale trade shows (see Volume 1, Section 3.19, "Events, Conferences, and Trade Shows," for more information about how to make your business shine) and distributors.

Fortunately, there are additional services that can help:

- **RangeMe:** helps retailers discover new products and connect with potential suppliers
- **IndieMe:** connects artists and retailers

- **NuOrder:** is an e-commerce platform that makes the wholesale process collaborative in the fashion and apparel industry while allowing buys to happen in real-time
- **Supplied:** offers an all-in-one platform to connect retailers with a wide variety of wholesale products
- **Tundra:** is an online wholesale marketplace where retailers and businesses can find products and make purchases
- **Abound:** has created a wholesale marketplace for independent retailers

Your business can also work directly with online retailers that focus on offering products from small businesses. For example:

- **The Grommet:** accepts applications from businesses offering unique, innovative, and useful products
- **Touch of Modern:** considers businesses that focus on the men's lifestyle space

Dropshipping

To expand their distribution, Guerrilla marketers also consider dropshipping. You can begin dropshipping your products yourself or work with an existing dropshipper to increase your distribution. How does it work?

The dropship business provides an FTP inventory feed that retailers connect with their systems to add in-stock items (with photos, descriptions, etc.) to their online stores. When an order is placed, it's transmitted to the dropshipper with the customer's shipping information.

The dropshipper charges the seller for the product(s), and the order is sent by the dropshipper directly to the customer. The dropshipper transmits the shipping tracking information to the seller so the seller can send a shipping notification (and a thank you) to their customer.

In addition to the product and shipping cost, a dropshipper typically charges a percentage of the sale and/or a flat fee per order, and the seller retains the remainder of the mark-up.

In the reverse, if your business is selling wholesale products, you could offer to dropship for other sellers. This harnesses their marketing efforts and increases your volume.

Third-Party Sellers

Guerrilla marketers have many options when they're selling retail products online, such as a third-party selling platform. What is a third-party selling platform?

There are a couple of different types of third-party selling platforms, for example:

- **Retailer Selling Platforms:** Walmart, Amazon, eBay, Etsy, etc.
- **Social Media Selling Platforms:** Instagram shops, Facebook shops, etc.
- **Television Shopping Channels:** Home Shopping Network (HSN), QVC, etc.

The advantage of third-party selling platforms is the ease of selling (from a technology perspective) and for some, their marketing efforts. The third-party selling platform takes on the responsibility for the technology and security that's required to run the site. That allows your business to focus on marketing your compelling products, answering questions from your prospects and customers, fulfilling orders, and providing excellent service for your customers.

The primary disadvantage can be a lack of a direct relationship with your customers (specifically on retailer selling platforms), which is critical to growing your business. Additionally, when using a third-party selling platform, your business is predicated on your flawless adherence to the current and changing rules (which can be extremely broad) of the selling platform provider. Your sales can be immediately stopped (including holding your payments for sales incurred) if your account is suspended or terminated at the determination of the platform provider.

White and Private Label

Manufacturers can increase their distribution with white labeling, which allows other businesses to put their name and/or logo (i.e., rebrand) on the product(s) your business produces. Equally, online businesses can sell their information products to other businesses, which then market them as their own.

On the other hand, private labeling is a product that is, typically, produced/manufactured, and customized exclusively for one retailer. Private labeling usually requires large orders and, therefore, can be more expensive. Grocery store chains and drug store chains often utilize private labeling for their branded products.

Licensing

If you hold a patent to a product, choosing to license the product, instead of manufacturing it yourself, can quickly help your business accomplish more. Equally, as your successful Guerrilla Marketing creates a desirable brand, you can license your brand name to expand your product line and broaden the appeal of your brand to a larger audience, thereby increasing your distribution.

Sports teams are a good example. They license their brand name to a multitude of manufacturers to expand their distribution. Instead of having products that only appear in sports-centric retail locations, they can expand to a variety of fashion retailers, automobile accessory retailers, drug stores, grocery stores, etc.

For more ideas, also reference:

- Volume 1, Section 7.6, "Fusion/Affiliate Marketing and Collaboration"
- Volume 1, Section 5.11, "Informercials"
- Section 4.50, "Digital Account-Based Marketing"

SECTION VIII

Guerrilla Company Attributes

GUERRILLA COMPANY ATTRIBUTES

Your company attributes are the characteristics and qualities that your business displays to your prospects and customers, whether you realize it or not. By defining, embracing, and being intentional about your company attributes, you have a broad array of Guerrilla Marketing tactics at the ready. Those tactics work together to create compelling and robust marketing for your business that appeals to your prospects and customers and delivers to their expectations.

Taking intentional ownership and taking the time to define and outline your Guerrilla Company Attributes puts your energy and Guerrilla Creativity to great use. Without awareness and ownership of the power of your company attributes, you're not engaging in intentional and intelligent marketing.

You're marketing with every bit of contact and interaction you have inside your company and that your business has with the outside world. When you're intentional with your marketing, you're the conductor of a world-class orchestra, with every instrument in perfect harmony and creating beautiful music together with audiences that are eager to hear more.

Guerrilla marketers know that being intentional means they're engaged in intelligent marketing. Therefore, you're focusing on the powerful details that most businesses are completely unaware of or choose to ignore. Fortunately, your Guerrilla Company Attributes are not difficult to define or create and market.

When your company attributes are defined, you benefit from your awareness, and you choose to harness the power of consistency. Consistency throughout each of your Guerrilla Company Attributes is a no-cost way to gain a competitive advantage that makes your prospects take notice.

That advantage is available to new and existing businesses. If you're starting a new business, you have the advantage of defining and creating your attributes with intention and consistency from the ground up. If you already have a business, you can review your Guerrilla Company Attributes to find the tactics you're currently missing. When you find inconsistencies, fix them, and reap the rewards.

The simple act of consistently and repeatedly leveraging your Guerrilla Company Attributes, such as your logo, tagline, meme, jingle, color palette, typeface, and fonts create and compel your prospects to notice your business, and it creates familiarity. Pair that with consistently marketing what makes your business unique (i.e., your USP), what it stands for, your stellar ratings and reviews, and your innovation and quality, and your business is creating greater familiarity. As that familiarity turns into trust and is paired with your motivating call to action, it creates sales, repeat purchases, and precious referrals, which fuels the long-term success of your business.

In Volume 1, we addressed many of the important components of your Guerrilla Company Attributes, such as:

8.1	Brand
8.2	Name
8.3	Identity
8.4	Logo
8.5	Memes and Jingles
8.6	Tagline
8.7	Color Palette, Typeface, and Fonts
8.8	Intelligent Positioning
8.9	What Your Business Stands For
8.10	How Your Business Delivers
8.11	Innovation
8.12	Quality
8.13	Efficiency
8.14	Credibility
8.15	Special Orders
8.16	Amazement
8.17	Writing, Copy, and Headlines
8.18	Subject Matter Expert (SME)
8.19	Product Placement
8.20	Testimonials, Reviews, and Ratings
8.21	Convenience
8.22	Service
8.23	Selection and Cross-Selling
8.24	Price and Upgrade Opportunities
8.25	Referral Programs
8.26	Awareness
8.27	Winning
8.28	Connecting and Interacting
8.29	Follow-Up
8.30	Payment Methods

8.31   Systems and Automation

8.32   Subliminal Marketing

8.33   Lead Buying

Now, we'll pick where we left off. Without further ado, let's get started.

8.34 * CONFLICT RESOLUTION

Conflict is inevitable when it comes to your business. The more your business grows, the greater the opportunity is for conflict with:

- Employees
- Investors
- Suppliers
- Vendors
- Competitors
- Government/Regulators
- Customers
- Prospects

Some of those conflicts will be behind closed doors, and others will be open to the world to see (e.g., a negative rating or review). Regardless of where conflict comes from, what is important is your successful conflict resolution skills. Some tension is ideal between work groups to drive maximum success. For example, you want your sales team selling so much that the fulfillment team is challenged to keep up and must scale up their operations and the profits of your business.

The key is healthy tension versus raging conflicts, so there are a number of considerations.

Training

There are numerous resources to help you and your business hone conflict management skills. From books to videos and even virtual reality (VR), there are resources at your fingertips. Regular role-playing exercises hone those skills and are an effective way to ensure that what you intend to happen is happening. Monitoring your employees is also important to ensure that what you intend to happen is happening.

Clarity

Providing simple and clear policies can help reduce and eliminate conflict. Equally establishing clear procedures with your employees (or representatives) will create consistency, which helps reduce and eliminate conflict.

No one enjoys interacting with a business that isn't transparent and applies different policies to different people and/or at different times. Transparency and clearly working from one set of rules will help reduce conflict and make resolving conflict far more successful. Equally, a clear chain of command for conflict resolution helps to utilize those with enhanced skills in your business, at the right time.

Listen

You can't successfully resolve a conflict if you haven't heard what the conflict is. By being calm, consistent, and non-confrontational, you can empathize and identify win-win opportunities to resolve the conflict.

Don't make assumptions; a dialogue with probing questions helps you to get to the root of an issue, which is necessary to effectively resolve a conflict. You may find there are multiple issues, and it's important to listen to all of them so you can effectively resolve the issues.

Be Responsive

Empathize and be accountable instead of being patronizing. Effective conflict resolution requires action. Just listening to the problem is only half the action that's needed. Your goal is resolution, which means finding compromise, opportunities, and a conclusion. Whenever possible, follow-up with the people involved to see if the problem is resolved or if it remains unresolved and requires more attention.

Make Changes

Repetitive conflicts can be avoided. If you need to break your own rules to resolve a conflict, take the time to evaluate your rules.

Doing things "the way you've always done them" can be destructive when it leads to repetitive conflict. For example, if your customers are continually having an issue with one of your business's policies, it's time to re-examine that policy. Equally, if you have a supplier or employee that is a constant source of conflict, separating ways may be the best way to resolve the conflict.

Follow-Up

Assumptions are expensive in your business. A Guerrilla marketer takes action to correct the situation and then invests the time to follow-up. Refer to Section 8.37, "Inspect What You Expect," for more information about the importance of inspection over assumptions.

Conclusion

Unresolved conflicts deplete energy, create tension, diminish morale, and reduce the success of the business. Guerrillas, on the other hand, know that effectively resolving conflict keeps energy, creativity, and satisfaction flowing throughout their business. Your ability to resolve conflicts, will keep your customers happy and your business on the path to success and profits.

When it comes to conflicts with your customers, according to Statista, 58 percent of customers report they have contacted a customer service department in the past month (in 2020). If you consider the expense of customer service and the greater expense of attracting new customers versus satisfying existing ones, avoiding and resolving conflicts is imperative for your long-term success. In Section 9.21 "Make Goods," we'll address additional ideas.

Conflicts are inevitable, and they are far more manageable when you look for the opportunities they represent. Guerrilla marketers don't let conflicts go unresolved. By doing so, they endanger their reputation, morale, and success. According to American Express, nine in ten Americans share their service experience with others. When conflicts arise, take action to successfully resolve them and not repeat them.

8.35 * COMPENSATION

Compensation motivates behavior, both positive and negative behavior. Therefore, your compensation plans need to be carefully created, monitored, and refined to ensure they are working for your business and not against your business.

For many small businesses, it can seem impossible to compete and attract great talent. Job seekers are typically looking for compensation with plush benefits, such as healthcare, financial plans (e.g., 401k or ESOP), and paid vacation time. Fortunately, Guerrilla marketers are creative.

Creative Approaches

You may be able to pay for a fraction of a talented person's time, instead of hiring a full-time employee. Fractional executives, including CEOs, CMOs, and COOs can bring the talent and experience that your business needs or would benefit from, whether it's short-term or long-term. With a fractional business arrangement, your business can benefit from a portion of the time of a more experienced and accomplished person than you could afford to hire someone full-time.

You can also be creative with typical employment arrangements. Your business might consider bringing on talented people as:
- Freelancers
- Independent contractors
- Self-employed workers
- An outsourced service

With these arrangements, you can compensate based on pre-arranged milestones, deliverables, or a share of profits. Those arrangements can help ensure your business receives a needed service without cost overruns (e.g., pre-arranged milestones) or time-consuming HR issues, especially for short-term services that may not be re-occurring.

Creative Compensation

When hiring employees, offering a mix of compensation elements can enhance the financial compensation that your business offers. Without breaking the bank, your business can add compensation elements that help you attract and retain happy employees.
- Work with other businesses in your area to create a shared discount program that benefits each of your employees
- Offer training that helps them improve their skills. The training is especially meaningful when it results in a certification or shareable badge
- Awards let the talent and achievements of your employees shine
- Free items, from the ordinary—such as food and beverages—to more unique, such as products and/or services

- Flexible pay options that allow your employees to receive their compensation in the way that's best for their needs (i.e., debit cards, direct deposit, etc.)
- Rewards and bonuses to keep your employee goals aligned with your business goals
- Time off motivates many employees. Extra time off, shortened workweeks, and holidays are attractive
- Flexible hours and days

Gravity Payments, according to CBS News, took a creative approach to their compensation when their CEO made a bold decision to raise the salary of everyone to $70,000 per year (which meant reducing his own to pay for the increases). The result was a thriving company and "fiercely loyal employees," whose experience and knowledge positively impact customer satisfaction.

Creative Work Environment

Putting your creativity and uniqueness to use in your work environment doesn't require breaking the bank, and it can attract and retain employees. Guerrillas consider a broad array of options, such as:

- Shared office locations, which offer compelling amenities and flexible space options without additional cost or effort for your business. Shared office locations such as Regus and WeWork offer engaging office environments to motivate your employees
- Flexible work locations, such as working from home instead of the office, is a valuable and money-saving option for many employees

Conclusion

When you look at your employees' expenses, you can find creative ways to add elements that help them reduce their expenses. For example, being able to work from home reduces their expense of commuting and perhaps child or pet care. What costs your business little to nothing is valuable compensation for your employees.

It's important to note that your employees will quickly find the best ways to make your compensation plan work for them. Unfortunately, that can be an invitation for bad behavior. Many a large business has found themselves in a scandal that was created by compensation that motivated bad behavior. The behavior may not have been intentionally motivated by the compensation, but the end result was still disastrous for the business.

8.36 * CROSS-PROMOTION

Guerrilla marketers know that achieving multiple channels of revenue sets their business up for long-term success. In Volume 1, Section 4.24, "Revenue Streams and Channels of Revenue," we addressed the ways that your business can find new revenue streams.

Multiple channels of revenue not only help your business grow but also help to insulate your business against the risk of unknown and unforeseen changes and disruptions. In Volume 1, Section 5.3, "By-Product," we addressed additional ways your business can leverage opportunities to grow and/or start an entirely new and separate business. Your by-product is an important opportunity for your business to be nimble, grow, profit, and succeed.

The challenge is, how do you efficiently promote multiple businesses, products, and/or services? It's certainly time for your Guerrilla Creativity to shine.

It's easier when your channels of revenue and/or by-product are tightly aligned to your current business. For example, a restaurant can easily cross-promote:

- Cooking classes
- Wine tastings
- Take-and-go meal kits from the restaurant
- Packaged food product sales through retail businesses or grocery stores
- Products, such as cookware, linens, serving items, and wine glasses
- Cookbooks
- Chef's tables
- Specialized events
- Memberships (see Volume 1, Section 7.5, "Memberships")
- Subscriptions (see Section 5.16, "Subscriptions")

Alternately, you may be familiar with examples of businesses that cross-promote their tightly aligned channels of revenue and/or by-product. For example, think of Gap, which cross-promotes—at the top of their website—their other brands (i.e., channels of revenue), such as Old Navy, Banana Republic, Athleta, etc. Equally, T.J.Maxx cross-promotes, also at the top of their website, their other brands (i.e., channels of revenue), such as Marshalls, Sierra, HomeGoods, Homesense, etc. For additional information, ideas, and examples, also refer to Volume 1, Section 8.23, "Selection and Cross-Selling."

The prospects and customers of those businesses have some tightly aligned similarities across their different brands, but there are significant differences, as well. When your channels of revenue and/or by-product are not tightly aligned (e.g., your prospects and customers have little to nothing in common), your Guerrilla Creativity will be put to the test. How do you cross-promote when your prospects and customers are not tightly aligned?

Let's look at an example. An ambitious ride-share driver (within the confines of their service agreement) can subtly promote (in their vehicle) their online business, private or white label products, Etsy shop, podcast, book, direct sales (e.g., Mary Kay, Pampered Chef, etc.), or other endeavors. They can do so by:

- Utilizing the products they're cross-promoting to demonstrate their value and usefulness (e.g., playing their podcast, utilizing their white-labeled car fragrance, etc.)
- Sampling
- Displaying a framed advertisement or offering a brochure, catalog, or business card with a QR code for easy access

In the example above, the ride-share driver only knows that they are marketing (in their vehicle) to people who want to get from one place to another hassle-free. Therefore, Guerrilla marketers are subtle because cross-promotion marketing for your business, service(s), and/or product(s) is focused on a broad and non-targeted audience.

By being subtle and delivering excellent service, the driver is connecting with their customers regarding their desire to get from one place to another hassle-free. With that connection, your creativity has an opportunity to be compelling, and your subtle marketing can open the door. If your subtle marketing compels your prospect to notice your business, product(s), or service(s), it's time to motivate them with your well-crafted call to action (e.g., to visit your website or social page, go to your podcast, download an ebook, make a purchase, etc.).

Guerrilla marketers know that asking prospects and customers to take an action first often falls flat. Your prospects or customers either ignore your call to action or are annoyed by it. Your subtle cross-promotion marketing must first be compelling and engaging. Only then, can your call to action motivate your prospects and customers to take the action you desire.

8.37 * INSPECT WHAT YOU EXPECT

Guerrilla marketers know their success hinges on inspecting what they expect. It's easy to make a decision and hand it off and assume that it was handled as you expected. Fortunately, it's widely known that assumptions can lead to disappointments and even disasters.

A Guerrilla marketer doesn't leave their success to chance and assumptions. Instead, Guerrilla marketers inspect what they expect. What does it mean to inspect what you expect? It's quite simple, but in the daily rush of other activities and to-dos, it's very easily ignored or overlooked.

Fortunately, when a Guerrilla marketer sets an expectation, they take the time to see if what they expected to happen does indeed happen. They leave assumptions to be the mistakes other businesses make. Why? There are many advantages to inspecting what you expect. For starters:

- **Evaluate**: the results are only part of the process and only a part of the story. Inspecting means looking at the entire process, along with the results when you're evaluating success or failure.
- **Recalibrate**: one simple error in the process can mean the idea didn't produce the anticipated results. Instead of scrapping the idea altogether, a simple inspection allows for recalibration. With a change to the process, you can turn that idea around and make it a profitable one.
- **Collaboration**: when people effectively work together, they accomplish more than they do on their own. A team that is focused on inspecting expectations is agile and focused. They develop efficient processes and successful results that boost the business for many years to come.
- **Replicate**: by inspecting what you expect, your business is boosting its ability to replicate winning ideas and processes, and that is a formula for long-term success and profits. Simply doing more of what works and less of what doesn't can be the difference between success and failure.

Guerrilla marketers think of inspecting what they expect akin to digging in and getting to the "why." Beyond knowing that an idea worked, they take the time to learn "why" that idea worked. Equally, they know "why" an idea didn't work.

Getting to the "why" prevents good ideas from being labeled as a bad idea and, therefore, slipping through the cracks, never being effective and/or implemented. Alternately, getting to the "why" prevents a seemingly good idea from going unchecked and, therefore, unnoticed when it turns out to be a bad idea. Omitting assumptions, inspecting what you expect, and getting to the "why" is fuel for the long-term success of your business.

8.38 * CAPITAL AND FUNDRAISING FOR YOUR BUSINESS/IDEA

As a creative Guerrilla business owner, you'll always have ideas regarding how to grow your business and how to branch off into new businesses or, perhaps, an unrelated business. Those options become easier with success; though, they often still require fundraising. The key is, build your business well, and the money will more easily flow to it.

If the success of your current business can help you fund a new business, you're in a great position to either self-finance or attract capital or a combination of both. However, if you need to attract capital and raise funds for your business or idea, there are many options.

While many business owners look only to their own bank accounts for that funding, Guerrilla marketers realize there are more opportunities available. By leveraging the option of having others contribute or invest in your business, you're providing them the chance to help get valuable ideas off the ground, which many investors find highly desirable.

Fortunately, if your business needs to (or wants to) rely on outside capital, there are several options available to you. When you begin with or create an agile and lean business structure/organization you can make your business desirable to outside capital, such as:

- Friends and family

- Competitions (e.g., FedEx Small Business Grant)
- Incubator and entrepreneurship organizations (e.g., International Business Innovation Association or INBIA)
- Grants
- Community development loan funds
- SBA loans
- Bank loans (including specialty lending, such as green banks that focus on environmentally focused businesses)
- Angel Investors
- Venture capital
- Peer-to-peer lending
- Crowdfunding (see Volume 1, Section 7.14, "Crowdfunding")
- Family Office
- Microlending
- Purchase order financing
- Merchant account financing
- Credit lines
- Investment reality TV (e.g., *Shark Tank* or *Unicorn Hunters*). See Section 5.13, "Reality TV," for more information.
- Capital raising using Regulation D of the U.S. securities law. Of the exemptions under Regulation D, 506B or 506C are most often completed with a private placement memorandum and used for both debt and equity types of securities. These regulations are subject to change, and you'll want to ensure that you're aware of the full details. In broad terms, currently, the differences between 506B and 506C are:
  - o 506B is most often used for friends and family rounds because you cannot publicly solicit, and you must have a substantial preexisting relationship. It currently allows up to thirty-five non-accredited investors and unlimited accredited investors.
  - o 506C limits you to accredited investors only but allows you to pitch in public as well as to promote, advertise, etc.

These rules are the United States securities rules and other countries differ, so refer to your country's rules. Also, each state in the United States has other rules. You'll want to talk to a securities attorney to make sure you know the laws and rules that govern a capital raise in your area.

Guerrilla marketers also embrace collaboration as a means of growing their business, attracting capital, and/or fundraising. When you look to other businesses, you can collaborate with a joint venture or a simple Guerrilla Fusion/Affiliate marketing arrangement (see Volume 1, Section 7.6, "Fusion/Affiliate Marketing and Collaboration," for more information).

When you're collaborating with other synergistic businesses, you're driving sales for your business (or both businesses) by harnessing one another's customer lists and/or prospects and online or physical business locations. Collaborating and cross-promoting with other businesses that share your ideal prospects and customers is a great way to create profits, raise capital, and build your success. You can also collaborate with referrals, such as:

- Attorneys, accountants, investment advisors, etc. working together to cross-promote or refer their prospects and customers to each other
- A car wash, automobile oil change/service provider, paint-less dent repair, etc., working together to cross-promote or refer their prospects and customers to each other
- A wedding planner, bakery, florist, and catering business working together to cross-promote or refer their prospects and customers to each other
- A dry cleaner, tailoring business, and shoe repair business working together to cross-promote or refer their prospects and customers to each other
- Referral sites (see Section 4.54, "Referral Sites")

Collaboration can be accomplished in many other ways to create mutually beneficial outcomes, such as expanding each other's business. Guerrilla marketers look for win-win options. For example:

- Joint ventures
- Acquiring another like-minded business
- Being acquired by another like-minded business

Those winning opportunities are brought to light with a Guerrilla marketer's relationship-building skills. As we addressed in Section 1.8, "Crucial Skills for Effectively Using Guerrilla Marketing," your ability to build strong relationships enhances your success. Guerrilla marketers realize their competitors today could be their joint venture or acquisition partners tomorrow. Beyond competitors, there are also potential synergistic opportunities with suppliers, diversified businesses, and many others, which means you're always on the lookout for creating win-win opportunities. See Volume 3, Section 9.29, "Relationship Builder," for more information.

Guerrilla marketers seeking an agile and lean business structure/organization, which can make their business more profitable and more desirable to outside capital, also turn to money-saving options with their marketing. For example, Google offers promotions within qualified Google Ads account. Those offers can be found in your account, under the "Partners program tab" and the "Promotional Offers" card. The offers vary, and they give you the opportunity to stretch your advertising investment. Other advertising platforms also offer promotions and incentives that you'll want to be on the lookout for.

Guerrilla marketers can also build a lean business with effective bartering. Your products and services have value, and your business can easily leverage that value to minimize your out-of-pocket and cash expenses while providing valuable products and services to your bartering partner.

In the process, bartering helps your business make and grow valuable relationships. You also receive valuable feedback about your products and services. Bartering partners are typically eager and willing to provide frank feedback, suggestions, and ideas. That information can be much more challenging to extract from your busy prospects and customers. Be sure to refer to Section 2.10, "Bartering," for ideas and examples of bartering that can help keep your business financials running lean while your bank accounts are flowing full.

Guerrilla marketers also seek to develop multiple streams of revenue to help their business grow and be desirable to outside capital. In Volume 1, Section 4.24, "Revenue Streams and Channels of Revenue," we addressed the ways that your business can find new revenue streams and channels. Additionally, in Volume 1, Section 5.3, "By-Product," and earlier in Section 8.36, "Cross-Promotion," we addressed many options that exist for your business. In Volume 3, Section 7.29, "Blockchain Solutions," you'll find more options. With a bit of effort, your business can identify where the opportunity is knocking so you can open the door.

8.39 ✳ Uniqueness

Guerrilla marketers are keenly aware of the power of uniqueness. Merriam-Webster defines unique as "being without a like or equal: unequaled."

Whether you realize it or not, there are things about your business that are one-of-a-kind, unlike anything else. Your job as a Guerrilla marketer is to identify and promote those unique attributes. After all, Guerrilla marketers are unique, and they know it and promote it.

When you market your uniqueness, you're marketing what no other business can compete with, and that's a great way to build your success and create more profits. The beginning point of finding what makes your business one-of-a-kind is your USP (see Volume 1, Section 1.3, "Unique Selling Proposition (USP)"). It's a powerful marketing and advertising message. However, the good news is that, as we mentioned in Volume 1, your business, likely, has multiple elements that make it unique, which means it's one-of-a-kind and unlike anything else.

Without question, you must walk the talk with your uniqueness. Your other Guerrilla Company Attributes must authentically encompass and promote your uniqueness. Unique businesses are often trailblazers. However, even a seemingly ordinary business can be extraordinarily unique.

Perhaps what makes your business unique is:
- Your charitable efforts (e.g., a portion of all sales benefit . . .)
- Your social consciousness
- Your environmentally friendly design, benefits, and/or advantages
- The only. . . (e.g., exclusivity, such as exclusive importer of [a specific] wine or coffee, the exclusive provider of . . .)
- Copyrights and patent-protected products and services
- A view like no other
- Historically significant
- The Top . . .
- The Highest Rated . . .
- Awarded the . . .
- More five-star ratings . . .
- Over a thousand five-star ratings
- Your only local . . .
- Cutting edge . . .
- Recommended by . . .
- Secret ingredient
- Exclusive ingredient(s) or materials
- Employee-owned, family-owned, locally-owned, etc.
- The most experienced . . .

- The first and only . . .
- Guaranteed . . .
- Lifetime warranty
- As seen on . . .
- In more homes than any other
- Unmatched quality, service, etc.

As you market your uniqueness, don't assume that your prospects know why your uniqueness is relevant. Guerrilla marketers are sure to make their uniqueness fascinating and then market it with consistency and repetition. That's how your marketing is guiding your business toward success.

Remember that Guerrilla Marketing shows your business how to perform 360 degrees of intelligent, impactful, and consistent marketing that drives profits for your business. As your unique attributes are woven 360 degrees throughout your business and marketing, you'll be both telling (see Volume 1, Section 6.5, "Stories Sell") and showing your unique, fascinating, and compelling story, product(s), and service(s).

The more compelling your business is to your prospects, the more likely they are to notice your business. At that point, your consistent and repeated marketing of your uniqueness is making your business recognizable and memorable. By being memorable, your business is top-of-mind when your prospects are ready to make a purchase.

The same is true for your customers. By being memorable, your business is top-of-mind when your customers are ready to make new or repeat purchases. The great news is that the benefits do not stop there.

Uniqueness also compels people to share and recommend your business. When your business is memorable (see Volume 3, Section 8.43, "Being Memorable"), you're top-of-mind when your customers are asked by their friends, family, and associates if they know of a business like yours. Receiving precious referrals from your prospects and customers is fuel for your long-term success.

At the same time, your uniqueness makes your business more valuable, especially when the day comes that you want to attract capital to grow your business or to sell or hand off your profitable business. Weaving your uniqueness 360 degrees throughout your business and marketing is putting your Guerrilla Marketing knowledge to profitable use.

8.40 * PROFIT OUT OF LEMONS

The reality of business is that things can, and likely will, go wrong at some point. The difference between success and failure during those times when things seem to be going wrong can come down to your mindset (see Section 9.25, "Owner Mindset," for more information).

When it seems that life is handing your business lemons, some people will fold. However, in that same situation, other people will see it as an opportunity because they know they are resilient (see Section 9.26, "Resilience") and, therefore, can adapt. It may not feel very fun at the time, but it's comforting to know that you are resilient, and you have the ability to adapt and find endless ways to make your Guerrilla Creativity shine.

Each volume of the all-new series of *Guerrilla Marketing* books is at your fingertips, with hundreds of ideas, tactics, and examples to inspire you to create profits out of lemons. When it seems that life is handing your business lemons, your business can focus instead on success. For example:

- Focus on your alternate opportunities. In Volume 1, Section 4.24, "Revenue Streams and Channels of Revenue," we addressed the ways your business can find new revenue streams
- Evaluate and develop your by-product, which can often be as successful as (or more successful than) your current business (see Volume 1, Section 5.3, "By-Product")
- Seek ways to expand your distribution (see Section 7.23, "Expanded Distribution")
- Work with other successful businesses that are like-minded and focused on delighting customers (see Volume 1, Section 7.6, "Fusion/Affiliate Marketing and Collaboration")
- Challenge your business model and be agile; maybe there is a better business model to meet your success goals

We talked about the importance of getting to the "why" in Section 8.37, "Inspect What You Expect." When things are going wrong, digging in and getting to the "why" is critical. Making assumptions, or only looking superficially, can make you miss the best option to turn the situation in your favor.

The unknown and unforeseen changes and disruptions in business are always a risk. Your ability to stay focused on the opportunities that always exist, remain nimble, and get to the "why" before significantly adapting will help to insulate your business against the natural risks you'll face as a business owner. With your knowledge, attitude, and skills, while others fold, you'll make profits out of lemons.

8.41 * SPIN-OFF

In various ways, we have addressed the importance of looking for opportunities to expand your business. Being focused on expansion and new opportunities is how you grow your business and create the much-needed fuel for long-term success.

When you come up with new ideas, many businesses think in terms of changing everything they're doing, Guerrilla marketers view opportunities differently. They see an opportunity for their existing business to continue *while* they develop their new idea into a possible spin-off business.

By maintaining your existing business, while developing a new idea and then spinning it off (online or offline), you're minimizing risk and maximizing opportunity. After all, your existing business can provide fuel (in terms of money and/or reduced costs that are gained with shared efficiencies) while it remains a successful business that delights its customers.

Spin-off opportunities can happen in several ways. For example:

- Organic opportunities arise as you grow your selection of product(s) and/or service(s). Your business may have a particular product or service that is so successful, it can be a better opportunity when you spin it off as a separate business
- Collaboration with another (or more than one) business to create a spin-off business, which is jointly owned and operated
- Acquisition also provides the opportunity to create a spin-off business related to a mutual or similar product(s) or service(s) or to create a new product or service
- The successful by-product (see Volume 1, Section 5.3, "By-Product") of your business also provides an opportunity for a spin-off business that could be consistent with your current business or completely different

Regardless of how a spin-off opportunity arises, you most likely will have a new set of marketing challenges. The spin-off business needs to be built on a strong foundation of Guerrilla Marketing success (see Section I, "Strong Foundation of Guerrilla Marketing Success") just as the one your existing business was built on. The same marketing research and decisions need to be made to build a strong business that is ready for long-term success.

For your spin-off business, unique marketing and advertising are needed if you want to compel your prospects to notice your business. That continued unique marketing and advertising are then needed for your call to action to motivate them to purchase your product(s) and/or service(s), make repeat purchases, and make precious referrals of their friends, family, and associates. Also refer back to Section 8.36, "Cross-Promotion."

Unique marketing and advertising for your spin-off businesses may be needed due to several factors. Your spin-off business may, for example, have identified a new style, an opportunity for a budget-conscious product, or a splurge-worthy product. Consider the following examples.

Different styles

The fashion industry provides good examples with businesses that offer different styles, and therefore, they need unique marketing and advertising, such as Gap Inc.

Gap Inc. sells as several different brands, including under their own name (Gap) and other brands/businesses, such as Old Navy, Banana Republic, and Athleta. Another example in the fashion industry is URBN group, which sells as several different brands/businesses, including Urban Outfitters, Free People, Anthropologie, Terrain, BHLDN, etc.

Different price points

Different price points easily require different marketing. The auto industry shows us some good examples by producing automobiles at several different price points and with different marketing. For example, the Volkswagen group sells automobiles as its own name and through other brands/businesses, including Audi, Bentley, Bugatti, Lamborghini, Porsche, etc. The Fiat Chrysler group sells automobiles as several brands/businesses, including Fiat, Chrysler, Dodge, Alfa Romeo, Jeep, Maserati, etc.

Different technology

Your prospects and customers may have different technology needs and desires. Your prospects looking for low-tech and no hassle does not have much interest in your robust technology. Equally, your prospects seeking high-tech and feature-rich products are not interested in low-tech products.

Conclusion

Guerrilla marketers look, first, to leverage their existing business to launch a spin-off business (or businesses). When they identify a product or service that could become a spin-off business, they can, for example, begin with creating a dedicated section in their store (online or offline) to test and grow their idea. In that dedicated section of their store, Guerrilla marketers have the opportunity to test different marketing. For example, email marketing or online advertising efforts utilize a link to a special landing page that features the new test marketing concept. With split testing, more than one marketing concept can be tested to find the best option (see Volume 1, Section 4.35, "Email Split Testing," for more information).

8.42 * LEVERAGING SOCIAL LIVE BROADCASTING

Social live broadcasting has proven to generate engagement for Guerrilla businesses. There are several social platforms to consider, such as:

- Facebook
- YouTube
- LinkedIn
- Instagram has IGTV
- Clubhouse (audio only)

Social platforms where your customers and prospects have a high level of engagement are ideal. When you consider that engagement and incorporate the ability to interact live (with audio and/or video), you have the ability to build relationships. You can build consistency, which builds familiarity, which builds trust; and trust creates sales, repeat purchases, and precious referrals, which is the fuel for long-term success.

Your business can leverage social live broadcasting to disseminate information, share your expertise with your customers and prospects, and convey what your business stands for (see Volume 1, Section 8.9, "What Your Business Stands For").

When choosing a platform, it's important to meet your prospects and customers where they are (see Section 6.16, "Meet Prospects and Customers Where They Are"). It's easy to get distracted by the reach of a social platform and put the importance of the quantity of the reach ahead of the quality of the reach. Therefore, keep in mind that a platform that reaches a lot of people may be far less effective than a platform that reaches fewer people, but those people are your customers and prospects.

At the same time, you want to match your reach with your content. For example, you may find it easier to reach your B2B prospect on Facebook vs. LinkedIn, but on Facebook, they don't want to talk business. Therefore, your community-minded (see Section 9.18, "Community-Minded") or purpose-minded (see Section 9.17, "Purpose-Minded") content is more engaging.

Should you find that your business can reach your prospects and customers effectively, using multiple social life broadcasting platforms, there are tools to help you be efficient. Become familiar with these platforms that allow you to simulcast across multiple social platforms:

- Restream
- Vimeo Livestream
- Dacast
- Streamyard
- BeLive
- Streamlabs

When your business is simultaneously broadcasting video content across multiple social platforms, you're efficiently using the same amount of effort while expanding your reach. That means your business is engaging with as many customers and prospects as possible. After all, your customers and prospects are not always where you expect them to be.

For example, consider that you may expect your followers, subscribers, and/or group members to engage with you on a particular platform. However, there are times when your prospects and customers might be active on LinkedIn and not on Facebook. Perhaps their employer allows them to use LinkedIn at work, but they don't allow them to access Facebook. Therefore, your 11:00 a.m. live broadcast may find a larger than expected audience on LinkedIn. At the same time, you're reaching your prospects and customers who are engaged with Facebook, Instagram, YouTube, etc.

According to Vimeo Livestream, "48% of consumers have shared a brand video on their social media platforms." Additionally, 80 percent of consumers they researched, along with *New York* Magazine, "would rather watch live video from a brand than read a blog" and "82% prefer live video from a brand to social posts."

Live video tends to attract more interaction than an uploaded prerecorded video. Uploaded prerecorded videos rely on algorithms to grow their reach and go viral. The more people who sample the video and watch approximately the first minute or longer, the more likely it is for the video to gain traction and be suggested to other people. To help your success, notify your subscribers and email recipients when you post a new video on YouTube. Their views will help trigger the algorithm to recognize that people are engaging with and enjoying your video.

SECTION IX

Guerrilla Company Attitudes

GUERRILLA COMPANY ATTITUDES

Your Guerrilla Company Attitudes are where the rubber meets the road for your customers and prospects. You can do everything right with your marketing and advertising efforts and attract prospects who want to become customers. However, if you forget, for even a second, that your company attitudes are a critical part of your marketing, your business can turn that hot prospect into a negative review or social post faster than you can say "social media."

Prospects and customers expect, consciously and subconsciously, consistency in everything your business does. If you're marketing and advertising the friendly and fast service of your business, you must consistently deliver the friendly and fast service that meets and exceeds your prospects' and customers' expectations.

When your Guerrilla Company Attitudes are consistent with all of your marketing and advertising efforts, your business is turning prospects into customers. It's also turning customers into repeat buyers and precious referrers of new prospects to your business.

When your company attitudes are inconsistent with your marketing, your business will need a lot more prospects because many will not become customers. Those that do become customers are not likely to be repeat customers, and your ratings and reviews will show it.

You don't need to look very far to find a rating or review that is directly tied to the attitudes of the business. Equally, you'll find a five-star review that says even though they had a problem with the product or service, they were delighted with the fantastic customer service they received. Customers will forgive a problem, but they won't forgive inconsistency.

Your Guerrilla Company Attitudes are on display at all times, so pay attention to the details and be intentional. It's as simple as the greeting your business offers when prospects and customers enter your business. From that point, everything they see, feel, and hear conveys the attitude of your business.

On the other hand, if your prospects and customers enter your business via your website, your company attitudes are also conveyed. If they are met with pop-ups, advertisements, auto-play videos, and slow to load content, you're conveying the attitudes of your business.

As we detailed in Volume 1, in the book *Guerrilla Marketing*, Jay Conrad Levinson pointed out some of the important unconscious factors that your prospects and customers process when it comes to doing business with you, which include:

- Speed
- Neatness
- Telephone demeanor
- Value
- Flexibility

Jay Conrad Levinson's observation of these important unconscious factors remains true today. Guerrilla Marketing's success spans decades because it focuses on the details that most businesses ignore. Guerrilla marketers tend to those tiny, supercharged details that can generate big profits.

It's simple and inexpensive to understand your Guerrilla Company Attitudes. It's worth a reminder that when those attitudes are consistent with all of your marketing and advertising efforts, your business is turning prospects into customers. It's also turning customers into repeat buyers and precious referrers of new prospects to your business.

Managing your Guerrilla Company Attitudes will put your business far ahead of most other businesses, including your competition. Think about businesses that you enjoy doing business with.

Take some time and dissect that business (or multiple businesses) that you enjoy doing business with. What are their company attitudes? Are their company attitudes consistent with their marketing and advertising? As you break down their marketing, it becomes easy to see that your business is marketing with every interaction, so be intentional about it and utilize every aspect of Guerrilla Marketing to your advantage.

In Volume 1, we addressed:

9.1	Passion and Enthusiasm
9.2	Easy to Do Business With
9.3	Technology Friendly
9.4	Your Employees' Voices
9.5	Responsive and Attentive
9.6	Honest Interest in People
9.7	Self-Confidence and Intention
9.8	Aggressiveness and Competitiveness
9.9	High Energy and Take Action
9.10	Focused

9.11   Consistency

9.12   Generosity

Now, we'll pick up where we left off. These factors and many more make up the Guerrilla Company Attitudes of your business, so let's dig a bit deeper.

9.13 * GUERRILLA AGILE MIND

An agile mind is defined by Merriam-Webster as "having a quick resourceful and adaptable character." A Guerrilla agile mind adds knowledge, time, energy, imagination, and unconventional tactics to the characteristics of an agile mind.

When you approach your business with the notion that "you never get it all done," it's easier to keep your focus, enjoy the everyday experiences, and delegate. After all, a successful business is built to change and evolve, and its day-to-day practices ensure that it's ever-evolving.

Many non-Guerrilla businesses find themselves surprised when they thought they completed every task that was needed to accomplish a goal. However, they didn't get the results they anticipated. For example, they launched their new product(s) or service(s) and opened their business doors expecting to find prospects lined up and ready to become customers. Unfortunately, their business, product(s), or service(s) were built in a vacuum, and there weren't any prospects lined up at the door.

What is the difference between a non-Guerrilla business and a business with a Guerrilla agile mind? A Guerrilla agile mind views their business, product(s), and/or service(s) as ever-evolving and nimble. The lines of communication are wide open, and they frequently ask questions, reassess, and adapt, as needed. As they evolve their ideas, product(s), and service(s), they rely on the right input throughout the journey. That input comes from:

- Research
- Prospects and customers
- Industry experts and associations
- Fusion/Affiliate partners (see Volume 1, Section 7.6, "Fusion/Affiliate Marketing and Collaboration")
- Employees and partners

- Experience and expertise (see Volume 1, Section 6.3, "Your Expertise and Credibility")
- Lateral thinking (see Section 9.23, "Lateral Thinking")
- Your business owner mindset (see Section 9.25, "Owner Mindset")

It's important to note that a Guerrilla agile and adaptable mindset is different from a solely reactive mindset. When your business reflects your mindset and is agile and adaptable, it takes careful consideration as it makes changes. Conversely, a reactive business often values action over deliberation, and doing something is more highly valued than doing the right (or best aligned) thing.

9.14 * INSPIRE

A business, and a business owner, that inspires people has a powerful and winning advantage, and it doesn't cost a dime. Merriam-Webster defines *inspire*, in part, as, "to spur on: impel, motivate" and "to exert an aminating, enlivening, or exalting influence on."

Guerrillas seek to inspire and, therefore, motivate many people, including:
- Employees
- Vendors
- Fusion/Affiliate partners (see Volume 1, Section 7.6, "Fusion/Affiliate Marketing and Collaboration")
- Prospects and customers
- Public and media relations partners

The key to inspiring others is to be inspired yourself. That sounds simple, but it takes intentional effort and action. Business owners are typically very inspired as they begin their businesses. However, it's easy for that inspiration to wane or fade away in the maze of your daily routine and in the ups, downs, and challenges that greet you along the way.

Finding what inspires you may be inside your business or outside of your business or a combination of both. It's what charges your batteries. You can easily identify when your inspiration batteries are running a bit low. It's easy to tell because, when people are inspired, they:
- Enjoy listening, learning, and developing

- See problems and easily find solutions
- Are committed to delighting their prospects and customers
- Develop innovative and unconventional systems, products, services, and solutions
- Are enthusiastic, full of creative ideas, and focused on success
- Are interested, engaged, and consistent

Keeping your inspiration batteries fully charged is a priority because it fuels your ability to inspire others, and that is a powerful advantage. When you and your business are inspired, it's a pleasure for everyone, including your prospects and customers.

Your ability to inspire people increases engagement, creativity, and action throughout your business. It also motivates people to care about your business. The ability to inspire people is fuel for long-term success, and it doesn't cost a dime.

9.15 * OPEN DOOR

Operating your business with an open-door attitude encourages interactions, communication, creativity, and relationship building (see Volume 3, Section 9.29, "Relationship Builder"). When your door is closed, you're relying on others to tell you what is going on in your business instead of observing it for yourself.

The challenge with a closed door is that you're hearing about what is going on with your business through other people's mindsets, opinions, and filters. That means you've created a barrier between you and your business by preferring to keep your door closed.

While it might be impossible to physically always have an open door, it's still very possible to achieve an open-door policy and attitude. What are the advantages of an open door?

An open-door policy and attitude enhance transparency and your ability to inspire (see Section 9.14, "Inspire") people to:
- Identify issues early to prevent them from becoming problems
- Identify opportunities for new product(s) and service(s)

- Identify competencies and efficiencies
- Identify roadblocks, inefficiencies, and disorganization
- Offer regular praise and rewards for jobs well done
- Embrace teamwork and collaboration
- Know, talk with, and interact with your customers and prospects
- Identify valuable by-product (see Volume 1, Section 5.3, "By-Product") opportunities that can help your business grow and succeed
- Implement your ideas, processes, and vision while you inspect what you expect (see Section 8.37, "Inspect What You Expect")

An open-door attitude and policy create an empowered workplace where people believe they are heard and can meaningfully contribute to the success of the business. They also know that always offering their best—through their own work and through the work of the team—is encouraged, appreciated, recognized, and rewarded.

To successfully have an open-door attitude and policy requires an open mind and an honest interest in people (see Volume 1, Section 9.6, "Honest Interest in People"). It also requires consistency with all of your other Guerrilla Company Attitudes, including those we addressed in Volume 1, those that we have addressed in this section, and those to be addressed in future volumes of the all-new series of *Guerrilla Marketing* books.

9.16 * AUTHENTICITY

Guerrilla businesses think of authenticity as "walking the talk" (see Section 9.19, "Demeanor") in all aspects of their business. Both consciously and subconsciously, people are always questioning and measuring your authenticity. Therefore, you're wise to:

- Not make promises you can't keep
- Promote only benefits that you offer
- Promote only solutions that you can deliver
- Be consistent throughout your marketing
- Offer warranties and guarantees (see Volume 1, Section 7.13, "Warranties, Guarantees, and Service Programs")

- Be easy to do business with (see Volume 1, Section 9.2, "Easy to Do Business With")
- Build relationships (see Volume 3, Section 9.29, "Relationship Builder")

Consistency and authenticity combine to build trust, authority, and respect. That's not easily achieved, but it is easily lost. Therefore, it's essential to monitor and manage your authenticity. But how can you measure your authenticity? Fortunately, you already have numerous measurements of your authenticity:

- Employee tenure/retention
- Product returns
- Refunds
- Ratings and reviews
- Negative social chatter

Your prospects, customers, potential employees, and suppliers look at your ratings and reviews as, in part, a measurement of your authenticity. For example, your marketing and advertising must first compel your prospects to notice your business. Then, your call to action motivates them to take a desired action.

However, many of your prospects will first rely on your ratings and reviews to measure your authenticity before they will make a purchase. If they like what they see in your ratings and reviews, they will proceed with purchasing your product(s) or service(s). Fortunately, when you have compelled and motivated your prospects to become your customers, your authenticity will also influence your positive customer satisfaction levels.

Those satisfied customers, often subconsciously, rely on your authenticity to determine if they will remain satisfied and make repeat purchases and provide precious referrals of their friends, family, and associates to your business. Guerrilla marketers understand the power of satisfied customers and how they put a business on the path to increased profits and long-term success.

9.17 * PURPOSE-MINDED

Guerrilla businesses have a purpose. That purpose is whatever they are passionate about and motivated by. A purpose-minded attitude is a no-cost, competitive advantage that focuses your work and your business around a clearly defined, core purpose.

Fortunately, Guerrilla businesses take an easy approach regarding their purpose. After all, they know there is no one "right" purpose for their business. Your purpose may be a noble cause, the desire to change the world, or in some way to improve, enhance, or simplify the lives of your prospects and customers. Perhaps it's to better your life and the lives of your family, employees, and community. There is no one "right" or "wrong" purpose; it's simply the objective that will be achieved with the revenue and profits that your business generates.

For your purpose to be an effective advantage for your business, take the time to define your purpose and share it. When you do, you're providing clarity and focus for everyone involved with your business, including your prospects and customers.

Where do you begin when you're defining your purpose? First, look to:

- The reason(s) you started the business
- The problems your business solves for your prospects and customers
- Your USP
- What your business stands for and what it will not compromise
  Then look to:
- The change that you want your business to create
- The change your business has already created
- The success story that you want to tell a decade from now

Some businesses call it a mission statement. You can choose to call it that or whatever else you want. Your clearly communicated purpose simply and powerfully acts as a compass for your business, keeping it pointed in the direction of the "right" accomplishments and success. As important questions pop up in your business, your simply defined purpose provides clarity and focus. When combined with your lateral thinking skill (see Section 9.23, "Lateral Thinking"), the right answer can be apparent while also being unconventional and perhaps even disruptive.

If that isn't powerful enough, the clarity and focus regarding your defined purpose make consistency come far more easily. With consistency, your purpose becomes woven, 360 degrees, throughout every aspect of your business, including your marketing efforts, as your product(s) and/or service(s) compel and motivate your prospects and customers.

9.18 * COMMUNITY-MINDED

In the last section (9.17, "Purpose-Minded") we addressed your purpose-minded attitude. In this section, we'll address your community-minded attitude. These attitudes are similar, in that:

- Your purpose-minded attitude is focused on "what your business stands for and wants to accomplish" and/or the "why" your business exists
- Your community-minded attitude is focused around "who is affected by your purpose"

Your community is made up of many people, such as:

- Your prospects and customers
- Those directly involved in your business, such as your employees, suppliers, business partners, lending partners, etc.
- Your Fusion/Affiliate marketing partners (see Volume 1, Section 7.6, "Fusion/Affiliate Marketing and Collaboration")
- Your neighborhood (which could be a section of your town or the entire globe)
- Your family and friends
- Your social connections
- Those involved in a charity or noble cause, which your business supports

A community-minded attitude keeps you focused on the people that matter to your business and those you want your business to positively impact. At the same time, your consistent and focused community-minded marketing is compelling when your community feels as if you're speaking directly to them while you promote your product(s) and/or service(s).

Think of St. Jude Children's Research Hospital as an example. They are purpose-driven and community-minded. They clearly market their purpose and do so with a broad community-minded approach. Their community includes, for example, medical professionals, the patients and their families who benefit from their expertise, the donors, and their potential donors that support their noble cause. Their marketing is compelling as it showcases the power of focusing on a purpose, along with the power of collaboration within a community and what purpose and community-mindedness can achieve.

Clarity, focus, consistency, and repetition, when combined with a purpose-minded and community-minded attitude, make it easier for your business to accomplish its goals. When it's woven 360 degrees, throughout every aspect of your business, including your marketing efforts, your prospects take notice, and they are motivated to become your loyal and satisfied customers.

9.19 * DEMEANOR

Demeanor is defined by Merriam-Webster as "behavior toward others: outward manner." For a Guerrilla marketer, it can be simply stated as "the rubber meeting the road."

Your business can be infused with consistent and aligned positive Guerrilla Company Attitudes. However, it's how those attitudes outwardly manifest in your behavior and everyone in your business's behavior that matters to your prospects and customers—and to the success of your business. It's the difference between understanding what you should do and believing in what you do; consequently, the positively aligned behavior comes naturally.

You and your employees' demeanors are the outward expressions of your company attitudes. Your prospects and customers are easily influenced by your demeanor. For example, in Volume 1, Section 9.6, "Honest Interest in People," we addressed the importance of focusing on the people (including your prospects and customers) that influence your success. You can say all the right things, but it's your demeanor that will signal to your prospects and customers if you authentically notice them and are also interested in their pain points, pleasure points, ideas, etc.

Alternately, if your business is selling product(s) or service(s) that are high energy (e.g., sporting gear, nutrition, recreational adventure experiences, etc.), and you've created an environment that is high energy (e.g., bold colors, music, images, videos, etc.), the demeanor of your employees will influence your prospects and customers. When your high-energy business is being represented by low-energy employees, their demeanor is costing your business sales, repeat purchases, and referrals.

Imagine if a fitness equipment company has an employee or owner who is introverted and/or displays low energy. They roll their eyes when they talk, they start each sentence with a long sigh and say "well . . ." as they speak slowly. Your prospect, who had been compelled by your marketing to notice your business and motivated by your call to action to visit your business, can quickly become unmotivated by the demeanor of that introverted and/or low-energy person.

Businesses that provide one-on-one services (e.g., salons, spas, barbershops, restaurants, etc.) are often the most impacted by demeanor. A five-star service business can be quickly derailed by a one-star demeanor. Demeanor will make or break sales, upgrades, repeat purchases, referrals, ratings, reviews, and the overall success of your business.

9.20 * CURIOSITY

Curiosity is a Guerrilla marketer's excellent friend, and it's an important attitude for your business. Merriam-Webster defines *curiosity* as "interest leading to inquiry." Guerrilla marketers are naturally interested in learning, and they're not afraid to ask questions and increase their knowledge with the information they receive.

Curiosity is a fantastic, free tool that is readily available to you. Inherent curiosity takes on many powerful forms, such as:

- The ability of your business to peak your prospects' and customers' curiosity, which motivates them to notice and interact with your business
- The ability of your business to learn about your customers and prospects
- The ability of your business to take calculated risks, solve problems, learn, adapt, innovate, and grow
- The joy that success, contribution, learning, growing, etc. produce to inspire your long-term success

Curiosity inspires a thirst for knowledge that keeps your business ahead of the competition by asking questions and seeking more knowledge and know-how with constant learning. Because Guerrilla marketers are curious, they have the opportunity to learn with market research, industry research, and by simply, asking questions, listening, and observing. Refer to Section I, "The Strong Foundation of Guerrilla Marketing Success" and Volume 1, Section 1.1, "Research and Knowing," for additional insights.

Curiosity motivates Guerrilla marketers to learn about the interests, likes, dislikes, pain points, and pleasure points of their prospects and customers. Curiosity motivates them to continually gain more knowledge about their expertise, products, and/or services. Curiosity also allows them to turn what others perceive as stress into an eager willingness to turn challenges into opportunities.

Your genuine curiosity, confidence, and inner amazement regarding your product(s) or service(s) will serve you well in an environment where opportunity abounds. From finding other businesses to create Fusion/Affiliate relationships (see Volume 1, Section 7.6, "Fusion/Affiliate Marketing and Collaboration") to talking to prospects and existing customers and learning precious and valuable new information, opportunities will easily present themselves.

The knowledge, motivation, excitement, and joy that a Guerrilla marketer gains from their curiosity help them build strong and long-lasting relationships with their prospects and customers while building a stronger business.

9.21 * MAKE GOODS

Let's face it, unexpected things can occur in your business, making it appear that something "went wrong." Whether something "goes wrong" inside your business, with your employees, vendors, and suppliers, or it "goes wrong" with your prospects and customers, for Guerrilla marketers, the key is for your *make good* (i.e., what you do to make things right) to be a longer memory than what "went wrong." In Section 8.40, "Profit Out of Lemons," we addressed the importance of turning situations to be advantageous for your business.

In Section 8.34, "Conflict Resolution," we addressed the components of resolving a conflict, but sometimes your business needs to go further and offer a make good. There is an endless number of ways that your business can offer make goods that result in your prospects or customers keeping all things that went "right" at the top of their minds. Guerrilla marketers want their prospects or customers to say, "I don't even remember what the issue was, but they were great about it, and they . . ."

For example, most of us have experienced a situation where we ordered several products from a company where one or some of them were not available, and we were not aware of them being unavailable until after the order was placed. Let's look at the multiple ways that a company can choose to handle that situation and their customers' likely reactions:

Company Response	Customers Likely Reaction (which they often share with friends, family and associates)
The company sends a message that: • Apologizes • Informs the customer that the item is on back-order and will ship when it's ready • The customer is charged for the product	"What's wrong with this company? They don't know what they're doing; I don't want to wait. Now, I have to contact them to cancel it. I'll never order from them again, and I'm unsubscribing."
The company sends a message that: • Apologizes • Informs the customer that the item is not available • Informs the customer that they were not charged	"What's wrong with this company? They don't know what they're doing, I don't know if I want to order from them again."
The company sends a message that: • Apologizes • Informs the customer that the item is not available • Explains why it's not available and when it will be available • Informs the customer that they were not charged	"What's wrong with this company? Good grief, what a hassle, let me see if I can order it from another company. I don't know if I want to order from them again."

The company sends a message that:	"Good grief, that's a hassle, but at least they're trying to make it right. Let me see if I can order it from another company . . . or maybe I'll wait. At least they're trying."
• Apologizes	
• Informs the customer that the item is not available	
• Explains why it's not available and when it will be available	
• Provides the customer with a discount or places a credit in their account for future purchases	
• Informs the customer that they were not charged	
The company sends a message that:	"That's too bad that it's not available. Maybe I'll wait. A credit in my account is fantastic; I'm going to choose that. This company does a great job. Let's see what other products they have and if they have . . ."
• Apologizes	
• Informs the customer that the item is not available	
• Explains why it's not available and when it will be available	
• Provides the customer with multiple make good options to choose from (e.g., a discount on future purchase, a credit in their account, free shipping on their next order, etc.) that the customer easily selects with one click	
• Informs the customer that they were not charged	

How your business makes good can make every bit of difference regarding how your customers perceive your business. When your make good is more powerful than what "went wrong," your business can turn a negative situation into a positive one.

Most customers don't expect your business to be perfect, but they do expect your business to be great. That means your business is:

• Making your customer feel noticed, recognized, heard, understood, important, and appreciated (see Volume 3, Section 9.29, "Relationship Builder," and Section 9.30, "A Superb Listener")

• Flexible to find a solution and/or make good that delights them. After all, their opinion is the one that matters. Their opinion is also the one they share on social media, in their ratings and reviews, and with their friends, family, and associates

- Offering a convenient make good that doesn't require the customer to invest more time and/or jump through hoops
- Following-up and focusing on the solution (instead of focusing on what "went wrong")
- Continually demonstrating your commitment to delivering experiences that delight your customers
- Tracking and fixing issues to prevent repeated problems that unnecessarily cause customer dissatisfaction

Make goods, when done well, are an opportunity for your business to let its creativity shine and, as we addressed in Section 8.40, to create profits out of lemons. However, the reason Guerrilla marketers can be creative and personalized with their make goods is that they stay focused on the goal, which is for your business to rarely need to rely on make goods.

It's important to track your make goods, and your CRM system is a great tool to assist with that tracking. It's also important to track, measure, and identify issues that your business is repeating. Your business must act to ensure that repeated issues are indeed fixed. This is a good time to refer back to Section 8.37, "Inspect What You Expect," to be sure that your business is getting to the "why." In doing so, what you intend to be a successful fix to an issue is evaluated to ensure that it is indeed the right fix.

If, as in the example in the last table, your business is regularly out of products, that's an issue to immediately fix. Equally, it's not a time to be naïve regarding some customers' intentions. Unfortunately, some customers do not have good intentions, and your creative make goods can attract them to take full advantage. Sometimes, the solution is for your business to thrive without those types of customers, and your CRM systems can help your business identify customers with repeated make goods.

9.22 * MENTORING

Guerrilla businesses embrace mentoring. They focus on both mentoring others and being mentored. After all, mentoring is the gift that keeps on giving. Why? Simply put, by motivating and inspiring others, we give that same gift back to ourselves, and we feel motivated and inspired.

Both having a mentor and being a mentor means taking time to step outside of your routine. That time outside of your routine stimulates your creativity, increases your knowledge, and refreshes your perspective. Giving and getting inspiration (see Section 9.14, "Inspire") not only fuels your passion, but it also fuels your purpose (see Section 9.17, "Purpose-Minded").

As a mentor or mentee, a mentoring relationship is made successful when you:

- Have common attributes, attitudes, and mindsets
- Are focused
- Are respectful of each other's time
- Clearly define and communicate goals
- Establish a schedule and communicate regularly

Also, as a mentor or a mentee, a mentoring relationship is successful with a few more considerations.

Mentoring Others

Mentoring is not teaching. The goal of mentoring is to listen and connect with the person you're mentoring and then provide your experience, ideas, and inspiration. Your goal is to first seek to understand and then to help them (by your example) find the path to the success they desire.

Being Mentored

When seeking a mentor, you can be focused on building your business, but you don't have to be solely focused on your business. You can focus on learning, developing, and improving your other interests. For example, utilizing a golf or tennis pro to improve your game or a private chef to expand your skills. Those outside interests stimulate your creativity while you're broadening your network.

If you reach the point where you don't feel you can gain anything more from your mentor, that's perfectly normal and acceptable, and it's a sign that you're ready to grow your circle and/or your interests, and it's time to move forward and find a new mentor.

9.23 * LATERAL THINKING

Lateral thinking is defined by Cambridge Dictionary as "a way of solving a problem by thinking about it in a different and original way and not using traditional or expected methods."

The term is linked to Dr. Edward de Bono, who has written several books on the topic and describes lateral thinking, in part, as: "We have learned that every step in our thinking has to be logical. We use judgement to reject illogical steps in our search for the right answer. Lateral Thinking uses a deliberately illogical step to provoke a new perspective." His books offer techniques ". . . encouraging people to approach thinking as a skill that can be learned and improved."

Lateral thinking can be learned with his well-regarded approach. It can also be thought of more broadly as thinking outside of a traditional logical approach.

You've likely noticed that great ideas come to you when you're getting ready to go to sleep or in your dreams. Additionally, they come to you in the shower, while you're brushing your teeth, or when driving your automobile. When you're enjoying some solitude and not thinking about solving your problems, solutions and creativity can more easily find you.

Business Insider related an interesting perspective from Todd Henry, author of *The Accidental Creative*: "We struggle with new ideas, new projects, and new things we want to pursue. We're terrible at saying no. If we're squeezing all of the white space out of our lives by filling it with activity, if we're not pruning and saying no to things on occasion, then we're not going to have the space that we need to innovate or think. We're not going to have those moments of serendipity or those insights that are just hanging there. We have to manage our energy and create space in our lives. This allows us to bring the best of who we are to what we do."

Guerrilla marketers understand the power of being unconventional and creative, which is often fueled by lateral thinking. Traditional thinking can lead to improvements, but lateral thinking often leads to innovation and disruptions.

For example, consider the story found in Volume 1, Case Study 3, "Function of Beauty." Their thinking disrupted the haircare industry, in part, by asking customers about their needs and wants and then creating and selling a personalized solution. In the process, they forged a powerful and precious direct relationship with their customers, which many other businesses in their industry lack.

You'll find similar examples in the other Case Studies, such as:

- Volume 1, Case Study 2: Whole Foods Market. Their thinking created a supermarket format in the natural foods industry.
- Volume 1, Case Study 4: Red Bull. Their thinking led to the first product in what is now known as the beverage category called energy drinks.
- Case Study 5: Sprinkles. Their thinking brought about a way to serve cupcakes, any time of day (at their stores or anywhere) when they developed the first Cupcake ATM.
- Case Study 7: Ace Hardware. Their thinking showed how competitors could work together to achieve far more.
- Case Study 8: Brooks Brothers. Their thinking brought forward ready-made, instead of tailor-made, suits.

Another way to consider lateral thinking is to spend a few minutes thinking about how you can get from point A to point B. You might think of traditional options, such as to:

- Drive
- Fly
- Walk
- Take a bus

You could also put aside logical and traditional thoughts. That would lead you to think of new possibilities, such as jet packs. Perhaps it could even make you think of new possibilities, such as designing a new form of transportation, such as:

- Elon Musk when he developed the hyperloop concept in 2012 or the innovative ways that he and his businesses have approached automobiles and space travel
- Jeff Bezos and Blue Origin, which have also developed innovative approaches to sub-orbital travel
- Sir Richard Branson and Virgin Galactic, which have developed innovative approaches to space flights

Given the challenge of rethinking the future of space travel, lateral thinking is a must, and it produced three different approaches for getting from point A to point B.

It's valuable to know that lateral thinking is sometimes referred to as divergent thinking. The American Psychology Association defines divergent thinking as, "creative thinking in which an individual solves a problem or reaches a decision using strategies that deviate from commonly used or previously taught strategies."

Lateral thinking is the skilled process of coming up with innovative, unconventional, and disruptive ideas. Fortunately, those ideas do not need to be complicated. Consider what lateral thinking can do for your business. After all, it's how Guerrilla marketers stand out from the competition. It's also how their businesses find what "can be" instead of simply "what is," and they elevate their success along the way.

In Volume 3, Section 9.28, "Skilled Thinking," we'll address more skills and options to help you solve problems, create opportunities, and set your business apart.

9.24 * ATTENTION TO DETAIL

Guerrilla marketers tend to the tiny, supercharged details that can generate big profits. In doing so, Guerrilla marketers realize the importance of those tiny, supercharged details because they can boost your success, and they can just as easily derail your business.

Whether you're detail-oriented by nature or must work at it, and if you have detail-oriented employees, it's a powerful characteristic to utilize in your favor. Here are a few key ideas for successfully paying attention to the details that Guerrilla marketers do:

Every Word Matters

Your goal with your marketing and advertising is to put words together carefully and creatively to compel your prospects and customers to notice your business. Once they do, your call to action must then motivate them to take a desired action. The selection of those words is one of those tiny, supercharged details that determines your success.

For example, as this book is being written, there is a law firm advertising on television with a commercial that talks about how they view their customers. The commercial says, ". . . you're not just a dollar sign . . ." Perhaps what they said is exactly what they meant, and they do view their clients as dollar signs. Perhaps it's not what they meant, and if not, by simply omitting, the word "just" the statement is different. Instead of telling their prospects, ". . . you're not just a dollar sign . . .," they would have told their prospects "You're not a dollar sign . . ." The word "just" can (and just might) determine whether or not their prospects are willing to walk through their doors.

Once the word "just" pops out as people view the commercial, the effect of that tiny, supercharged detail compounds every time their prospects and clients hear and see the commercial.

Every Image Matters

Just as every word matters, Guerrilla marketers also know that every image matters. For example, if you're featuring people in your advertising and marketing, do they represent your prospects and customers? When your images represent both who your prospects and customers are and who they want to be, your business is making a powerful connection. Whether your business is online or offline, taking the time to know how to effectively represent your customers and prospects is a tiny, supercharged detail that can generate big profits.

Your product images are also a tiny, supercharged detail. When you're paying attention to the tiny, supercharged details, your images are appealing, clear, and detailed. Those appealing images turn prospects into satisfied customers, who then become repeat buyers. Those satisfied customers provide positive reviews and ratings, and they recommend your business, product(s), and/or service(s) to their friends, family, and associates. This is a formula for long-term success.

Just as easily, images that don't represent your business, product(s), or service(s) can derail your business. When you're not paying attention or you're misrepresenting your business, product(s), or service(s) with the images that your business advertises and markets, it results in dissatisfaction, returns, distrust, negative ratings, and negative reviews.

Conclusion

In a skeptical world that is all too willing to share mistakes (even turning them viral), your attention to detail is critical for your success. The reality is that when it comes to marketing and advertising, mistakes can easily happen.

Perhaps the mistake occurred because your business used the wrong word, the wrong image, the wrong date, the wrong price, etc. While mistakes are human, the key is to avoid as many mistakes as possible. When you are taking the time and putting in the effort, such as hiring professionals (e.g., an editor and/or proofreader) to pay attention to details, your focus can prevent mistakes. Services such as these can help:

- **Grammarly:** offers a digital writing assistant tool powered by AI (artificial intelligence)
- **Scribendi:** offers both editing and proofreading
- **ProofreadingPal:** offer both editing and a two-proofreading model

Mistakes are nearly inevitable, but they also create unnecessary roadblocks between your business and your customers and prospects. The more roadblocks you create, the less likely your customers and prospects are to maneuver around them.

Guerrilla marketers view attention to detail as an opportunity to turbo-charge their effectiveness and their success. Therefore, they take the extra time and engage additional resources for needed help. In doing so, it's easy to make it a priority to tend to those tiny, supercharged details that can generate big profits.

9.25 ✳ OWNER MINDSET

In Section 6.17, "Consumer Mindset," we addressed the importance of understanding mindsets to better understand how to market to your prospects and customers. It's just as important to understand how your mindset, as the business owner, affects your business.

As a reminder, mindset is defined by *Psychology Today* as "a belief that orients the way we handle situations—the way we sort out what is going on and what we should do. Our mindsets help us spot opportunities, but they can also trap us in self-defeating cycles."

Psychology Today offers additional insight into numerous different mindsets. Two important categories to be aware of which make up most business owners is:

- **Fixed mindset**: these business owners think their ability is innate. They think failures are mistakes, and it's unsettling, which creates doubt and defensiveness. These business owners are more focused on being perfect because they want to prevent failures
- **Growth mindset**: these business owners expect they can improve so failures create a motivating force for them to bounce back and work harder to grow and improve. These business owners are less focused on failures because they believe they can find solutions and become better because of the experience

People can easily switch between these mindsets in various situations. However, mindsets can become a habit, and being aware of both mindsets can be helpful when it comes to your reactions, lateral thinking (see Section 9.23, "Lateral Thinking"), and decision making. That is especially true in challenging times when it's possible to find yourself reacting based on habit.

It's equally important to understand the mindset of the people in your business. If you've established a team of growth mindset employees, and you introduce one (or more) fixed mindset employees, you can expect challenges. Equally, if you've established a team of fixed mindset employees, you can also expect to have challenges when a growth mindset employee is introduced.

While differing mindsets can be empowering to a business, they can also be divisive. That can be well managed with your knowledge of mindsets and knowing what to expect. On the positive side, just as your prospects and customers have differing mindsets, a well-balanced mix of employees can help your business be widely appealing to various mindsets.

9.26 * RESILIENCE

Resilience is a part of the DNA of a Guerrilla marketer. Taking an idea and turning it into a thriving business is not an easy task. It requires a great deal of pivoting and adjusting for the unexpected. Resilience is a crucial skill, as we addressed in Section 1.8, "Crucial Skills for Effectively Using Guerrilla Marketing."

Resilient is defined by Merriam-Webster as "tending to recover from or adjust easily to misfortune or change." The word to emphasize in that definition is *easily*. The longer it takes you to recover or adjust from misfortune or change, the more opportunity passes you by.

Because Guerrilla marketers are resilient, they easily spot opportunities, especially when others don't see opportunities. They also know change is constant, so the expectation that there will be roadblocks, unexpected twists, and turns all along their success path is natural. By embracing those changes and being unaffected by setbacks, your resilience keeps you ahead of the competition.

Those who don't possess resilience, struggle with change and waste time and energy working against change instead of adapting to it and capitalizing on the opportunities that change delivers. They also easily give up and close the doors when the going gets challenging.

Guerrilla marketers, on the other hand, are:

- Not hindered by mistakes or misfortunes
- Keeping their eye on trends and looking for changes
- Looking to their by-product (see Volume 1, Section 5.3, "By-Product") to help their business and/or portfolio of businesses expand and thrive
- Asking their customers about their needs, listening to their answers, and taking action

It's extremely easy to become complacent and get into a pattern of being in "selling mode," which means you're talking *to* your customers instead of having a conversation with them and listening to them. The needs of your customers and prospects grow and change over time, and your active listening keeps opportunity knocking. Your resilience makes you eager to open that knocking door, knowing that you can easily adjust to whatever you find on the other side.

In Volume 3, Section 9.31, "Focused on Success," we'll help you keep yourself and your business focused in the right direction.

SECTION X

Guerrilla Marketing Case Studies

INTRODUCTION

As you are now aware, Guerrilla Marketing is a 360-degree, consistent methodology that weaves through every aspect of your business. Guerrilla Marketing is intelligent marketing that utilizes a strategy and a plan that is supported with knowledge and low-cost, unconventional, creative tactics to convey and promote a compelling product(s) or idea(s).

Guerrilla Marketing succeeds as it makes the truth fascinating and compelling. It also helps your business identify and market your USP so your prospects and customers take notice of what makes your business unique.

In the following four Guerrilla Marketing Case Studies, we'll look at some well-known companies and outline how Guerrilla Marketing tactics can take an idea and turn it into limitless success. The companies we'll cover are:

- Sprinkles
- Barnes & Noble
- Ace Hardware
- Brooks Brothers

You'll see that many successful businesses utilize these tactics, and they combine them with the values of clarity, focus, and consistency.

These businesses began where every business begins—with an idea and a dream. That idea and dream are precious and so is the opportunity to turn that idea and/or dream into a small business. With Guerrilla Marketing, they turn knowledge, time, energy, and imagination into profits, and you can do the same with your idea, dream, and/or business.

With compelling messages and tactics, along with an authentic and consistent identity, small businesses grow. By consistently repeating and improving upon the compelling messages and winning tactics, businesses turn their prospects into customers. Their success grows as their growing customer base makes repeat purchases and provides precious referrals, which is the fuel for the long-term success of the business.

Guerrilla marketers understand how marketing works, and they constantly put that knowledge and their creativity to work . . . along with the power of consistency, tracking, analysis, and repetition. The simple act of repeating what's working and improving or eliminating what's not can set their success apart. Let's take a look at Guerrilla Marketing in action!

GUERRILLA MARKETING CASE STUDY 5

Sprinkles

Sprinkles began as a baked-fresh-daily cupcake bakery. They took what was considered an ordinary product and made it interesting and unique. That's not an easy task but they put time, energy, imagination, and innovation—and so much more—to work to set their business apart from the competition, which, for the most part, was ordinary.

Today, Sprinkles also makes cakes, chocolates, and cookies. According to Sprinkles, "Since 2005, Sprinkles has innovated their way to an ever-growing, loyal fan base for their unexpected flavors, on-demand Cupcake ATMs, convenient online ordering and steadily expanding the footprint of design-forward bakeries coast to coast. Today, the brand proudly leverages its platform to support the empowerment of women and continuously put their guests first."

Sprinkles took something ordinary and made it extraordinary. Innovation and design are at the foundation of Sprinkles. According to *Inc* and Candace Nelson, founder of Sprinkles, "Sprinkles was the world's first cupcake bakery and is credited with starting a worldwide cupcake craze."

Taking the ordinary and making it extraordinary is exactly what Guerrilla Marketing helps you do. Is your idea, business, product(s), or service(s) ready to break through the ordinary and become extraordinary?

The list of evident Guerrilla Marketing tactics at play with Sprinkles is long. Let's outline some of the most successful Guerrilla Marketing tactics at play:

- Innovation (see Volume 1, Section 8.11)
- Convenience (see Volume 1, Section 8.21)
- Name (see Volume 1, Section 8.2)
- Identity (see Volume 1, Section 8.3)
- Brand (see Volume 1, Section 8.1)
- Television Appearances (see Volume 1, Section 2.5)
- By-Product (see Volume 1, Section 5.3)
- Amazement (see Volume 1, Section 8.16)
- Passion and Enthusiasm (see Volume 1, Section 9.1)
- Selection and Cross-Selling (see Volume 1, Section 8.23)
- Unique Selling Proposition (USP) (see Volume 1, Section 1.3)

- Fusion/Affiliate Marketing and Collaboration (see Volume 1, Section 7.6)
- Public Relations (see Volume 1, Section 7.8)
- Guerrilla Creativity (see Volume 1, Section 1.2)
- Intelligent Positioning (see Volume 1, Section 8.8)
- Product Displays/Experiences (see Volume 1, Section 3.1)
- Purpose-Minded (see Section 9.17)
- Consistency (see Section 1.9 and Volume 1, Sections 2.8 and 9.11)
- Repetition (see Section 1.10 and Volume 1, Section 2.8)

Let's dive a bit deeper into some of those Guerrilla Marketing tactics as they relate to Sprinkles. For those tactics that you decide are well-suited for your prospects and customers, and therefore, you decide to incorporate them into your Guerrilla Marketing plan, be sure to take the time to re-review the details of each tactic.

Innovation Convenience and Unique Selling Proposition (USP)

From the beginning, Sprinkles focused on innovation as the world's first cupcake bakery. Cupcakes had competition; they were already sold at grocery stores and bakeries. Cupcakes were also made (from scratch or box mixes) at home by bakers that served them at/after school, at birthdays, and at other parties. Therefore, Sprinkles had to focus on being unique and innovative.

Sprinkles introduced the convenient and innovative world's first cupcake truck and the world's first Cupcake ATM. What makes them unique makes them memorable and relevant as they consistently promote their uniqueness.

Guerrilla Creativity, Brand, Identity, Intelligent Positioning, Consistency, Product Displays/Experiences, Selection, and Cross-Selling

Sprinkles reaps the benefits from utilizing a consistent name, logo, color palette, design, etc., in their marketing and advertising. That consistency flows through to their packaging and retail operations, including their interior and exterior design and signage, as well as their color-coded cupcakes that coordinate with their color-coded menu.

Sprinkles continues to expand their selection with cookies, brownies, layer cakes, and chocolates to appeal to more customers and promote cross-selling. They also offer gift and special occasion options to extend their appeal.

Fusion/Affiliate Marketing and Collaboration, Selection, and Cross-Selling

Though Sprinkles currently directly sells their cupcake mixes, initially, they partnered with Williams-Sonoma to distribute their cupcake mixes. They also now offer franchising and licensing to expand their reach by partnering with other businesses to help them grow and increase their access and convenience for their customers and prospects.

Television Appearances, Passion and Enthusiasm, and Public Relations

According to *Inc* and Candace Nelson, founder of Sprinkles, "We had been open for a few months, and my husband Charles and I were literally sleeping on the bakery floor some nights after 18-hour workdays. It was true #startuplife! One afternoon, we got a call from Harpo Studios asking if we could be in Chicago the next morning with 300 cupcakes for The Oprah Winfrey Show. We said "yes!" not knowing how we were going to get it done. But when Oprah calls, you know you've made it. Needless to say, we revved up our mixers, bought some red-eye tickets, and hand-carried all those cupcakes onto the plane. A couple of months later when the episode aired, our business increased by 50%!"

Candace Nelson has also regularly appeared as a judge on *Cupcake Wars,* which airs on Food Network and her Netflix show called *Sugar Rush.* Those television appearances give her credibility and are low-to-no-cost opportunities to promote the business.

By-Product

Sprinkles has expanded their business with the utilization of its by-product. Their cookbook (*The Sprinkles Baking Book*) is a *New York Times* bestseller. They also created baking mixes, which they distribute nationwide.

Purpose Minded

Your business might start with a noble cause and/or a purpose in mind. Alternately, your business might not start that way, but you find along the journey that it can accomplish more than anticipated. Therefore, you take the time to define the purpose of the business, and perhaps it aligns with a noble cause. There isn't a right or wrong way.

Consistency and Repetition

Sprinkles has created marketing that is applied consistently and with repetition. From the cupcakes to the packaging and retail location (e.g., stores and/or ATMs), it's a consistent and distinctive look. With repetition, they make their brand memorable for their customers, and that works for their success.

Conclusion

Remember, Guerrilla marketers seek to disrupt and innovate every day as they pave their path to profits. The moment you stop innovating and asking the important questions of yourself and your customers and prospects, your business becomes less compelling. When your business is less compelling your business needs to spend more on marketing, oftentimes, while you're getting fewer results.

GUERRILLA MARKETING CASE STUDY 6
Barnes & Noble

Barnes & Noble began in 1873 in the home of Charles M. Barnes. *Business Insider* reports that "It wasn't until Barnes' son traveled to New York in 1917 and joined forces with G. Clifford Noble that the company was officially established. During the Great Depression, the company opened its flagship location in New York on Fifth Avenue."

According to Barnes & Noble, "Nearly a century later, Leonard Riggio acquired the flagship Barnes & Noble trade name and over the next four decades transformed the company into the bookselling giant that it is today."

Leonard Riggio retired in 2016, after decades of guiding Barnes & Noble with resilience through growth, innovation, and constant change. NPR stated it well: "Riggio steered Barnes & Noble from an era of bonded leather books through the proliferation of free information in the Internet age, and the advent of online booksellers. Yes, he's watched his industry wrestle with digital publishing and the popularity of e-books and the rise of Amazon."

According to NPR, Leonard Riggio planned to pursue engineering until a job as a clerk in a bookstore changed his direction. He founded the Student Book Exchange in 1965, which he turned into a successful retailer and later acquired the Barnes & Noble bookstore in New York City.

As Leonard Riggio stated, "We were the first retail in America to have a super store of any kind. The first retail in America to have public restrooms. The first major retailer to open Sundays." Riggio believes that the Internet, and the access to books and free information online, was a source of great change and he said ". . . I think that technology component had more to do with the suppression of book store sales than Amazon did."

Today Barnes & Noble is "the internet's largest bookstore." They have expanded beyond books to sell music, toys, and more. Additionally, in-store, their Barnes & Noble café offers free wi-fi along with tasty food and beverages.

The list of evident Guerrilla Marketing tactics at play with Barnes & Noble is long. Let's outline some of the most successful Guerrilla Marketing tactics at play:
- Name (see Volume 1, Section 8.2)
- Identity (see Volume 1, Section 8.3)

- Brand (see Volume 1, Section 8.1)
- Consistency (see Section 1.9 and Volume 1, Sections 2.8 and 9.11)
- Passion and Enthusiasm (see Volume 1, Section 9.1)
- Connect and Interact (see Volume 1, Section 6.15)
- Selection and Cross-Selling (see Volume 1, Section 8.23)
- Product Displays/Experiences (see Volume 1, Section 3.1)
- Collaboration (see Volume 1, Section 7.6)
- Convenience (see Volume 1, Section 8.21)
- Innovation (see Volume 1, Section 8.11)
- Systems and Automation (see Volume 1, Section 8.31)
- Easy to Do Business With (see Volume 1, Section 9.2)
- Guerrilla Creativity (see Volume 1, Section 1.2)
- Resilience (see Sections 1.8 and 9.26)

Let's dive a bit deeper into some of those Guerrilla Marketing tactics as they relate to Barnes & Noble. For those tactics that you decide are well-suited for your prospects and customers, and you decide to incorporate them into your Guerrilla Marketing plan, be sure to take the time to re-review the details of each tactic.

Name, Identity, Brand, Consistency, Passion, and Enthusiasm

Barnes & Noble reaps the benefits of utilizing a consistent business name. Much to Leonard Riggio's credit, he didn't change the name when he acquired the Barnes & Noble store in New York City in 1965, which many others may have been tempted to do.

They also reap the benefits of a consistent name, logo, color palette, design, etc., in their marketing and advertising. That consistency flows through their retail operations, including in their interior and exterior design and signage, which makes their retail stores easily identifiable.

Selection and Cross-Selling, Convenience, Product Displays/ Experiences

In their retail locations, Barnes & Noble has stayed committed to offering an experiential environment that invites cross-selling. Their customers can, for example, enjoy coffee and snacks while they connect with other people and/or read an ebook or have a seat in a comfortable chair while exploring and reading books.

It's not always easy to create memorable experiences in a physical business location. However, sometimes, it's as simple as a comfortable chair and an invitation to relax and enjoy a bit of a good read.

They also offer a selection of non-book products (e.g., journals, gift cards, toys, music, and accessories) that appeal to their customers and expand their selection for easy gift shopping. The more you know about your customers, the easier it is to add products and services to your selection that interest them and motivate them to make initial and repeat purchases.

Connect and Interact

Barnes & Noble also offers a help desk that encourages its employees to interact with and assist their customers and prospects. Those interactions provide valuable insights regarding their customers' and prospects' needs, pain points, and pleasure points while helping them find the solutions they seek.

Collaboration

Barnes & Noble works with countless publishers to bring their books into the hands of Barnes & Nobles' readers. They also collaborate with brands, including Starbucks and Godiva, to offer desirable treats that engage their customers and prospects.

Innovation and Resilience

Without the ability to adapt and innovate, Barnes & Noble would not be here today. When they began, books were leather-bound, and retailers did not offer public restrooms.

They have maneuvered their way through the introduction and innovation of the Internet and intense competition, which put many bookstores out of business. Today, they sell food, beverages, books (physical and electronic), music, and video—online and in brick-and-mortar locations.

Systems and Automation

Today they continue to refine their systems and operations. According to the *Wall Street Journal*, Barnes & Noble is moving away from its centralized approach and "uniformity designed to create economies of scale and simplify the shopping experience." Their goal is to put decision-making back in the hands of their stores and "the company is empowering store managers to curate their shelves based on local tastes."

The competitive landscape and technology have dramatically changed since Barnes & Noble began blazing its path as a bookseller. Today, they are a book-selling giant and belong to an elite club of the oldest US retailers. They are in good company with retail businesses, such as Brooks Brothers (opened in 1818), Macy's (opened in 1858), Saks Fifth Avenue (opened in 1867), and Walgreens (opened in 1901).

Conclusion

Whether you're starting your business or you've been in business for decades, how can you rethink your business from the customers' point of view? If you're not constantly thinking about convenience, innovation, technology, or learning your customers' problems, needs, and experiences, be aware that someone else is. That someone else could be your competition or a start-up business with its sights set on your customers because they think it's possible to compete with and win against your business.

Guerrilla marketers seek to innovate and disrupt traditional businesses every day. Your Guerrilla Creativity is always a strength for you to draw upon. Never stop asking and challenging yourself and your business. In your weekly or daily meetings, be sure that you're asking questions to improve your success, such as:

- Can purchasing be made easier?
- Can our business, product(s), or service(s) be more convenient?
- How can we compel customers to buy more products?
- Can we offer an experience (or experiences) that result in greater customer satisfaction, higher ratings, positive reviews, sales, and profits?
- How can we be more irresistible to our prospects?
- If employees were more satisfied in their jobs, what would be the positive impact on the business?
- How can we improve our ratings and reviews?
- Can we do more while spending less?
- What can be done to make our customers love us more?
- What other problems/pain points do our prospects and customers have that we can solve?
- Are we using Guerrilla Creativity to our full advantage?
- Are we using the power of consistency and repetition in our marketing?

While change for the sake of change is rarely a good use of your resources, change for the sake of progress is a good use of your resources. The moment you stop asking the important questions, your business becomes less innovative, convenient, and compelling to your customers and prospects, which means your business is spending more on marketing and getting fewer results.

Ace Hardware

Ace Hardware was founded in 1924. From the beginning, they utilized the power of collaboration. According to Ace Hardware, they were founded by a "small group of Chicago hardware store owners, Ace changed the retail landscape by allowing individual stores to purchase merchandise in bulk to save money and buy at the lowest possible price. This partnership enabled even the smaller stores to compete effectively at retail despite larger stores in their market. And to this very day, Ace Hardware Corporation is still owned solely and exclusively by the local Ace retail entrepreneurs."

In a challenging retail year—2020—Ace Hardware saw double-digit growth in same-store sales, average transaction sizes, and triple-digit growth in the number of new stores and online revenues. Nearly a century after their beginning, their business remains appealing and compelling to their prospects and customers.

Guerrilla Marketing is about knowledge, creativity, imagination, and the ability to dare to be different and take new approaches to meet the needs of prospects and customers. Guerrilla marketers are unconventional, not only in their marketing efforts but also in their approach to building their business. Guerrilla marketers understand the power of being different and promoting it. Being different makes you stand out.

Ace Hardware consists of over 5,400 stores around the world. While the retail hardware space is dominated by big-box retailers (e.g., Home Depot and Lowes), Ace Hardware has stayed focused on its uniqueness (USP), and they promote it well.

The list of evident Guerrilla Marketing tactics at play with Ace Hardware is long. Let's outline some of the most successful ones:

- Collaboration (see Volume 1, Section 7.6)
- Selection and Cross-Selling (see Volume 1, Section 8.23)
- Convenience (see Volume 1, Section 8.21)
- Unique Selling Proposition (USP) (see Volume 1, Section 1.3)
- Name (see Volume 1, Section 8.2)
- Identity (see Volume 1, Section 8.3)

- Brand (see Volume 1, Section 8.1)
- Uniforms (see Volume 1, Section 6.2)
- Tagline (see Volume 1, Section 8.6)
- Personalization (see Volume 1, Section 3.6)
- Be the Solution (see Volume 1, Section 6.4)
- Intelligent Positioning (see Volume 1, Section 8.8)
- Satisfied and Delighted Customers (see Volume 1, Section 6.11)
- Guerrilla Creativity (see Volume 1, Section 1.2)
- Consistency (see Section 1.9 and Volume 1, Sections 2.8 and 9.11)
- Repetition (see Section 1.10 and Volume 1, Section 2.8)
- Meet Prospects and Customers Where They Are (see Section 6.16)
- Touch Points (see Section 6.19)

Let's dive a bit deeper into some of those Guerrilla Marketing tactics, as they relate to Ace Hardware. For those tactics that you decide are well-suited for your prospects and customers, and you decide to incorporate them into your Guerrilla Marketing plan, be sure to take the time to re-review the details of each tactic.

Collaboration and Convenience

From the beginning, they utilized the power of collaboration to redefine the retail landscape. By collaborating, those Chicago hardware store owners found greater buying power to deliver a wide array of desirable products at reasonable prices. At the same time, they maintained the appeal of their businesses as a convenient and local hardware store.

Ace Hardware also franchises, which allows them to grow the business by partnering with others (e.g., existing hardware stores that want to convert and/ or new businesses). Because ". . . Ace Hardware Corporation is still owned solely and exclusively by the local Ace retail entrepreneurs," their franchises are invested in their locations and the wellbeing of the entire business.

Selection and Cross-Selling

With the right selection, cross-selling becomes an important part of creating relationships with your customers and motivating them to make additional and repeat purchases. A customer values the expertise and suggestions of a business that is eager to help and knowledgeable. Prospects and customers want to find well-suited products that solve their problems and relieve their pain points.

A Unique Selling Proposition (USP), Brand, Name, Identity, Uniforms, and Tagline

Guerrilla marketers think about their business with the end in mind. In the case of Ace Hardware, they use the power of intentional marketing as they align their company attributes and attitudes in their marketing. Their tagline is "Ace is the place with the helpful hardware folks." That tagline is memorable, and it contains their business name, which works to their advantage. Their tagline also clearly conveys their USP, and their stores back it up (earning service awards to prove it).

Their stores share a common and easily identifiable logo, name, and identity. At the same time, their employees are easily recognizable by the red vests they wear. Their strong brand allows them to sell many of their products packaged with their brand name.

Personalization, Be the Solution, Touch Points, Satisfied and Delighted Customers, and Intelligent Positioning

Ace Hardware focuses on personal attention with their customers. They strive to make their prospects and customers feel welcome, and they are readily available to assist with knowledge, helpful advice, and lending a hand as they take you right to the product, rather than simply pointing or telling you the isle number.

Ace Hardware clearly satisfies and delights their customers because in 2020, "Ace Hardware Ranks Highest In Customer Satisfaction By J.D. Power. The world's largest retailer-owned hardware cooperative has achieved this ranking 13 out of the last 14 years."

Guerrilla Creativity, Repetition, and Consistency

Ace Hardware fully utilizes one of the most powerful Guerrilla Marketing tactics with their television advertising, which is marketing a consistent, clear, and compelling message. Their message is focused (i.e., no gimmicks or distractions) on their USP, convenience, and problem-solving capabilities. Their marketing also conveys consistent company attributes (e.g., brand, name, logo, tagline, etc.) and consistent company attitudes (e.g., easy to do business with, responsive and attentive, passion and enthusiasm, etc.)

Telling their story with consistency and repetition pays dividends. Consistency builds familiarity; familiarity builds trust, and trust creates sales, repeat purchases, and precious referrals, which is the fuel for long-term success.

Conclusion

In the case of Ace Hardware, a small group of competing business owners unconventionally found a way to collaborate. By doing so, they dared to show that they understand their customers' needs and could deliver compelling solutions.

They seek every opportunity to create personal connections while offering knowledge and experience to their prospects and customers. They have found a way to keep their smaller neighborhood hardware stores thriving in a retail market that often focuses on "bigger is better." Remember, Guerrilla marketers seek to disrupt traditional businesses every day as they pave their path to profits.

GUERRILLA MARKETING CASE STUDY 8
Brooks Brothers

According to Brooks Brothers, they are the oldest clothing retailer in the US. They opened their first store in 1818 under the name H. & D.H. Brooks & Co. in New York City. The business passed from a father to his four sons and, in 1850, it became Brooks Brothers.

Brooks Brothers has a long history of innovation. For example, in 1849, Brooks Brothers was innovative when they introduced ready-made clothing, an alternative to tailor-made clothing. In 1896, the innovation continued when they introduced the first button-down polo shirt, and in 1900, they began importing and producing clothing with Harris Tweed. In 1902, they were also the first to offer madras fabric for warm-weather wear, and in 1904, they brought the Shetland sweater to America, which later helped to grow their business to include women's wear. They also introduced America to seersucker in the 1920s, which became quite popular in the mid-1930s.

In 1850, they began using the golden fleece symbol as their logo. In 1903, they began their expansion by sending out, what they called, "The Roadman" to various cities to set up trunk shows. In 1979, they opened their first international location in Tokyo. They had grown their business to more than 500 locations worldwide. Though the current times are challenging for Brooks Brothers, their long history demonstrates resilience.

The list of evident Guerrilla Marketing tactics at play with Brooks Brothers is long. Let's outline some of the most successful ones for them:

- Consistency (see Section 1.9 and Volume 1, Sections 2.8 and 9.11)
- Repetition (see Section 1.10 and Volume 1, Section 2.8)
- Name (see Volume 1, Section 8.2)
- Logo (see Volume 1, Section 8.4)
- Selection and Cross-Selling (see Volume 1, Section 8.23)
- Brand (see Volume 1, Section 8.1)
- Innovation (see Volume 1, Section 8.11)
- Unique Selling Proposition (USP) (see Volume 1, Section 1.3)
- Benefits and Competitive Advantages (see Volume 1, Section 7.2)
- Guerrilla Creativity (see Volume 1, Section 1.2)

- Resilience (see Section 1.8 and 9.26)
- Passion and Enthusiasm (see Volume 1, Section 9.1)
- Product Displays/Experiences (see Volume 1, Section 3.1)

Let's dive a bit deeper into some of those Guerrilla Marketing tactics, as it relates to Brooks Brothers. For those tactics that you decide are well-suited for your prospects and customers, and you decide to incorporate them into your Guerrilla Marketing plan, be sure to take the time to re-review the details of each tactic

Consistency, Repetition, Name, and Logo

Brooks Brothers is a company that embraces and profits from the power of consistency. Guerrilla marketers give their advertising and marketing an enormous boost when they simply employ the no-cost, turbo-charged, profit-generating marketing tactics of consistency and repetition.

"Brooks" has been in their name since 1818, and they have operated as Brooks Brothers since 1850. In that same year, they began using the golden fleece symbol as their logo. Their name and logo are highly recognizable because of their consistency and repetition.

When your customers are willing to wear your visible brand name and/or logo on their clothing, you're enjoying the benefits of powerful Guerrilla Marketing. Each customer is a human billboard for your company, and your consistency makes that even more powerful. With a consistent logo, there is recognition. Brooks Brothers has been reaping the multiplying benefits of their consistency for well over 170 years.

Selection and Cross-Selling, Brand, Innovation, USP, and Benefits and Competitive Advantages

Through a long history of innovation, Brooks Brothers created a strong brand that compels their customers, motivating them to make repeat purchases. By offering everything from shorts to formal wear, they appeal to a broad array of prospects. To increase their appeal and cross-selling, they increased their selection to include shoes, accessories, women's apparel, children's apparel, etc.

The highly recognizable brand they have built is also a benefit and competitive advantage. Because they rely on their own designs, their customers find their clothing and accessories appealing and unique.

Resilience

It goes without saying that a business that has been in operation since 1818 knows a lot about resilience. They have been through the best of times, the worst of times, and more changes than most of us can imagine.

Resilience is a part of the DNA of a Guerrilla marketer. Taking an idea and turning it into a thriving business is not an easy task. It requires a great deal of pivoting and adjusting for the unexpected. Resilience is a crucial skill for effectively using Guerrilla Marketing for your success.

Conclusion

For a retail business to thrive for over 200 years is indeed a rarity. They have seen the best of times and worst of times . . . multiple times. Through it all, they have innovated, adapted, and been resilient as they have marketed appealing apparel and accessories and continue to build their brand.

Now that you've seen four more great examples of Guerrilla Marketing success (also see Volume 1, Case Studies 1–4), it's time to develop and execute your Guerrilla Marketing plan and Guerrilla Creative and Advertising Strategy and over-achieve the success of these businesses. Guerrilla marketers understand that this is their dream, and they will never settle. What do you plan to do with your precious dream and your precious opportunity?

SECTION XI

100+ Free Tools

100+ FREE TOOLS TO PROPEL YOUR GUERRILLA MARKETING SUCCESS INTO PROFITS

Refer to gMarketing.com/Club for convenient links.

Business Operations Resources and Tools

From accounting to communications, customer relations, HR, project management, data analytics, and more, there are high-quality tools at your fingertips, which a Guerrilla marketer can use to put their business on the path to profitable growth. Note: Any offers or services shown are subject to change by that business.

Refer to gMarketing.com/Club for convenient links.

Agiloft	"Agiloft, Inc. is a trusted provider of agile software for contract and commerce lifecycle management. Our unique platform enables our pre-built and custom modules to be tailored to your exact needs without writing custom code, so deployment times and costs are a fraction of those required for other systems."
	Get started with the free Agiloft edition, which is designed to meet the needs of growing organizations. You'll be able to select the functions you need and their robust options (paid) are ready to grow with your business.
Avast	"We believe everyone has the right to be safe online, which is why we offer our award-winning free antivirus to millions of people around the world. Using real-time intelligence from over 400 million Avast users, we prevent more than 66 million threats every day."
	Get started for free with Avast and add (paid) features and services to meet the needs of your business.
BlogTalk Radio	"Effortless Broadcasting. Why make things harder than they need to be? That's the thinking behind our comprehensive studio, which makes managing multiple elements simultaneously child's play."
	BlogTalkRadio allows you to get started for free to create your radio broadcasts anywhere in the world. As your needs grow, they will help you scale with paid options with more callers, hours, storage, and live studio sessions.

BP Simulator	"Free business process simulation modeling software . . ." With BP Simulator, you can map out your business process to ensure that your goals and plans are aligned to give you the results you're expecting. It's a great way to develop new business processes or improve existing processes to create efficiency, improved customer experiences, and cost reductions.
Diagrams	"Diagram with anyone, anywhere. Diagrams is open source, online, desktop and container deployable diagramming software." With Diagrams, you can create professional diagrams for free that work with your existing tools, such as G Suite, Google Drive, Dropbox, Github, OneDrive, Office 365, and more.
EdX	"Access 2500+ online courses from 140 institutions." Guerrilla marketers are curious and thrive with knowledge. With thousands of courses to choose from, EdX provides the opportunity to learn from institutions, such as Harvard University, Massachusetts Institute of Technology (MIT), Princeton University, and many more. The courses (free and paid) are offered individually or in a series for those that want to gain in-depth knowledge about a subject.
Evernote	"Evernote helps people focus on what matters most to them. It's where ideas become answers, where individuals organize their daily lives, and where teams come to create and share work together." Turn your "To-do" chaos into streamlined productivity. With the free Evernote Basic program, you can get started with organizing your notetaking, lists, reminders, and ideas with notebooks, tags, and searching and sharing capabilities. With robust features, you can upgrade (paid) to add more features to help you become streamlined and productive.
Evernote Scannable	"Scannable - Scanner app for documents. Scannable captures the paper in your life quickly and beautifully, transforming it into high-quality scans ready to save or share. Whether on the go or at the office, send paper on its way and move on." Evernote Scannable is a convenient way to scan documents, receipts, business cards, and more while you're on the go with your mobile device. With easy editing features, you'll be ready to share your document via email, text, or exported as a PDF or JPG.

Free-Confer-ence-Call	"FreeConferenceCall.com, an award-winning conferencing solution, is everything you want it to be—from phone conferencing service with international teleconferences to free video conferencing and free screen sharing."
	It may sound too good to be true, but it's true. Started in 2001, FreeConferenceCall helps businesses around the globe. With robust features and offerings, these free tools will help your business function like a top-tier company.
Genius Scan	"Genius Scan is a scanner in your pocket. It helps users digitize millions of documents on the go every day. Discover how it will help you too!"
	With Genius Scan, your phone camera becomes your scanner. Simply use Genius Scan to automatically detect your document using your camera. Your scan is turned into a PDF file that you can edit, keep, or share (email, cloud storage services, social media, etc.) with just a few clicks. Enhanced features are available in the paid edition.
GitHub	"GitHub is a development platform inspired by the way you work. From open source to business, you can host and review code, manage projects, and build software alongside 50 million developers."
	Get started for free with public/private repositories, storage, collaborators, community support, and more. As your collaboration and the needs of your team grow, GitHub is ready to grow (paid) with you.
Gmail	Gmail, provided by Google, is a staple for SMBs. Gmail is free and you can easily and affordably upgrade to a G Suite account to access valuable features, such as a professional email address with your domain, chat, video and voice conferencing, storage, and many other tools to make your business productive.

Google Account	Your free Google account includes a number of productivity tools that can save you a lot of money. Here are a few: **Google Drive**: Google offers a set number of GBs for free, and that storage is used by Google Drive, Gmail, and Google Photos. You can upgrade to Google One to increase your capacity. Your Google Drive files are private, but you can choose to share them with an invitation. A shared file allows others to view, comment, and edit any file or folder you choose, making online collaboration easy. **Google Docs, Sheets, and Slides**: Google provides you with tools to create documents, spreadsheets, and presentations to move your business forward. **Google Forms**: put together a form in minutes to conduct a survey or offer an online form. The collected data is accumulated in a spreadsheet to give you the answers and the data that you need. **Google Drawings**: create easy diagrams and flow charts for your documents or to embed them on your website. **Google Apps**: choose from the numerous productivity, collaboration, and creativity apps in the Google Drive collection in the Chrome Web Store.
Microsoft Power BI Desktop	"Bring your data to life with Power BI Desktop." "Dig deeper into data and find patterns you may have otherwise missed that lead to actionable insights." "Explore your data, automatically find patterns, understand what your data means, and predict future outcomes to drive business results." Let Microsoft help do the heavy lifting when it comes to visualizing and analyzing your business data. With Power BI Desktop, free from Microsoft, you can pull your data (from hundreds of supported services) and easily prep and model your data to find patterns and insights to drive your business forward. Microsoft Power BI Pro (paid service) is available as you grow your business.
Miro	"Where . . . teams get work done. The online collaborative whiteboard platform to bring teams together, anytime, anywhere." Get started for free with editable boards and unlimited team members. Miro is integrated with Slack, Microsoft One Drive and Teams, Google Drive, Dropbox, and more to give you the ease you need and the productivity and creativity you desire.

PandaDoc	"Take the work out of your document workflow. Finally, enable your fast-moving teams with a simple, sophisticated all-in-one solution to easily manage the creation, editing, and signing of documents."
	PandaDoc helps businesses simplify processes, such as proposals, quotes, contracts, forms, and e-signatures. With their free plan, you can begin with e-signatures. You can then upgrade with valuable features, such as templates, tracking, CRM integration, workflow approvals, etc.
Podbean	"Podbean is an easy and powerful way to start a podcast. Everything you need for a successful podcast. No difficult technology to learn."
	Get started for free, and Podbean will scale (paid) with your business to include more storage space, monetization, video, etc.
Proposify	"Discover the proposal software that gives control and insight into the most important stage of your sales process. From design to sign-off, get the confidence and consistency to dominate your deals."
	Proposify helps businesses that rely on proposals thrive. With consistent, accurate, and powerful content, your proposals will stand out. With popular integrations, your prospects will find it easy to become your customers while your business has key insights along the way. While their free plan is ideal for solo deals, they offer (paid) solutions for all levels.
Slack	"Work more easily with everyone. Stay on the same page and make decisions faster by bringing all of your work communication into one place."
	Slack offers an innovative channels system that will help your business stay organized and focused with your conversations, files, and tools. Collaboration is made easy, even with voice and video calls, and workflows become automated for routine actions.
	Slack provides a scalable framework to grow with your business. You can get started for free with a limited plan and move into a paid plan as your business grows.

Trello	"Trello lets you work more collaboratively and get more done. Trello's boards, lists, and cards enable you to organize and prioritize your projects in a fun, flexible, and rewarding way."
	Forget boring spreadsheets and make productivity, organization, and teamwork a snap. With Trello you get an easy interface and automation tools; you'll get more done with ease. You can get started with a free plan, and Trello is then ready to help your business soar with the additional tools offered with their paid plans.
Ultradox	"Automate Your Business . . . With Ultradox you can automate tedious tasks and create your own enterprise apps without hiring a team of developers. The unique combination of workflow and template engine allows you to merge, send and print documents, generate websites or send out responsive emails as part of your process."
	Stop allowing your business to be slowed down by repetitive tasks. You can get started with a free Ultradox plan and add (paid) automation features as your needs grow. If you use G Suite, you'll enjoy additional benefits.
Wave Apps	"Wave is an award-winning financial management software company that is changing how entrepreneurs make money, move money and track money. Wave provides solutions that empower small business owners to simplify their finances while giving them more confidence to run their businesses."
	Wave offers free accounting software to help you with income and expense tracking, invoicing, sales tax tracking, financial statements, reporting, integrations, a performance dashboard, and more. Get started with their free program, and as your needs grow, they will grow with your business (with a paid service).
Wrike	"Project management is easy and efficient with Wrike. All-in-one collaboration software for leading productive, happy teams."
	Get started for free with features that every business needs, including task management, file sharing, storage space, activity streams, desktop and mobile apps, and more. As your business grows, Wrike can grow with your business and offer additional (paid) features to keep your productivity soaring.

Yahoo Mail	"Show the world you mean business."
	Yahoo offers free email with improved organization and helpful tools to allow you to be more productive and efficient. With their subscriptions tab, you can easily unsubscribe from unwanted lists. For a low monthly fee, a Guerrilla marketer will get a business email address that matches their domain to enhance their professional image and build trust with their prospects and customers.
ZipBooks	"Simple accounting software that makes you even smarter. Simple, beautiful, and powerful, ZipBooks gives you the tools and intelligence to take your business to the next level."
	With ZipBooks, you can send custom quotes, estimates, and invoices and get paid with major credit cards or PayPal. With auto-billing and automated payment reminders, you can take the heavy lifting out of your recurring invoicing while providing a polished experience for your customers. ZipBooks offers a variety of additional features to make your bookkeeping easier with their free service. As your business grows, upgrade to a paid version and benefit from even more productivity features.
Zoho Desk	"Put customer service at the heart of your company. Zoho Desk is the industry's first context-aware help desk software that helps businesses focus on the customer."
	Get your important customer service activities organized and working for your customers with email ticketing, customer management, a knowledge base to ensure consistency, a help center, a mobile app, and more with the free version of Zoho Desk. As your business and customer needs grow, Zoho Desk offers a robust set of (paid) features, from integrations to AI, to help you grow and excel at customer service.
Zoho Docs	"Online file management for teams and individuals. Bring your team to a secure and collaborative workspace where everything is available to everyone in real time. Create, collaborate, and get work done, securely."
	Have the documents you need at your fingertips wherever you go. Start with a free Zoho Docs account for a small team and expand into a paid service as your data needs and team size grow.

Zoho Recruit	"An ATS (or applicant tracking system) is a software that manages your entire hiring and recruitment process. It helps you to speed up candidate management and significantly reduce time-to-fill. From posting the job online to making the job offer an ATS keeps track of all the activity that takes place in the recruiting department."
	Zoho Recruit lets you get started for free with a basic program to test out the process with your job opening. They then grow with you (with paid services) as you need to add more positions.
Zoom	"One consistent enterprise experience for all use cases. Engineered & optimized to work reliably." "Easy-to-use, buy & scale. Most affordable, straightforward pricing."
	Whether you need online meetings, video webinars, virtual conference rooms, phone systems, or cross-platform messaging and file sharing, Zoom makes it easy. Get started for free, and upgrade (paid) to meet the needs of your growing business.

Marketing Resources and Tools

From PR to surveys, search, content, social media, email marketing, and more, there are high-quality tools at your fingertips. A Guerrilla marketer can put these to use to ensure their marketing is on the path to profitable growth for their business. Note: Any offers or services shown are subject to change by that business.

Refer to gMarketing.com/Club for convenient links.

Agorapulse Facebook Barometer	"The Barometer will determine how many fans this page has and will compare it to thousands of other pages with a similar fan range. You will see how your last 50 Facebook posts compare in terms of: Facebook Reach…Facebook Engagement…Facebook Click-through rate."
	This free tool is to help you gauge your performance and to understand which pages you need to work on to improve your score.

Agorapulse Ads-Report	"Getting important statistics and data regarding your Facebook campaigns and accounts can be exhausting and a drain on your workday. The format on Facebook itself is confusing and not as streamlined and efficient as it can be. Enter AdsReport, Agorapulse's free tool for helping social media managers and agencies easily and efficiently get the analytics they need regarding their Facebook Ad accounts and ad campaigns." This free tool helps you analyze your spend, conversions, reach, impressions, clicks, CTR, CPC, and CPM. Guerrilla marketers know their careful analysis helps them do more of what's working and less of what's not, which helps pave their path to profits.
Agorapulse Twitter Report Card	"Do you perform better than your competitors on Twitter? Compare Twitter accounts with each other and gain new insights into your Twitter performance." This free tool provides a report card to help you understand how you compare to the accounts you choose. You'll be able to examine your audience quality, brand engagement, and content performance.
Airtable	"Orchestrate powerful business solutions with a single source of truth. The only limit is your imagination." "Get started in a snap. From day one, your team will love the familiarity of a spreadsheet, and the power of a database." Airtable is a strong planning and performance tool to help your marketing succeed. See and track all your marketing efforts and collaborate, all in one place. With numerous available integrations, you can get more out of the tools you're already using. Get started with their free plan and grow your capabilities with their advanced (paid) options.
AnswerThePublic	"Discover an untapped goldmine of content ideas. AnswerThePublic listens into autocomplete data from search engines like Google then quickly cranks out every useful phrase and question people are asking around your keyword. It's a goldmine of consumer insight you can use to create fresh, ultra-useful content, products, and services. The kind your customers really want." AnswerThePublic will tell you every question people are asking on a given topic, which is invaluable for building your business. For example, if you simply type in "dog grooming," they will generate hundreds of questions that people are asking related to dog grooming across numerous search engines.

Apptivo	"Connect to your favorite services. Everything you need in one cloud solution: CRM, Project Management, Invoicing & more." Apptivo is customizable and flexible to provide the apps that are necessary for your business. Small businesses can get started for free with their Starter package, which includes sales automation and business management, data management, and analytics tools. Their (paid) services grow with you as you move from a small business to an enterprise business.
BuzzStream	"Use our free tools to find link opportunities, conduct link research or automate link building tasks." From email research tools to link-building query generators and extraction tools, you'll find numerous free tools on Buzz-Stream to increase your productivity.
Canva	"Canva, your secret weapon for stunning design. Design anything in minutes with thousands of beautiful templates and images." Canva offers a basic program to get started for free. Canva Basic includes free templates, photos, elements, fonts, design types, and storage. When your business is ready to take it to the next level, you can move to a paid plan that provides even more of what's included in the basic program, along with more storage, a brand-building kit, priority support, and more.
Coupon Sites	Along with social media, these coupon sites—that feature online coupon codes and printable coupons—give your business added exposure and are worth getting to know: • Groupon • RetailMeNot • Coupons • Shop Savvy • Smart Source • Sunday Saver • Coupon Cactus • Extrabux • Rakuten—formerly Ebates Some of these sites require an account and a fee to post your coupons, and others do not, so be sure to do your homework to find the right fit for your business and its customers and prospects.

Crowdfire	"Social media management, simplified. Crowdfire helps you discover and schedule content and manage all your social accounts from one place." "Crowdfire is a powerful social media tool used by businesses and individuals all over the world to drive social media engagement and growth." Get started for free with select supported social networks. You'll be able to schedule posts and benefit from content curation tools and analytics tools. As your needs grow, so do their (paid) capabilities to help your business succeed.
Email Copy Checker	"This is a free email spam checking tool, which looks at your email copy or your entire email sequence to ensure you aren't triggering any spam words or spam keywords." Email Copy Checker is a great free tool to check your email copy and receive guidance that helps you improve your deliverability rate.
Fanpage Karma	"With Fanpage Karma you have everything you need for professional social media management: analyzing, publishing, communicating, researching and presenting. Everything in one tool." Fanpage Karma is a social media analytics and monitoring tool. They support Facebook, Instagram, Twitter, LinkedIn, YouTube, and more. The performance knowledge you'll gain will help you determine the most valuable posts/content. You can get started with a free account that lets you analyze Facebook and upgrade (paid) from there.
Feedly	"Goodbye information overload. Keep up with the topics and trends you care about, without the overwhelm." "Organize all your trusted sources in one place." Feedly gives you the control to organize and prioritize what matters to you. Feedly offers a free plan on the web and mobile to help you follow a select number of sources and organize them into feeds. You can then upgrade (paid) to include more sources, notes, highlights, organized and curated team sharing, and so much more.
Flowcode	"Create a free, customer QR code in 60 seconds." Begin with three free Flowcodes, which last forever, allow for unlimited scans, and offer free analytics. You can then choose a (paid) plan that fits the needs of your growing business.

Followerwonk	"Followerwonk is a social analytics mega-tool that digs through Twitter data. Use it to track your follower gains and losses, compare Twitter accounts, do global searches in Twitter bios, and analyze any account's followers!"
	Get started for free with this analytics and discovery tool for Twitter and optimize one profile. You can then increase (paid) the number of profiles as needed.
Free Business Profiles	Being listed in as many directories as possible helps your business build credibility. When your prospects reach the point of researching your business, you can build trust by being everywhere they look, or you can create doubt with your absence. Guerrillas tend to the small details, which build valuable trust. Be sure to build out your profiles with: • Google My Business • Bing Places for Business • Foursquare • Yahoo! • Apple Maps • MapQuest • Yelp • Angie's List (Angi) • Home Advisor • Nextdoor • Manta • Trip Advisor • Better Business Bureau • LinkedIn • Facebook • HubSpot • Superpages and Yellow Pages • Yellowbook • Thumbtack • MerchantCircle

Free Classified Ads/Listings	These online services provide an opportunity to increase the reach of those businesses that are selling products or services: • Classified Ads • Craigslist • Oodle • Global-free-classified-ads • Letgo • Facebook Shops
Guerrilla Marketing	Your source for ever-expanding Guerrilla Marketing tactics, tools, and tips. Be connected to all the latest information to help you continually grow your profits and success. Join us at gMarketing.com/Club.
Google Alerts	"Monitor the web for interesting new content." A great tool to keep you in the know is at your fingertips, and it's free. You can get email alerts for any topic you choose using Google Alerts. Google searches news, blogs, the web, videos, books, discussions, and finance information to bring you the alerts you need about a particular topic (e.g., your business, products and services, your competitors, your industry, etc.).
Google Analytics	Google Analytics requires a simple snippet of code that you will add to your website. That snippet of code tracks all the visitors to your website and, thereby, provides you with a wealth of valuable information. The information is provided in Google Analytics to help you understand how to turn more prospects into customers and how to compel customers to make repeat purchases.
Google Analytics - Social Interactions	"You can use social interaction analytics to measure the number of times users click on social buttons embedded in webpages. For example, you might measure a Facebook 'Like' or a Twitter 'Tweet.'" Extend the benefit of Google Analytics by utilizing this free tool to measure and analyze your important social shares/interactions.

Google Analytics - App/Screen Measurement	"Screens in Google Analytics represent content users are viewing within an app." "Measuring screen views allows you to see which content is being viewed most by your users, and how are they are navigating between different pieces of content."
	If your business is using an app, this valuable and free tool will help you analyze how your prospects and customers are moving through and interacting with your app.
Google for Small Business	"Get help for your business with simple steps and free resources. Help people find you online, know that you're open, and stay connected to customers with simple steps and free resources."
	Google for Small Business offers tools, such as the Digital Toolkit. With the Digital Toolkit, you can create surveys, explore new markets for your business, test your websites speeds, receive insights and recommendations for improvement, and even create a personalized marketing kit with content from your business profile on Google.
Google My Business	"Engage with customers on Google for free. With a Google Business account, you get more than a business listing. Your free Business Profile lets you easily connect with customers across Google Search and Maps."
	Actively managing and leveraging all the benefits of your Google Business Profile is "must-do" marketing every Guerrilla business utilizes to its full benefit. You can set your business hours and phone number and add photos of your products, as well as include Q&As. If your business takes appointments or reservations, you can take your convenience to the next level by linking those services.
Google Optimize	"Whether it's a custom-tailored message at checkout or a completely revamped homepage, Optimize shows you which site experiences engage and delight your customers, and gives you the solutions you need to deliver them."
	Google Optimize uses your existing Google Analytics data to help you target areas of your site to improve. Model your experiments with statistical methods to get more accurate results that lead to the right experience for your customers and prospects.

Google Postmaster Tools	"If you send a large volume of emails to Gmail users, you can use Postmaster Tools to see: • If users are marking your emails as spam • How to prevent your emails from being blocked by Gmail • Why your emails might not be delivered • If your emails are being sent securely" Google Postmaster Tools are a great way to improve your email deliverability rate to Gmail users.
Google Search Console	"Search Console tools and reports help you measure your site's Search traffic and performance, fix issues, and make your site shine in Google Search results." Guerrilla marketers embrace tools, such as the Google Search Console, which make it easy to optimize content with search analytics, understand how Google sees pages, and receive alerts when there are issues. Then, it lets Google know when the business has fixed them.
Google Trends	"Google Trends provides access to a largely unfiltered sample of actual search requests made to Google. It's anonymized (no one is personally identified), categorized (determining the topic for a search query) and aggregated (grouped together)." Google Trends allows you to see what the world is searching for by term or topic. With that information, you can be aware of searches related to your business, and you can write about trending topics.
Grammarly	"Great Writing, Simplified. Compose bold, clear, mistake-free writing with Grammarly's AI-powered writing assistant." Grammarly is a free Chrome extension to help you write more clearly and effectively across many of your favorite sites. Get started for free and become familiar with their (paid) business program that can help your team communicate consistently and more quickly to increase satisfaction with your prospects and customers.
H5P	"Create richer html5 content in existing publishing platforms. Share content seamlessly across any H5P capable site. Reuse and modify content in your browser at any time." With a variety of available integrations, H5P is "free and open technology, licensed with the MIT license." Create rich, interactive, and mobile-friendly content to make your website more engaging.

HARO	"HARO connects journalists seeking expertise to include in their content with sources who have that expertise."
	Similar to ProfNet, Help A Reporter Out (HARO) is a great free resource to boost your content (for journalists and bloggers) and/or boost your public and media relations efforts (for experts and sources). You'll have daily opportunities to respond to requests for experts or to post requests for experts to provide content. HARO offers a free membership that allows you to receive or post requests for media content.
Hootsuite	"Discover what's possible when you unite your social campaigns on one platform. Schedule and publish content to the right channels at the right time, track effectiveness in real time, and crank the volume on your top-performing content."
	Guerrilla marketers know that consistency is one of the most powerful marketing tools to put to work for their businesses. Hootsuite makes it easy to create consistent marketing messages across multiple social platforms and keep a consistent presence with scheduled posts. Hootsuite offers a limited free plan that lets you get started with a few social profiles and scheduled messages. When you find that Hootsuite is delivering benefits for your business, you can then upgrade to a paid plan to unleash the power of what Hootsuite can do for your business and social presence.
Hotjar	"We help you better understand user behavior so you can make the right changes, improve UX, and grow conversions."
	With the free personal Basic account, you can begin to understand how your prospects and customers interact with your site. You can create Heatmaps and on-demand, manual reports, get users' feedback, and more.
Hubspot	"Think CRM software is just about contact management? Think again. HubSpot CRM has free tools for everyone on your team, and it's 100% free." "You have a lot on your plate. Make things easier on yourself by tracking your contacts and customers and sending bulk email — all using the same tool. It's easy to use, and completely free."
	Hubspot offers the tools you need to manage and organize your contacts in one CRM database. You'll benefit from free features, such as lead management and tracking, document tracking, pipeline management, and ticketing. As your business needs advance, they have a robust line-up of (paid) features and tools to help your business grow.

JotForm	"Easy-to-use online form builder for every business. Create online forms and publish them. Get an email for each response. Collect data."
	JotForm is a great resource for simple or advanced forms. With a broad array of templates to choose from—or customized forms with a drag-and-drop interface—they make getting started easy. Their free plan is full of features to start creating online surveys, applications, contact and request forms, and much more.
Latest	"We automatically collect the links posted by a bunch of the most interesting people on Twitter. You know the people that always tweet the best links - first. We take all the links they tweet and compile a real-time updated list of the 10 most popular links right now. Plus, all links are automatically posted to our Twitter feed too. Pretty useful, right?"
	If staying up to date is important for your business, Latest is a great free tool to keep you informed of the latest links from Twitter.
Leadfeeder	"Generate more leads by seeing which companies visit your site. Leadfeeder shows you the companies visiting your website, how they found you and what they're interested in."
	Take the mystery out of your website traffic and turn that information into valuable leads for your follow-up. Leadfeeder offers a free, "lite" package. Although it offers limited functionality, you can begin by seeing the last three days' worth of leads (with a maximum number of leads provided). As your needs and success grow, they offer a wide array of (paid) features and robust solutions.
MailChimp	"With Mailchimp, you can promote your business across email, social, landing pages, shoppable landing pages, postcards, and more—all from a single platform."
	Get started for free with MailChimp with templates, CRM, surveys, and more. As your business grows, you can upgrade (paid) your features to include split testing, retargeting, segmentation, multivariate testing, and much more.

Mail-Tester	"We needed a cheap, simple and efficient way to quickly test the quality of our own newsletters. We simply built on our own tool. Now we're sharing it for free via our web-interface and enable you to include our tests in your own app and whitelist our service by creating an account. We're geeky email software engineers."
	With Mail-Tester, you'll send a test email to the email address they generate for you, and you'll then receive a score for your email. You can continue to refine your email to score a perfect ten prior to sending your email to your audience.
ManyChat	"Turn Conversations Into Conversions. Automate two-way, interactive conversations in Instagram Direct Messages, Facebook Messenger, and SMS to grow your brand."
	If your business can benefit from connecting with your customers and prospects via chat, take the time to become familiar with ManyChat. You can begin with a free account that accesses Facebook Messenger to help you automate conversations, segment your audience, and more.
MeetUp	"Discover events for all the things you love." "Starting a Meetup group connects you with passionate people looking to share experiences in real life. It's simple to start a group and schedule events, and we'll help promote your group to interested people who are ready to join you."
	MeetUp is an essential way for Guerrilla marketers to join and host like-minded individuals who want to collaborate to solve problems and/or grow their businesses. It's also a great way to host your prospects and customers.
Mentionmapp	"Social Network Analysis & Insights. See what you're missing. Identify critical online relationships and conversations with our network visualization tool." "Mentionmapp collects the last 200 Tweets for any profile or hashtag searched for."
	Mentionmapp will help you, for free, search and find more people and conversations on Twitter.

Moz	"At Moz, we believe there is a better way to do marketing. A more valuable way where customers are earned rather than bought. We're obsessively passionate about it, and our mission is to help people achieve it. We focus on search engine optimization." "Try the best free SEO tools for link building and analysis, keyword research, webpage performance, local listing audits, and more!" Select from numerous free tools, including keyword explorer, link explorer, MozBar (to analyze search, social and page metrics), domain analysis, MozCast, and more.
Namecheckr	". . . an online service designed to permit Users to check the availability of domain names and social usernames across multiple networks." Namecheckr allows you to check domain and social username availability across multiple networks. With this free tool, you can be sure that you own your identity across countless platforms.
Pixabay	"Stunning free images & royalty free stock. Over 1.8 million+ high quality stock images and videos shared by our talented community." Pixabay is a fantastic resource for otherwise difficult to find, free images, and royalty-free stock. Members of the community freely share their great works in this easy-to-search platform. Pixabay provides an attribution option if you wish to give photo credits. Additionally, you can follow and donate to your favorite contributors in the community. You can learn about the Pixabay license on their website.
Popurls	"Popurls encapsulates headlines from the most popular websites on a single page and is also known as the mother of all news aggregators." Popurls is a trending topic website that's easy to use and provides great insight and information. They aggregate all kinds of pop viral news from the most popular websites. With their data, you can write about current events.
Portent's Content Idea Generator	"Portent's Content Idea Generator lets you create catchy titles for your next blog post, podcast, or video. Simply type in your subject and the Idea Generator will spin up a creative title and advice to take it to the next level." This is a fantastic tool to expand your creativity as you develop compelling titles for your well-crafted content.

ProfNet	"There is a real opportunity for your organization to tap into the news coming out of your industry. When your experts become quotable sources for journalists, not only do they earn your organization a lot of free and often high-profile PR, but they also help you develop relationships with the members of the media you need in your corner."
	Similar to HARO, ProfNet offers a free membership that allows you to receive regular updates with media opportunities that you can preview and respond to, or you have the ability to request that experts respond and provide their content to your publication or blog.
Segment	"The leading Customer Data Platform. Join 20,000+ businesses that use Segment's software and APIs to collect, clean, and control their customer data."
	Guerrilla marketers embrace opportunities to better understand their prospects and customers. With Segment, you can get started collecting your data and turning it into powerful experiences for your prospects and customers. You can begin with their free plan and as your business grows, their (paid) plans are designed to scale with your success.
Shareaholic	"Shareaholic provides you with a comprehensive set of marketing tools to engage with your audience, get found across search and social, and grow your following. All for Free. Code-free Customization."
	Shareaholic offers valuable tools that can be used with multiple platforms to make your content easily shared, compelling, consumable, and revenue-generating with ads and affiliate links.
SharedCount	"Created in 2010, SharedCount was the first API tool capable of giving you holistic engagement data on your website content. From simple use with WordPress, to larger API integrations, SharedCount makes it easy to see what content is connecting, what content is not, and where you should focus your efforts to maximize ROI."
	SharedCount offers a free account with 500 free API calls per day, to learn about the shares of your website content. For more API calls per day, you can choose from the best (paid) plan to fit your needs.

Social Media Sites and Networks	Take the time to manage your presence on the social media sites/networks that are compatible with your prospects and customers. Social media is your opportunity to connect with your prospects and customers in an environment that they find favorable. Facebook, Instagram, Pinterest, Snapchat, LinkedIn, Twitter, YouTube, and Clubhouse are great places to start, and you can add on with TikTok, Flickr, Tumblr, Medium, MeetUp, and Nextdoor. Be sure to use services such as Namecheckr to make sure your business is well represented within the vast pool of available social media sites and networks.
Sumo	"We've noticed lots of people struggle to collect emails because the tools just aren't available or are too expensive. So, we thought, why not make our tools available for you? Our goal, plain and simple, is to help you grow your website." Sumo can help your business grow your list and communicate with your customers as well as provide analytics. Get started with their free account to grow your business and then upgrade (paid) to benefit from their enhanced features to help grow your relationship with your customers.
SurveyGizmo	"SurveyGizmo provides the best and most affordable tools to connect you with your customers and employees. We also help you identify the actions to take to support them. Now more than ever, staying close to people is critical to the well-being of your company." SurveyGizmo offers a free account to get started with your small and basic survey needs. Perfect for a small or new business with a small number of customers and employees to get started with the benefits of surveying. As your business expands, SurveyGizmo has robust features (paid) to grow with your business.
SurveyLegend	"Create engaging surveys on your tablet or computer with ease. No matter who you are, we make creating a survey as easy as breathing." With SurveyLegend, you choose from designed themes and then customize them to reflect the look and feel of the marketing for your business. You can then share your survey via email, SMS, Facebook, Twitter, blogs, and more. Best of all, you can get started for free, and you can receive unlimited responses. Try a few surveys before you decide if it's the right fit for your business.

Tableau Public	"Tableau Public is a free service that lets anyone publish interactive data visualizations to the web. Visualizations that have been published to Tableau Public ("vizzes") can be embedded into web pages and blogs, they can be shared via social media or email, and they can be made available for download to other users."
	For businesses that have broadly appealing data, which they want to present creatively and make public, Tableau Public allows you to create interactive graphs, maps, and dashboards—called a Viz—and share them anywhere on the web. Additionally, if your business needs data, you can search for a Viz created by others to convey the data in an appealing way. Additional paid services are available for businesses needing a robust analytics platform.
Tiny URL	Tiny URL takes your long URLs and shortens them for redirection on your website and for easy linking in emails. This free service helps your business look polished and effortless.
Unsplash	"The internet's source of freely-usable images." "Unsplash is a platform powered by an amazing community that has gifted hundreds of thousands of their own photos to fuel creativity around the world. So, sign up for free, or don't. Either way, you've got access to over a million photos under the Unsplash license—which makes them free to do-whatever-you-want with."
	Unsplash is a great resource for photos, which you can download for free and use for commercial or non-commercial purposes without needing permission. Image contributors, of course, appreciate your attributions. You can learn about the Unsplash license on their website.
Vimeo	"The world's leading all-in-one video solution." "We enable professional-quality video for all." "Simple tools for you and your team to create, manage and share high-quality videos."
	You can get started with Vimeo Basic for free. As your needs grow, and you want to store more videos, customize, live stream, and benefit from analytics, you can upgrade (paid) to a plan suited to your success.

Website Grader	"Grade your website in seconds. Then learn how to improve it for free." This free tool is provided by HubSpot. When you enter your website and email address, you will receive information regarding their relevant content, products, and services, designed to improve your website.
Wistia	"The video host with the most." "One easy-to-use platform that turns your videos and podcasts into marketing machines." Wistia offers a customizable player, lead generation tools, embeddable channels, integrations, analytics, and more to help your videos and podcasts work for your business. You can get started with the free package that offers their standard features and the ability to embed a select number of videos or podcasts and a channel to share. You can then easily upgrade (paid) to enjoy more valuable features.
WordPress	"Beautiful designs, powerful features, and the freedom to build anything you want. WordPress is both free and priceless at the same time." WordPress is indeed priceless, especially for SMBs. It's the open-source software platform that has allowed everyone from bloggers to new sites to retailers to thrive online. With countless available plug-ins (free and paid) and a community of developers, content creators, and website owners, you can build a website that fits your needs and your budget now . . . and also grows with you into the future.
Wordtracker	"Our own proprietary data and toolset means you can get 10,000 keywords per search as well as related keywords, so your pages can be optimized more effectively to outrank the competition." Wordtracker allows you to get started with a few free keyword searches before you move into a paid plan.
Wufoo	"Easy-to-Use Online Form Builder For Every Organization. Cloud-based form builder that makes it easy to create registration forms, application forms, surveys, contact forms, payment forms and more." With an easy-to-use, drag-and-drop form builder, you'll be creating beautiful online forms with ease. Get started with a few forms with their free plan and move up (paid) to enjoy more features and conveniences.

Zoho Social	"The easiest way to manage your brands on social media. Schedule unlimited posts, monitor what matters, and create custom-reports to analyze your social media performance with Zoho Social." Zoho Social offers a free edition, with limited features, to help you get started. They also offer numerous (paid) options for growing businesses that can benefit from more robust features.

SMB Resources and Organizations

These resources and organizations are designed for your success. Whether you get to know them as a subscriber or as a member, be sure to know these free resources that drive Guerrilla business success. Note: Any offers or services shown are subject to change by that business.

Refer to gMarketing.com/Club for convenient links.

Better Business Bureau (BBB)	"BBB's Vision: An ethical marketplace where buyers and sellers trust each other." The Better Business Bureau (BBB) offers the National Programs Insights, which outlines best practices to help businesses succeed with information on a variety of helpful topics. For example, they provide Data Protection information covering a wide range of topics. They also offer the Better Business Bureau (BBB) Cybersecurity, which is a resource to help educate SMBs and provide tools and tips to manage their cyber risks, thereby learning best practices.
Federal Trade Commission (FTC)	"Protecting consumers and competition by preventing anti-competitive, deceptive, and unfair business practices through law enforcement, advocacy, and education without unduly burdening legitimate business activity." The FTC business center is an important resource for your business to learn about topics from advertising and marketing to protecting your business and finding legal resources. For example, the FTC offers tips and tools for cybersecurity for small businesses. The Small Biz Cyber Planner will help you create a customized cybersecurity plan. To learn more, visit their website.

Guerrilla Marketing	"We exist for your success. Guerrilla Marketing has been producing results since its introduction in 1984. There is no other source for Guerrilla Marketing success." Visit gMarketing.com/Club for more information. Guerrilla Marketing exists to give you the tactics, tools, and tips you need to succeed beyond your wildest expectations. The simple question is: Will you react and claim your success, or will you fold? We think you're ready to react and claim your success. You've nearly reached the end of the book, so we know you're ready for success.
National Cyber Security Alliance	The vision of the National Cyber Security Alliance is: "Empowering a more secure, interconnected world." The National Cyber Security Alliance focuses on helping SMBs conduct business safely and securely online. They offer free checkups, tools, and education to help your business be secure and manage privacy.
National Federation of Independent Business (NFIB)	"NFIB is the voice of small business, advocating on behalf of America's small and independent business owners, both in Washington, D.C., and in all 50 state capitals. NFIB is non-profit, nonpartisan, and member-driven. Since our founding in 1943, NFIB has been exclusively dedicated to small and independent businesses, and remains so today." The NFIB has been leading the way for small businesses for decades. They offer countless resources to help small businesses succeed. You can subscribe for free and join as your business grows.
National Retail Federation	"The National Retail Federation has represented retail for over a century. Every day, we passionately stand up for the people, policies and ideas that help retail thrive." The NRF is a membership-based organization that offers valuable insight and research regarding consumers and retail businesses in their blog and podcast. As your business grows, joining the NRF will give you even more valuable information and opportunities, such as research findings and live events.

SCORE	"SCORE, the nation's largest network of volunteer, expert business mentors, is dedicated to helping small businesses get off the ground, grow and achieve their goals."
	SCORE offers mentoring access to experts in entrepreneurship, webinars, courses on demand, online resources, and local events. Whether you're starting your business or growing your business, SCORE provides invaluable resources and networking opportunities.
Small Business & Entrepreneurship Council (SBE Council)	"The Small Business & Entrepreneurship Council (SBE Council) is an influential voice and advocate for entrepreneurs and small business owners . . . Our network of supporters, including entrepreneurs and small business owners, state and local business organizations, corporate partners and associations work with us to strengthen the environment for entrepreneurship, investment, innovation and quality job creation."
	The SBE Council is focused on the key issues that matter to small businesses and entrepreneurs. Their news and resources can help you and your business stay ahead of the curve. You can subscribe for free and join as your business grows.
Small Business Administration (SBA)	"Created in 1953, the U.S. Small Business Administration (SBA continues to help small business owners and entrepreneurs pursue the American dream."
	The SBA is a great resource for SMBs . . . from business funding to education and local assistance. Whether you're just starting your business, building your business, or you want to grow your business, the SBA is a great resource. Though it's often only thought of for business funding, there are many more resources available for businesses. Take advantage of the numerous free opportunities to learn all that's available—right at your fingertips.
	For help with staying legally compliant with state and federal business laws, see a list of courses, and more, visit the SBA website.
The International Association of Privacy Professionals (IAPP)	The International Association of Privacy Professionals (IAPP) describes themselves as: "the world's largest and most comprehensive global information privacy community."
	In a world filled with new and constantly changing laws and regulations, you need a source like the IAPP to help keep you on top of the latest developments.

SECTION XII

Guerrilla Marketing Definitions

THE DEFINITIONS

TERM	DEFINITION
80/20 Rule	The Pareto principle, also known as the 80/20 Rule, has been translated into many meanings since it was first introduced in the late 1800s. For Guerrilla businesses, the 80/20 Rule teaches simplicity, and it applies throughout your business, for example: • 20 percent of your marketing generates 80 percent of your sales. • 20 percent of the time you spend working generates 80 percent of what you achieve at work. • 20 percent of a company's products usually account for 80 percent of its sales. • 20 percent of a company's employees contribute to 80 percent of the work that generates profits Therefore, Guerrilla marketers seek to continually prune the 80 percent, and they delegate to people in their business to carry out the necessary workload so they focus on the critical 20 percent that's difficult to delegate.
Advanced TV	Advanced TV, according to Cuebiq, is a term that includes: • Connected TV (CTV), which is an internet-connected television, such as a smart TV • Over-the-top (OTT) devices, such as Roku, Amazon Fire, Apple TV, smartphones, tablets, computers, and media players (like video game consoles) • Subscription video-on-demand services (SVoD), such as Amazon Prime and Netflix, and partially ad-supported services, such as Hulu, CBS All Access, and Amazon's IMDb TV • Addressable TV via network providers (e.g., Comcast, Dish, Direct TV, etc.)

Agencies	The services that an agency provides can vary widely. From full service to niche services, it's important to understand their expertise and match that expertise with your needs. Common agencies are: • Social Media Agencies • Digital Media Agencies • Public Relations Agencies • Branding Agencies • Direct Response or Promotional Agencies • Media Agencies
Agile	A Guerrilla agile mind views their business, product(s), and/or service(s) as ever-evolving and nimble. The lines of communication are wide-open, and they frequently reassess and adapt as needed.
Amazement	Guerrilla marketers make their prospects hear and feel what is amazing, exciting, unique, and compelling about their business, product, or service
Apathy	Apathy is a lack of interest or a sense of indifference. In terms of marketing, a Guerrilla is focused on moving their prospects from apathy to interest and excitement about a purchase.
Augmented Reality (AR)	With a smartphone or tablet camera, your prospect or customer can focus on a designated image and turn it into an engaging and interactive product experience. The image can be printed and featured in countless ways, such as in your direct mail, business cards, brochures, vehicle wrap (for events when the vehicle is stationary and on display), etc. Also, your website can feature virtual try-on technology that allows them to experience your product as if they were wearing or seeing it (e.g., eyeglasses, cosmetics, furniture, paint colors, tailoring/clothing, etc.). ARKIT by Apple and ARCore by Google help you develop new augmented reality experiences to transform how your prospects and customers shop and experience your product(s) and service(s).
Awareness	Guerrilla marketers pride themselves on being the "first to know." A business that's informed is a wise business that's utilizing the low-cost opportunities Guerrilla Marketing presents.
B2B	Business-to-business

Bartering	In lieu of money, negotiating the products, services, or capabilities of your business in exchange for something of value, such as advertising, marketing and/or media exposure that increases your success.
Brand Awareness /Recognition	First, your prospects become aware of your business (i.e., brand awareness) and second, they recognize your business and the product(s) and/or service(s) associated with it (i.e., brand recognition). Once they do, your call to action must then motivate them to take a desired action (e.g., download an ebook, make a purchase, etc.). Your marketing efforts are ideal when they appeal to each aspect (brand awareness, brand recognition and action), at the same time.
Better Business Bureau (BBB)	The Better Business Bureau (BBB) is a business performance rating service designed to give consumers a trusted resource and a voice related to business performance. The BBB National Programs offer best practices to help businesses succeed with information on a variety of helpful topics.
Brand	Your brand is generally recognizable by your visual and graphic representation (e.g., name, logo, tagline, etc.), but all elements of your company attributes and attitudes make up the components of your brand. Your brand is the entirety of your business that you're marketing to your prospects and customers.
Broadcasting	The largest possible audience for your business to share your compelling and engaging information, products, and/or services with (e.g., Advanced TV, social live broadcasts, etc.). When choosing a smaller audience, you're narrowcasting.
Buying Language	Buying language is the collection of words and phrases that motivate and compel your prospects and customers to purchase your product(s) or service(s). Understanding and speaking to their pain points and pleasure points in a way that allows them to visualize how you will solve their problems and the pleasure they will feel with their problems solved is speaking their buying language.
Call to Action (CTA)	Guerrilla marketers use a call to action—a clear and motivating message that tells prospects and customers exactly what you want them to do next (e.g., click here, call before May 1st, shop online before May 1st, enter promo code "ABC" at checkout, etc.).

Click-Through Rates (CTR)	A click-through occurs when your ad or link is clicked. That number is divided by the number of times the ad is seen to determine the click-through rate. The goal of CTR is to understand how many times your ad is seen as compared to how many are compelled to click it. The higher your CTR is, the more compelling, engaging, and effective your ad is.
Collaboration	Businesses working together, such as joint ventures, partnerships, mergers, acquisitions, or other arrangements, to share resources and assets and create greater growth together.
Color Palette	A selection of up to six complimentary colors that a business uses consistently and in every bit of its marketing. The chosen colors should be defined in each of the various systems, such as: PMS, CMYK, RGB, HSB, and HEX.
Commitment	Guerrillas learn by doing, imagining, experimenting, being realistic, keeping track, paying attention, improving, and committing to their successful experiments. The simple difference between many successes and failures is a simple marketing plan and a commitment to continue to do what's working.
Compelling	A no-cost tactic for Guerrilla Advertising and marketing that is irresistible, powerful, and motivates prospects to take action.
Competitive Advantages	Guerrilla marketers keep and maintain an ongoing list of their advantages versus their competitors. The list is utilized by everyone in the business to share their advantages (without specifically mentioning a competitor) with prospects, customers, community leaders, public relations contacts, etc.
Complacency	The enemies of Guerrilla Marketing and business success is complacency, rigidity, and sluggishness. When we speak of the importance of consistency, people can mistakenly confuse consistency and complacency. Consistency should not be confused with complacency. "Doing it the way we've always done it" is not the way of Guerrilla Marketing. "Doing it in a way that evolves and builds on what you've already done to continually grow your success" is the way of Guerrilla Marketing.
Connections and Interacting	Guerrilla marketers pride themselves on their relationship skills. It's a characteristic that costs zero dollars and when mixed with your energy and imagination, it drives profits.

Consistency, Familiarity and Trust	A no or low-cost way Guerrilla marketers multiply their marketing effectiveness. You're marketing with every bit of contact your company has with anyone. Guerrilla marketers are intentional with that contact, fully utilizing the power of consistency. Consistency builds familiarity; familiarity builds trust, and trust creates sales, repeat purchases, and precious referrals.
Consumer Packaged Goods (CPG)	Consumer packaged goods are products that are packaged to be sold via distribution to retailers for regular and repeat consumption. For example, consumer package goods can be vitamins, toothpaste, deodorant, etc.
Convenience	What is convenient for your prospects and customers is determined by your prospects and customers. Therefore, convenience means being there when and where your prospects need or want your product(s) or service(s).
Conversion Rate Optimization (CRO)	CRO is the art and science of taking the prospects and customers that come to your site and turning them into buyers.
Conversions	The people that view your ad and respond by taking a desired action. This can be measured across your advertising by tracking web clicks, phone calls, and coupon (or other offer) redemptions.
Co-Op Funds	Advertising and marketing funds that your suppliers or vendors offer for mentioning or showcasing their products in your advertising.
Cost Per Action (CPA)	Online advertising or Fusion/Affiliate Marketing arrangements are typically structured as CPA, and the action could be a sale, lead (CPL), or click (CPC), as determined by the product owner. A trackable link is provided by the product owner and used by the affiliate partner so the transaction is recorded within the affiliate network. The agreed upon commissions (flat rate or a percentage) is then paid for completed transactions.

Cost-Per-Click (CPC)	Online advertising or Fusion/Affiliate Marketing arrangements may be structured as cost-per-click (CPC). The product owner determines the parameters that constitute a lead, and you want to be aware of those parameters. A trackable link is provided by the product owner and used by the affiliate partner so the transaction is recorded within the affiliate network. The agreed upon commissions (flat rate or a percentage) are then paid for completed transactions.
Cost-Per-Lead (CPL)	Online advertising or Fusion/Affiliate Marketing arrangements may be structured as cost-per-lead (CPL). The product owner determines the parameters that constitute a lead (e.g., filling out form, signing up for a trial, etc.), and you want to be aware of those parameters. A trackable link is provided by the product owner and used by the affiliate partner so the transaction is recorded within the affiliate network. The agreed upon commissions (flat rate or a percentage) are then paid for completed transactions.
Cost-Per-Thousand (CPM) advertising	Cost-per-thousand (CPM) advertising is based on the number of impressions that an ad generates. Guerrilla marketers are wise to focus on viewable impressions to maximize their investment.
Cost-Per-View (CPV) advertising	Cost-per-view (CPV) advertising is for video advertising campaigns. A view is determined by a defined period of time or an action taken, such as clicking the call to action (CTA).
Credibility	Guerrillas should know that two significant factors that influence a purchase decision for your prospects are confidence and trust. An easy way to build confidence and trust is with authentic credibility.
Cross-Selling	Offering compatible and complimentary products to your customers is a way to offer convenience and solutions that your prospects and customers appreciate. Making a cross-selling suggestion in a way that's friendly and engaging can stimulate a valuable conversation for you to learn more about your customers.
Customer	The people that buy your product(s) or service(s). The goal of a Guerrilla marketer is to have highly satisfied customers that make repeat purchases and precious referrals of their friends, family, and associates to their business.

Customer Lifetime Value (CLV) or Lifetime Value (LTV)	Guerrilla marketers understand the power of measuring and tracking a customer's lifetime value as a KPI (key performance indicator). Looking at a customer's lifetime value goes beyond their initial purchase. It accounts for what you deem to be important to the long-term success of your business, such as shares, likes, repeat purchases, referrals, etc.
	Measuring the value of your customers over their "lifetime" with your business, by accounting for the revenue they generate and the associated costs, gives you two valuable pieces of your success puzzle. One, which customers should be handled with the greatest care and, two, which customers you want to clone (e.g., demographics, psychographics, etc.) and/or attract more of.
	See Volume 3, Section 8.44, "Customer Lifetime Value (CLV or LTV)," for more information.
Customer Relationship Management (CRM)	Technology systems to manage your business and customer interactions and data (from customer service to marketing and sales). CRM systems are a more robust version of marketing automation systems. CRM tools can range from robust to lighter versions that will help you manage your marketing, customers, and transactions.
Delegate	Guerrilla marketers engage like-minded experts to shine in the areas of the business that are either not the Guerrilla marketers' strengths or are too time-consuming. A Guerrilla marketer seeks to be true to the 80/20 Rule. Therefore, Guerrilla marketers seek to continually prune the 80 percent, and they delegate to people in their business to carry out the necessary workload so they focus on the critical 20 percent that's difficult to delegate.
	By doing so, together, they drive the success of the business further than the Guerrilla marketer ever could on their own.
Demographics	As defined by Dictionary.com, demographics are "the statistical data of a population, especially those showing average age, income, education, etc."
Digital Account-Based Marketing	Digital account-based marketing is a B2B marketing strategy that allows your business to target an entire company or the people in a certain division or functional role in a company.

Directories (online)	Online businesses that produce searchable business listings broadly (e.g., Manta, Super Pages, or Yellow Book) or by interest (e.g., Trip Advisor, Yelp, etc.) or by industry (e.g., Angi, Home Advisor, etc.). These businesses typically allow the businesses that are listed to claim and manage their profiles (either for free or for a fee).
Discovery Ads	With Discovery ads, a single ad campaign allows your business to reach your prospects as they interact across the different Google platforms.
Display Advertising	Display advertising, such as banner ads, use photos, videos, graphics, and rich media to promote engagement with your business by placing your business in front of people on targeted websites or social platforms.
Domain Name	Your domain name is the web address for your business.
Dots per inch (DPI)	Web images are usually 72 dpi (i.e., dots per inch) resolution, and images used for print are typically 300 ppi (i.e., pixels per inch) or more.
Ebooks	Ebooks are electronic books that can stand alone or are the electronic version of a printed book. An ebook is extremely easy to create and can be downloaded from your website for free or sold on your website or third-party ebook seller platforms.
Efficiency	For Guerrilla businesses, beyond the traditional definitions, efficiency means increased customer satisfaction and increased profits.
Email Autoresponder Platforms	To send email broadcasts to your prospects and/or customers, you'll need to use a software (email autoresponder) platform. Software platforms offer many advantages for a Guerrilla marketer, such as automation, results tracking, personalization, and customization.
Email Deliverability	Email deliverability is the challenging skill of getting your emails to reach your prospects' or customers' inboxes (rather than bouncing or being delivered to the spam or promotions folder, etc.).

Engagement	A combination of web traffic, ratings/reviews, and social media interactions that determine, in part, your brand favorability and interaction among your prospects and customers.
Engaging	A no-cost tactic for Guerrillas in their advertising and marketing that makes your prospect want to connect and know more.
Ethical Bribes	Ethical bribes mean your business is giving your prospects and customers an ethical incentive to take a particular and ethical action.
Evergreen Content	Your audio and video content that has a useful long-life (e.g., recipes) and will continue to work for your business for years.
Firmographics	Firmographic data helps to segment businesses for B2B marketing. Hubspot breaks down firmographic data into industry type, organizational size, total sales and revenue, current location, ownership framework and growth trends.
Follow-up	Tenacity is a trait that Guerrilla marketers embrace. It makes skills, like follow-up, a natural part of their business mindset. Relentless follow-up can be the simple difference that turns a prospect into a customer and a customer into a repeat buyer.
Friendly Picketers	Friendly picketers are a Guerrilla Marketing tactic to garner attention and pique the interest of your prospects and customers. Friendly picketers appear to be real picketers, but they are holding clever signs, which promote the business and ask "passer buyers" to honk because they love the business. They may also hand out samples or direct people to a booth at an event.
Fusion/Affiliate Marketing	Businesses working together to create a compelling marketing offer to increase the sales and profits for one or both businesses.
Geofencing	Geofencing is a location-based service. It can work with B2B advertising or with consumers. Geofencing gives you the ability to create a boundary around a physical location and send targeted messages (e.g., alert, advertising, etc.) to your prospects and customers that are within that boundary. It can also be used with your app to send messages to your prospects and customers who have your app and receive notifications.

Google My Business	A powerful Google service that every Guerrilla marketer fully utilizes. Google My Business allows you to be in control (with your Google Business Profile) of the details and services that people see when they Google search or Google Map your business when searching from their phone, tablet, or computer.
Guerrilla Creative and Advertising Strategy	An amazingly simple plan designed to align your advertising efforts to your overall Guerrilla Marketing plan. A Guerrilla Creative and Advertising strategy creates clarity about what you're offering (the benefits), to whom you're making your offer (your target audience, prospects, and customers), and the action you want them to take. See Volume 1, Section 1.6, "Guerrilla Creative and Advertising Strategy Challenge," for more information.
Guerrilla Creativity	The combination of thoughts, ideas, and approaches that create powerful marketing and business ideas. See Volume 1, Section 1.2, "Guerrilla Creativity," for more information.
Guerrilla Marketing	Intelligent marketing that utilizes a plan and strategy along with knowledge, low-cost, unconventional, creative tactics to convey or promote a compelling product or idea. Guerrilla Marketing was introduced to the world in a self-titled book by Jay Conrad Levinson, written in 1984, as an unconventional system of marketing that relies on knowledge, time, energy, imagination, and information rather than a big marketing budget. Visit gMarketing.com/Club for more resources and information.
Guerrilla Marketing Calendar	The way Guerrilla marketers track their efforts and move their successes forward into the next year. Equally, it's the way to ensure they're not continuing to do what is not working. See Volume 1, Section 1.7, "Guerrilla Marketing Calendar," for more information.
Guerrilla Marketing Plan	An amazingly simple plan focused on a core idea that always comes before you engage in any marketing tactics. Your plan makes your Guerrilla Marketing focused, impactful, consistent, compelling, engaging, and profitable. See Volume 1, Section 1.5, "Guerrilla Marketing Plan Challenge," for more information.
High definition	For videos posted online, it's best to use high definition, 1024x768 or better.

Hot Leads	Prospects that have been referred to your business (e.g., one-on-one, through your referral program, from a referral site, etc.) and have a high propensity to buy. Therefore, a hot lead deserves specialized, consistent, and immediate attention to turn them into a customer.
Identity	Your business identity defines what your business is about and how you go about doing your business.
Impressions	The number of people who have seen (or had the opportunity to see) your advertising, plus how many times they have seen it (e.g., if one person has the opportunity to see your advertising four times, that is four impressions). Guerrilla marketers seek clarity with any advertising partner regarding how they define impressions.
Influencer Marketing	Influencer marketing can be an effective means of paid advertising for Guerrilla marketers. With influencer marketing, you pay (or barter with) an influencer on social media, such as YouTube, Twitter, Instagram, Pinterest, Talk, or other platforms to promote your product(s), service(s) or business.
Innovation	Guerrilla businesses succeed when they focus on desirable innovations—especially those that relate to the pain points of their prospects and customers—and thereby inspire and motivate their customers to make repeat or additional purchases and prospects to make new purchases.
Intelligent Marketing	Guerrilla Marketing is intelligent marketing. A Guerrilla marketer uses knowledge and intentional and intelligent marketing to produce profits, which allows their business to grow, expand, evolve, thrive, and make a difference in their community or the world.
Jingle	Your jingle is an audio trigger for your customers and prospects. This Guerrilla Marketing tactic, with consistent repetition, is designed to help people recognize, remember, and have a favorable view of your business, its name, and, ideally, your condensed USP (i.e., brand awareness and brand recognition).

Key Performance Indicators (KPIs)	Key performance indicators are the metrics that businesses use to measure their success. Examples, as we've defined in our volumes of the all-new series of *Guerrilla Marketing* books, are ROI, ROAS, CRO, CPA, CPC, CPL, CPM, LTV/CLV, CPV, PPC, etc.
Leads	Leads are prospects that are a result of lead buying and/or those prospects that have interacted (organically or as a result of your marketing) with your business. Cold leads are prospects that are not familiar with your business. It's your job to warm those leads and interest them in your product(s) or service(s) by giving them a compelling desire to purchase your product(s) or service(s) and become your customer. Medium leads are prospects that you are marketing to as a part of a marketing arrangement with Fusion/Affiliate Marketing partners. These prospects have a relationship with your Fusion/Affiliate Marketing partner, who is recommending or endorsing your business, product, or service. Hot leads are prospects that have been referred by your customers, a referral site, etc. They could also be prospects that opted into your quiz or survey, downloaded your ebook or white paper, or requested your updates/newsletter and, therefore, have provided their information. Hot leads have a high propensity to buy.
Lead Buying	Purchasing lists of targeted prospects to market to, as well as marketing to the customers and prospects of other businesses (see Fusion/Affiliate Marketing), are both long-time, proven ways to attract more prospects and customers to your business.
Lead Magnets	Discount or give away something valuable (free trials, an ebook, a free course, an assessment, personalized report, a consultation, etc.) to entice your prospects to buy additional products or services.
Left Brain	People with left-brain tendencies are motivated by logical and sequential reasoning.
List Building	List building is the art and science of deploying multiple tactics (blogs, lead magnets, etc.) to have people opt-in to connect with your business and receive your email communications.

Logo	A clean and distinct graphic representation of your business name that helps to build recall and familiarity with your prospects and customers.
Market Research	Guerrillas engage in ongoing marketing research to stay informed of trends, their target audience, advertising options, the competition, the industry, the economy (local and national), and their business and social community.
Marketing Automation	These tools allow you to set up your online marketing, from newsletters to promotional mailings, with triggers that allow greater personalization based on the actions your prospects and customers take and/or the information they provide.
Media Contacts	Each reporter, author, blogger, and other public relations contact that you meet and interact with becomes part of your important network of media contacts. Guerrilla marketers realize that building these relationships will help them create more media coverage for their business and, thereby, grow their public relations reach.
Meme	Much like a stop sign or a traffic light, a meme is an instantly recognizable idea without words. In business marketing, it's an image that compliments your name and logo. Your meme is a visual trigger for your customers and prospects. This Guerrilla Marketing tactic, with consistent repetition, is designed to help people recognize, remember, and form a favorable view of your business, its name, and, ideally, your condensed USP (i.e., brand awareness and brand recognition). Examples are: • Pillsbury Doughboy • Michelin Man • The Green Giant • The Energizer Bunny • M&M Characters
Message Bots	Message bots are a form of artificial intelligence (AI). They can boost sales and satisfaction while reducing your costs by providing a variety of services. Message bots can add to your appeal and help your business build and grow relationships with your prospects and customers.

Native Advertising	Native ads can be text, display, video, slideshows, or carousel, and they flow with the look, feel, and content of the site or social platform on which they are placed while being marked as "sponsored."
Native and Social Outstream Advertising	According to AdAge: "Social outstream is video ads that autoplay on mute with headlines and formats that match the look and feel of social feeds on Facebook, Instagram, Twitter, etc. Native outstream is the same as social but made to match the look and feel of editorial feeds."
Opt-In	The right opt-in offer enables a Guerrilla marketer to turn curious prospects into customers. An opt-in form on your website allows your prospects or customers to enter their information and email addresses to be added to your mailing list and/or take advantage of an offer you have made.
Pain Points	Guerrilla businesses are in the problem-solving business. Your prospects and customers are seeking solutions to their problems. The more effectively your business connects with your prospects and customers by speaking their buying language and relating to their pain points (physically or emotionally), the more likely your business is able to motivate them to buy. Once you've related to their pain points, and you've shown them the pleasure (i.e., pleasure points) they can experience when their problem is solved—and the more they believe you can provide that solution—the more motivated they are to buy.
Pay-Per-Click (PPC) or Cost-Per-Click (CPC) Advertising	Pay-per-click (PPC) or cost-per-click (CPC) ads are based on the number of clicks on your ad. Therefore, you will pay for each click on your ad.
Personalization	Addressing and connecting with your prospects and customers in a knowledgeable, caring, and attentive manner that makes them feel recognized, noticed, important, and, ultimately, engaged.
Pixels per inch (PPI)	Images used for print are typically 300 ppi (i.e., pixels per inch) or more and web images are usually 72 dpi (i.e., dots per inch) resolution..

Positioning	Your positioning defines what your business, product, or service stands for, its value, and why it should be purchased.
Private Labeling	A product that is typically produced/manufactured and customized exclusively for one retailer. Grocery store chains and drug store chains often utilize private labeling for their branded products.
Prospect	A target market or segment (people or businesses) that has the demographic, geographic, and/or psychographic characteristics you have identified as being the most likely to purchase your product(s) or service(s) and become a customer. Also referred to as a prospective customer.
Psychographics	As defined by the American Psychological Association, psychographics is, "an extended form of demographic analysis that surveys the values, activities, interests, and opinions of populations or population segments (psychographic segmentation) to predict consumer preferences and behavior."
Public Relations (PR)	Guerrilla public relations (PR) is a low-cost method of garnering high-quality exposure for your business by building strong, collaborative relationships with leading people. Guerrilla PR helps establish the identity of your business (or yourself) and gives you authority and credibility.
Push Notifications	Push notifications are an opportunity to notify your customers with ease. VWO offers, "Push notifications are clickable pop-up messages that appear on your users' browsers irrespective of the device they're using or the browser they're on. They serve as a quick communication channel enabling companies to convey messages, offers, or other information to their customers."
QR Code	A quick response code (QR Code) is a matrix barcode. QR codes (created using a QR code generator) are used in marketing as a convenient and fast way to direct your prospect or customer to a specified URL. When the barcode is scanned, using a QR Code scanner app or a camera on a smartphone or tablet, it directs people to a specified URL that you defined with the QR code generator.

Quality	A hallmark of a Guerrilla business. Guerrillas understand that the quality of their product(s) or service(s) is measured by their customers and prospects. The measurement of quality encompasses the entire customer experience. High-quality products and services typically require less marketing investment because positive ratings and reviews, along with customer referrals, attract prospects to your business.
Radio DJ or On-air Personality Endorsements.	Radio personalities can be hired to make direct (scripted or unscripted) endorsements of your product (often referred to as "DJ chatter"). Those endorsements are, ideally, given as an authentically satisfied customer, who's sharing their exceptional experience with their listeners. Keep in mind that those endorsements can be partially or fully paid by bartering (i.e., providing products or services, instead of money, in exchange for paid endorsements.).
Reach	Reach is the number of unique people that are exposed to your marketing and/or advertising.
Referral Programs	Referral programs are a must for a Guerrilla business, as they are the path to profits and a leading indicator that your business is performing well. The referral of a friend, family, or associate to your business, by your customers, is a precious gift that makes Guerrilla marketers extremely grateful and focused on an exceptional experience.
Referral Sites	Referral sites curate compelling content, offers, and solutions for their prospects and customers. They create revenue and profits with a combination of advertising and referral/affiliate commissions. They can be a great source of hot leads and customers for your business.
Referrals	Meaningful endorsements provided by your customers put powerful word-of-mouth marketing to work for your business. Referrals are the precious gift that customers bestow upon grateful Guerrilla marketers. Whether you have a paid (money, credits, or points) or unpaid referral program, the endorsement that your satisfied customers (or affiliate referral partners) provide is one of the most powerful and low-cost methods of marketing your business possesses. Guerrilla marketers maximize the opportunity that a strong referral program provides. Many successful businesses have been built using, primarily, referral marketing.

Relationship Builder	Guerrillas place an emphasis on creating relationships with prospects, customers, employees, other businesses, media contacts, industry leaders, community leaders, etc. Their listening skills and honest interest in people boost their relationship-building skills and those relationships are a source of endless knowledge and opportunities. See Volume 3, Section 9.29, "Relationship Builder," for more information.
Repeat Purchases	A powerful opportunity that many businesses do not pay attention to is the repeat purchase. Fortunately, Guerrilla marketers know that when their customers are making additional and repeat purchases, it's an indicator that their customers are happy, and the marketing is working profitably well.
Repetition	Repetition, when done correctly (i.e., with consistency), is at the core of successful Guerrilla Marketing. It's a low-cost method of creating recognition, familiarity, interest, trust, and motivation among your prospects to turn them into customers.
Research	In most cases, great advertising and marketing are preceded by great research. Research helps you identify the demographics and psychographics of your target market, which helps you save time and money (by focusing on prospects that are most likely to buy) and be more personal with your marketing messages.
Retargeting (or Remarketing) Advertising	Retargeting is a tremendously effective Guerrilla Marketing tactic that allows you to target your prospects as they move around the Internet after they've engaged with your brand.
Return on Investment (ROI)	Return on investment (ROI) is an important metric for determining the success of your marketing efforts. The formula is: Revenue from the transaction - Minus - The expenses incurred to acquire and fulfill the transaction. *Expenses include operations, marketing, sales, and product costs.* To accurately determine your ROI, you need appropriate tracking systems for expenses, production, marketing, and sales. Additionally, if your product is subscription-based, your ROI will account for the increased revenue and expenses over time.

Return on Ad Spend (ROAS)	Return on ad spend (ROAS) is an important metric for determining the success of your advertising spend. The formula is a percentage resulting from: Revenue from the transaction - Divided By - The expenses incurred in advertising. *Expenses include creative costs, agency fees, and media spending.* To accurately determine your ROAS, you need appropriate tracking systems. ROAS is a comparison metric to determine advertising efficiency. Successful Guerrilla ROAS is always over 100 percent or expressed as 1.0 ROAS.
Right Brain	People with right-brain tendencies are motivated by emotional and aesthetic appeal.
Search Engine	Search engines allow you to search the web for answers to whatever query you enter. Search engines can be broad, such as Google, Bing, or Yahoo. Or they can be niche, like travel or entertainment (e.g., Yelp) or maps (e.g., Google Maps or Apple Maps).
Search Engine Keywords	Search engine keywords are the words and phrases your prospects and customers might use in their search for businesses like yours.
Search Engine Optimization (SEO)	Simply put, SEO is the practice of making sure that your website is optimized for the unpaid results of search engines. Search engines exist for the benefit of their searchers. On-page SEO allows your website to boost its ranking in the search engine results when your site addresses and answers the questions and words that your customers and prospects are searching for with quality information. Off-page SEO is the practice of getting content on other sites to link back to your website in the right context.
Service	Your prospects and customers define what is excellent service for them. Excellent service may be defined by your prospects and customers as a seamless experience that's free of resistance and has minimal interaction or it might be a hands-on and high-touch service.

SMBs	Small- and medium-sized (or midsized) businesses
Social Media Monitoring	Social media monitoring is valuable to spot trends, problems, opportunities, and online chatter regarding your business, product(s), service(s), and competitors so you can improve engagement while managing your reputation.
Solopreneurs	Business owners who are the only person in their business (i.e., they don't have employees, a business partner, etc.).
Solutions and Problems	Guerrilla marketers are in the business of developing and selling solutions to their prospects' and customers' problems.
Sponsorships	Providing money, goods, or services to a desirable activity (news broadcasts, targeted information segments, etc.) or event (local events, venues, etc.) in exchange for them promoting your business via advertising, marketing, and/or endorsements.
Stories That Sell	Guerrilla marketers sell through storytelling. For example, telling the story of the problem they had that set them on the path to finding a solution. In the process, they turned it into a business, and now they can solve that problem for you.
Strategy	The high-level plan that you create for meeting or exceeding your goals.
Street Teams	Hired promotional teams that are attention-getting and engaging, that attend events and heavy pedestrian traffic areas, handing out samples of your product.
Subconscious or Unconscious Mind	The activity of your mind that you are not aware of (or conscious of) but are impacted or influenced by. In terms of marketing, the subconscious or unconscious mind is taking in all kinds of marketing information. Guerrilla marketers utilize well-crafted marketing and advertising, along with repetition and consistency because they understand the value of the subconscious mind.
Subliminal Marketing	Subliminal marketing is marketing messages, images, and sensations that only the subconscious mind absorbs but the conscious mind is influenced by. Guerrilla marketers focus their attention on the transparent methods of subliminal marketing that influence the purchase decision.

Tactics	The actionable marketing techniques you employ to achieve your strategy.
Tagline	Your tagline expresses your compelling, competitive advantage, company attitude, or USP in just a few powerful words. This Guerrilla Marketing tactic, with consistent repetition, is designed to help people recognize, remember, and form a favorable view of your business (i.e., brand awareness and brand recognition).
Target Audience or Target Market	The research- and experience-based demographic and psychographic characteristics of your prospects and customers.
Technographics	The technology utilized by a business. The information helps your business segment its B2B prospects to those most likely to become your customers, based on the technology they are currently using.
Testimonials, Endorsements, and Referrals	The precious gift that happy and loyal customers bestow on a Guerrilla business that has met and exceeded their expectations. When customers recommend your business to their friends, family, and associates, you're utilizing one of the lowest-cost and highest-satisfaction methods for generating profits.
Top-of-mind	Being top-of-mind is critical to Guerrilla marketers. For example, when you go to buy a CPG (consumer packaged good), you likely have an idea about the exact product you want to buy. That product is top-of-mind. For example, you likely have a top-of-mind product when you're going to buy toothpaste, deodorant, a beverage, or a sweet treat. Your every marketing effort is to make your business top-of-mind when your prospects and customers are shopping for your product(s) or service(s).
Tracking and Measuring	Guerrilla Marketing evolves and succeeds when the resulting activity (views, sales, and inquiries) is tagged, followed, recorded, and analyzed to determine the value of your investment.

Unconventional	Guerrilla Marketing is a strategy in which knowledge and low-cost unconventional means are utilized to convey or promote a product or an idea. Those unconventional means compel your prospects to notice your business. Once they do, your call to action must then motivate them to take a desired action (e.g., download an ebook, make a purchase, etc.). Your existing customers also need to be motivated to make repeat purchases and precious referrals of their friends, family, and associates.
Unique Selling Proposition (USP)	Your USP represents one of your greatest marketing opportunities, and most businesses neither promote nor have identified theirs. It's your proprietary competitive edge stated clearly and succinctly. See Volume 1, Section 1.3, "Unique Selling Proposition (USP)," for more information.
Upgrade Opportunities	When you design an engaging pricing model you can increase your sales by selling similar products at various prices.
Uniform Resource Locator (URL)	A URL is your web address. It's a good practice, alongside a promotional offer, to use a specific sales page on your website that ties directly to a marketing piece or offer (e.g., direct mail, radio advertisement, social media ad, etc.) to seamlessly continue your message while being able to track the results of that dedicated URL.
Video Advertising	Video ads are immensely powerful and an effective way to market your product(s) or service(s) on platforms, such as YouTube.
Viral Marketing	When stories, images, and/or videos have widespread appeal, people love to share them. When those stories, images, and/or videos hit at just the right moment, and they have broad appeal, the magic begins. As the number of shares grows over a short period of time, the story, image, and/or video reaches critical mass and is considered to have "gone viral."
Webinars	Webinars can be live or recorded. They are your opportunity to host countless people online for the purpose of educating, interacting with, and/or selling your product(s) or service(s).
White Labeling	Allows other businesses to put their name and/or logo (i.e., rebrand) on the product(s) your business manufactures. Equally, online businesses can sell their information products to other businesses, who then market them as their own.

AUTHORS NOTE

When starting the all-new series of *Guerrilla Marketing* books, we had to ask ourselves some important questions:

- Did Jay Conrad Levinson want the world of SMBs to continue to thrive with Guerrilla Marketing?
- Could we build upon his vision and continually evolve the tactics, tools, and tips that SMBs need to thrive?
- Is Guerrilla Marketing as effective today as it was when it was introduced decades ago?
- Could we deliver a complete experience for everyone, regardless of whether they are new to Guerrilla Marketing or have been using it for decades?

When we answered yes to every question, we knew it was time to get to work. It's been no small task, but when you're fueled by a passion for SMBs to succeed, it's a worthy task.

Guerrilla Marketing has always been about you:

- The person with an idea and a dream of being self-employed, their own boss, and/or a business owner
- The SMB that needs help understanding and using intelligent marketing and realizing how it can help them thrive
- The established business that is not meeting its potential and craves support to get it where it knows it can be (or beyond)

We were fortunate to, individually, be born to hard-working parents with tenacity, focus, relentlessness, pride, generosity, and compassion. Those are the foundational energy sources that make SMBs thrive.

As we, individually, grew up with their examples and set out to create our own paths, we intersected at the same Fortune 50 corporate environment. We've never lost the tenacity of our parents' examples, and we've had the good fortune to also engage in large-scale businesses. The contrast was exciting and noteworthy, and it answered several important questions:

- How do start-up companies upend the Goliath of their industries?
- Why does the tiniest decision make or break a business and a dream?
- Does a big budget mean big results?
- Is a large-scale company more capable of driving a higher ROI with their marketing investment than an SMB?

- What are the shared secrets of success that large-scale and SMBs hold?

Ultimately, it's the leveling of the playing field that allows SMBs to take on Goliath and come out victorious. Guerrilla Marketing has always been about not only leveling the playing field but also tilting it in favor of SMBs, and we intend to keep it that way. However, we want your involvement. Don't just read this book—join us. Let's all talk, collaborate, grow, and succeed together. Join us at gMarketing.com/Club.

Know this:

- Collaboration takes an idea and turns it into a movement
- Energy alone is not enough to succeed
- When you continually add knowledge and focused action, you succeed
- Learning is like breathing; it's necessary and exhilarating, and you can't exist without it

We've been fortunate to experience vast backgrounds of success. We, along with you, look forward to helping your ideas and SMBs turn into million-, billion-, or trillion-dollar companies that never forget that Guerrilla Marketing is the path that delivered you there.

GUERRILLA CLUB

THE GUERRILLA CLUB AWAITS YOU WITH FREE TOOLS, EXAMPLES, RESOURCES, AND SO MUCH MORE

Imagine what you'll find to help you succeed!

We know you're ready for success right now, and we're ready to help you make it happen. The best place to start is by building a strong foundation of Guerrilla Marketing. Our FREE companion course will help you build your rock-solid Guerrilla Marketing foundation. Regardless of whether you're currently using Guerrilla Marketing tactics in your business and a great refresher will ensure your foundation is solid, or you're new to Guerrilla Marketing and need a good overview, a few minutes is all you need.

In our FREE companion course, we'll dive in with video tutorials, exercises, and the tools you'll need to build that crucial foundation from which your Guerrilla Marketing success will be born. Remember, businesses that fail have a poor foundation. If you build your castle on a poor foundation, don't be surprised when it collapses into rubble.

Beyond the tools you need to build your strong foundation, our Guerrilla Club members will find a growing list of tools, examples, and resources to help your success going forward.

Scan this QR code with your app or smartphone camera:

Or go to gMarketing.com/Club
We are looking forward to further connecting with you!

WHAT THE GUERRILLA MARKETING BOOK SERIES WILL DO FOR YOU AND YOUR BUSINESS

Guerrilla Marketing, since the original *Guerrilla Marketing* book was introduced in 1984, has supported and empowered entrepreneurs, small and medium-sized businesses, solopreneurs, and people with ideas they think can be a business to:

- Start and/or build successful Guerrilla businesses
- Understand why and how marketing works and why Guerrilla Marketing is intelligent marketing
- Weave the consistent methodology of Guerrilla Marketing through every aspect of their business
- Create profits for the benefit of themselves, their families, their employees, their community, and the world at large
- Tap into their Guerrilla Creativity to create highly profitable marketing
- Utilize Guerrilla Creative Strategies to ensure their Guerrilla Marketing tactics hit the target
- Create and execute their Guerrilla Marketing plan and Guerrilla Creative and Advertising strategy

- Utilize consistency in their marketing to build familiarity, which, in turn, builds trust; and that trust creates sales, repeat purchases, and precious referrals from their customers
- Define the authentic attitudes of their business and use the power of authenticity in their marketing
- Identify their company attributes and consistently make their prospects and customers aware of them in their marketing and advertising
- Track their marketing to build on their successes and remove their unsuccessful efforts
- Make the truth fascinating
- Thrive with low-cost tactics
- Thrive with unconventional tactics
- Deliver their marketing tactics with creative, low-cost, and unconventional methods
- Upend their competition, big and small
- Sell their successful businesses and start all over again or perfect their favorite pastime as their full-time endeavor
- Win, on purpose

Guerrilla Marketing is a combination of knowledge, unchanging fundamentals and ever-changing ideas, examples, tactics and tools. Our job is to keep you aware of the latest of each of those, to help you succeed.

**Your *Guerrilla Marketing* know-how and toolbox are
ever-expanding. Be sure to pick up:**
Guerrilla Marketing Volume 1
Guerrilla Marketing Volume 3
**We are hard at work to keep you and your business
far ahead of the competition.
Visit gMarketing.com/Club now.**

ABOUT THE AUTHORS

Jason Myers

Chairman, Guerrilla Marketing Global, LLC

My journey into Guerrilla Marketing started while in high school in the 1980s, shortly after Jay published the first book. The timing was perfect, and I embraced the concept immediately. However, I was pretty much always a Guerrilla, perhaps by necessity.

You see, I grew up as a child of parents that were construction workers. They moved us all over the country, from one project to another, and we had times of feast and times of famine. This instability, living in the cycle of being middle-class then dropping into barely scraping by, meant that I had to always be creative, curious, and committed to lifelong learning. I wanted "more," and I knew I could achieve it.

I learned sales and marketing—as many kids did—by reselling candy to my classmates. Often, I would get lunch money on Mondays, with a promise that the lunch money for the rest of the week would come later. To be sure that it did, I would invest my Monday lunch money into a pile of candy, and by Monday at lunchtime, I would have earned the entire week's lunch money. I still remember the first time I told my mom that I didn't need the rest of the week's lunch money. The marketing aspect came in the packaging and positioning. I would try different types of candy and combinations. I would try telling compelling stories of the origin or my adventures acquiring the candy. I learned that people want to buy a story; they would pay more for that than they would for a commodity. I went on to learn to sell many things using these important lessons.

My first business was a Guerrilla fusion marketing experiment. It started when I learned computer programming; I'd buy a computer video game, modify the game, and sell those re-engineered copies to my friends. This led to an intense interest in video games and an introduction to a local amusement company that owned the full-sized coin-operated video games. I inquired about how the business worked for an arcade and before I knew it, I had organized the delivery of a truckload of video games to my new arcade business. We had agreed to split the revenue, and the entire setup cost me nothing to get started. It was a true fusion, joint-venture relationship. As a teenager with an arcade, the next step was to develop my marketing plan. Fortunately, I discovered the first *Guerrilla Marketing* book and the genius idea that Jay Conrad Levinson brought forward to help small businesses implement intelligent marketing.

My first fifteen minutes of fame came when, inspired by *Guerrilla Marketing's* concepts, I covered my car with refrigerator magnets for a pizza shop. As I drove around, people stared. When I parked the car, people would "borrow" the magnets. The pizza shop saw an increase in sales. Then, the local newspaper decided to run a small article with a photo of the car covered completely in magnets. The pizza shop was incredibly happy to get the free press, and I became small-town "famous" for a minute. I felt *so* Guerrilla!

Those early lessons allowed me to start a second business, which grew quickly and had more business activity than I could handle at times. I learned so much from applying the methods and concepts in the first edition of *Guerrilla Marketing*. Eventually, when that business ran its course, I found my way into a management/leadership position in the telecom industry, and my marketing and sales skills allowed me to stand out in a rapidly growing industry, and I achieved many successes.

As I transitioned back into entrepreneurship, my decades worth of Guerrilla skills—be it marketing, mindset, management, and money-making skills— really paid off. I have started, invested in, grown, and sold dozens of businesses and am often called upon to help others grow their businesses. I'm passionate about mentorship, coaching, and applying Guerrilla techniques.

Since starting to learn and apply Guerrilla Marketing back in the '80s, I've dedicated a chunk of my life to perpetually pursuing knowledge and experience. I think you should, too.

During this journey, I've discovered that anyone who has learned effective sales and marketing skills will never go hungry. These two skills are the most important, self-empowering skills that exist, and they form the foundation for entrepreneurship. I encourage everyone to learn these as early as possible and take control of their financial futures.

I consider Jay to be one of my most significant mentors. His lessons helped form who I am today. To honor him, I have dedicated myself to carrying on his legacy by ensuring that the entire concept of Guerrilla is relevant today and tomorrow for millions more people.

I encourage you to learn as much as you can about Guerrilla Marketing and apply those lessons to your business and share your successes with others. This book is a great next step, and we'll be providing many more steps going forward, to help you and your business grow and succeed—now and long into the future.

I'll see you at the top!

Merrilee Kimble

Chief Creative Officer, Guerrilla Marketing Global, LLC

I had the incredible privilege of being raised in a thriving small-to-medium-sized business success story (from a start-up company that grew into a medium-sized business before being successfully sold), for which I'm very grateful. My father utilized many Guerrilla Marketing tactics, and he combined them with relentless energy. I'm grateful for the experience I had in his business from cleaning the office to sales/customer service and whatever else needed to be done.

My parents insisted that I have a college education, perhaps because they thought it would make my life easier, and what parent doesn't generously want that for their child? I'm also grateful they both wanted me to push myself further. When I graduated college, I had no idea how this was supposed to come together. An entrepreneurial up-bringing, a marketing education, and options of working for large corporations.

Decades later, I not only secured incredibly large corporation experiences under my belt—from managing multi-million-dollar advertising and marketing budgets to executing every aspect of multi-language marketing—but I also earned the priceless experience of my own boot-strapped entrepreneurial endeavors.

I'm excited to share my broad marketing experience with you as we, from here, advance *Guerrilla Marketing* and your success. There is nothing more satisfying when it comes to work than being your own boss. Guerrilla Marketing is intelligent marketing that can help you stay successful or become successful as your own satisfied boss.

Marketing is getting more complex by the day. Fortunately, Guerrilla Marketing is here for you now and long into the future to reduce the complexity.

We're here to help you build a strong marketing foundation from which you'll be prepared to continually execute fresh marketing tactics with easy-to-use tools.

Guerrilla Marketing helps you turn complicated marketing into the simple and delightful task of knowing, attracting, and connecting with your customers. We're here for, and excited about, your success.

ENDNOTES

Preface
Levinson, J.C. (2007). *Guerrilla Marketing*, 4th Edition. In J.C. Levinson, *Guerrilla Marketing*, 4th Edition. Houghton Mifflin Harcourt.

Introduction
Levinson, J.C. (2007). *Guerrilla Marketing*, 4th Edition. In J.C. Levinson, *Guerrilla Marketing*, 4th Edition. Houghton Mifflin Harcourt.

1.8
Mohamed, T. (2021, August 10). "Warren Buffett warned the Bill & Melinda Gates Foundation's CEO about the 'ABCs.'". Retrieved from Markets. BusinessInsider.com: https://markets.businessinsider.com/news/stocks/warren-buffett-bill-melinda-gates-foundation-ceo-abcs-philanthropy-dangers-2021-7.

Section II
Levinson, J.C. (2007). *Guerrilla Marketing*, 4th Edition. In J.C. Levinson, *Guerrilla Marketing*, 4th Edition. Houghton Mifflin Harcourt.

2.11
Shepherd, M. (2021, May 11). "Small Business Marketing Statistics." Retrieved from fundera.com: https://www.fundera.com/resources/small-business-marketing-statistics.

2.15
PBS. (2021, May 07). PBS Sponsors. Retrieved from SGPTV.org: https://www.sgptv.org/pbs-sponsors/.

3.25
Google. (2021, May 23). "How Smart Campaigns are Helping You Reach More Customers." Retrieved from Google.com, https://support.google.com/google-ads/answer/9934637?hl=en.

Support.google.com. (2021, May 29). "Increase In-Store Sales With Your Online Ads." Retrieved from Support.google.com, https://support.google.com/google-ads/answer/10724985.

4.45

Developer.Amazon.com. (2021, June 6). "Understanding Custom Skills." Retrieved from https://developer.amazon.com/en-US/docs/alexa/custom-skills/understanding-custom-skills.html.

Google.com. (2021, June 6). "How Google's Featured Snippets Work." Retrieved from Support.Google.com, https://support.google.com/websearch/answer/9351707?hl=en.

Tankovska, H. (2021, June 6). "Smart speakers: Statistics & Facts." Retrieved from Statista.com, https://www.statista.com/topics/4748/smart-speakers.

4.47

Intercom.com. (2021, June 7). Intercom.com. Retrieved from https://www.intercom.com/.

ManyChat.com. (2021, June 7). ManyChat.com. Retrieved from https://manychat.com.

4.48

Ads.Google.com. (2021, June 16). Reach Planner. Retrieved from https://ads.google.com/home/tools/reach-planner/.

Falkner, C. (2020, April 04). "Linear vs. Advanced TV: The Current State of Television Advertising." Retrieved from https://www.cuebiq.com/resource-center/resources/linear-vs-advanced-tv/.

McDonald, M. (2021, June 16). "Connected TV Ads." Retrieved from ThinkWithGoogle.com, https://www.thinkwithgoogle.com/marketing-strategies/video/connected-tv-ads.

Weinstein, D. (2021, July 29). "5 Ways Brands are Adapting To Shifts in Video Viewership to Drive Results." Retrieved from ThinkWithGoogle.com, https://www.thinkwithgoogle.com/marketing-strategies/video/video-results/.

YouTube.com. (2021, June 16). Ads. Retrieved from https://www.youtube.com/intl/en_us/ads/.

4.49

Statista.com. (2021, June 7). Number of Monthly Active WhatsApp Users as of 2013–2020. Retrieved from https://www.statista.com/statistics/260819/number-of-monthly-active-whatsapp-users/.

Statista.com. (2021, July 25). WhatsApp: Statistics & Facts. Retrieved from https://www.statista.com/topics/2018/whatsapp/.

WhatsApp.com. (2021, June 7). WhatsApp.com/business. Retrieved from https://www.whatsapp.com/business/?lang=en.

4.50

Forsey, C. (2021, July 7). "The Complete Guide to Firmographic Data." Retrieved from www.Blog.HubSpot.com, https://blog.hubspot.com/marketing/firmographics.

Jabmo.com. (2021, June 7). Jabmo.com. Retrieved from https://jabmo.com/.

Leadfeeder.com. (2021, June 7). Leadfeeder.com. Retrieved from https://www.leadfeeder.com/.

N.rich. (2021, June 7). N.rich. Retrieved from https://n.rich.

RocketReach.co. (2021, June 7). RocketReach.co. Retrieved from https://rocketreach.co/.

Seamless.ai. (2021, June 7). Seamless.ai. Retrieved from https://www.seamless.ai/.

Terminus.com. (2021, June 7). Terminus.com. Retrieved from https://terminus.com/.

4.51

Callloop.com. (2021, July 25). Callloop.com. Retrieved from https://www.callloop.com/.

EZTexting.com. (2021, July 25). EZTexting.com. Retrieved from https://www.eztexting.com/.

Text-em-all.com. (2021, July 25). Text-em-all.com. Retrieved from https://www.text-em-all.com/.

4.52

Business.Twitter.com. (2021, August 5). "4 Recommendations for Tweeting During COVID-19." Retrieved from https://business.twitter.com/en/resources/small-business.html.

Twitter.com. (2021, June 7). "How to use TweetDeck." Retrieved from Help. twitter.com: https://help.twitter.com/en/using-twitter/how-to-use-tweet-deck.

4.53

VWO.com. (2021, June 7). Push Notifications. Retrieved from https://vwo. com/push-notifications/.

4.55

AgoraPulse.com. (2021, June 7). AgoraPulse.com. Retrieved from https://www. agorapulse.com/.

Later.com. (2021, June 7). Later.com. Retrieved from https://later.com/.

Newberry, C. (2021, May 25). "15 of the Best Social Media Monitoring Tools to Save You Time." Retrieved from blog.hootsuite.com, https://blog.hoot-suite.com/social-media-monitoring-tools/.

Zoho.com. (2021, May 25). "Social Media Monitoring Software." Retrieved from https://www.zoho.com/social/social-media-monitoring-software.html.

4.56

Support.Google.com. (2021, June 23). "About Discovery Cam-paigns." Retrieved from https://support.google.com/google-ads/ answer/9176876?hl=en.

5.14

Inspire Education. (2021, May 24). "The Seven Learning Styles – How do you learn?" Retrieved from https://www.inspireeducation.net.au/blog/the-sev-en-learning-styles/.

5.15

About.LinkedIn.com. (2021, August 6). About. Retrieved from https://about. linkedin.com/.

5.17

Maguire, F. (2021, August 6). "Reaching Consumers With Video: The Inter-ruptiblity Myth." Retrieved from adage.com, https://adage.com/article/ sharethrough/reaching-consumers-video-interruptibility-myth/313945.

5.18

ContentStudio.io. (2021, May 25). ContentStudio.io. Retrieved from https://contentstudio.io/.

Google. (2021, May 25). About Social Plugins and Interactions. Retrieved from https://support.google.com/analytics/answer/6209874?hl=en&ref_topic=1316551#zippy=%2Cin-this-article.

Shareaholic. (2021, May 25). Website Tools. Retrieved from https://www.shareaholic.com/website-tools.

Statista. (2021, May 25). Reddit Monthly Visitors. Retrieved from https://www.statista.com/statistics/443332/reddit-monthly-visitors/.

Statista. (2021, May 25). Social Sharing. Retrieved from https://www.statista.com/topics/2539/social-sharing/.

6.17

Curtis, M., Quiring, K., Theofilou, B., & Björnsjö, A. (2021, July 31). "Life Reimagined: Mapping the motivations that matter for today's consumers." Retrieved from https://www.accenture.com/us-en/insights/strategy/reimagined-consumer-expectations.

Klien Ph.D., G. (2021, May 26). "Seeing What Others Don't." Psychologytoday.com. Retrieved from https://www.psychologytoday.com/us/blog/seeing-what-others-dont/201605/mindsets.

6.20

JFKLibrary.org. (2021, June 11). John F Kennedy Quotations, JFKLibrary.org. Retrieved from https://www.jfklibrary.org/learn/about-jfk/life-of-john-f-kennedy/john-f-kennedy-quotations.

7.18

Guttmann, A. (2021, May 27). Average loyalty program membership in the United States as of March 2020. Retrieved from Statista.com, https://www.statista.com/statistics/618744/average-number-of-loyalty-programs-us-consumers-belong-to/.

Markey, R. (2021, June 27). "Why Customer Loyalty Beats Quarterly Earnings." Retrieved from Bain.com, https://www.bain.com/insights/why-customer-loyalty-beats-quarterly-earnings-snap-chart/.

8.34

American Express. (2021, June 17). American Express Study. Retrieved from Templatelab.com, https://templatelab.com/american-express-study/.

Statista.com. (2021, June 17). Customers who have contacted customer service in the past month U.S. 2015–2020. Retrieved from https://www.statista.com/statistics/815526/customers-who-have-contacted-customer-service-in-the-past-month-us/.

8.35

CBS News. (2021, September 20). CEO on why giving all employees minimum salary of $70,000 still "works" six years later: "Our turnover rate was cut in half." Retrieved from CBSnews.com: https://www.cbsnews.com/news/dan-price-gravity-payments-ceo-70000-employee-minimum-wage/

8.38

Support.Google.com. (2021, July 22). About Google Partners Promotional Offers. Retrieved from https://support.google.com/google-ads/answer/7624810?hl=en.

8.39

Merriam-Webster.com. (2021, June 28). Definition of Unique. Retrieved from https://www.merriam-webster.com/dictionary/unique.

8.41

fcagroup.com. (2021, June 4). Home. Retrieved from https://www.fcagroup.com/en-US/Pages/home.aspx#.

Gapinc.com. (2021, June 4). About Us. Retrieved from https://www.gapinc.com/en-us/about.

Urbn.com. (2021, June 4). Our Brands. Retrieved from https://www.urbn.com/our-brands.

Volkswagenag.com. (2021, June 4). Group. Retrieved from https://www.volkswagenag.com/en/group.html.

8.42

Golum, C. (2021, July 22). Live Video Stats: What Consumers Want [Infographic]. Retrieved from Livestream.com, https://livestream.com/blog/live-video-statistics-livestream.

Livestream.com. (2021, July 22). "47 Must-Know Live Video Streaming Statistics (Updated)." Retrieved from https://livestream.com/blog/62-must-know-stats-live-video-streaming.

Section IX

Levinson, J.C. (2007). *Guerrilla Marketing*, 4th Edition. In J.C. Levinson, *Guerrilla Marketing*, 4th Edition. Houghton Mifflin Harcourt.

9.13

Merriam-Webster.com. (2021, June 4). Definition of Agile. Retrieved from https://www.merriam-webster.com/dictionary/agile.

9.14

Merriam-Webster. (2021, June 5). Definition of Inspire. Retrieved from https://www.merriam-webster.com/dictionary/inspire.

9.19

Merriam-Webster.com . (2021, August 9). Definition of Demeanor. Retrieved from https://www.merriam-webster.com/dictionary/demeanor.

9.20

Merriam-Webster.com. (2021, August 3). Definition of Curiosity. Retrieved from https://www.merriam-webster.com/dictionary/curiosity.

9.23

LateralThinking.com. (2021, June 26). "Lateral Thinking." Retrieved from LateralThinking.com: https://www.lateralthinking.com/what-is-lateralthinking

DeCross, M., & Didier, K.-J. (2021, June 26). Hyperloop. Retrieved from Brilliant.org: https://brilliant.org/wiki/hyperloop/.

Dictionary.Cambridge.org. (2021, June 5). Definition of Lateral Thinking. Retrieved from https://dictionary.cambridge.org/us/dictionary/english/lateral-thinking.

Smith, J. (2021, June 5). "Why People Get their Best Ideas In the Shower."
Retrieved from BusinessInsider.com, https://www.businessinsider.com/
why-people-get-their-best-ideas-in-the-shower-2016-1.

American Psychological Association. (2021, September 16). APA Dictionary of
Psychology. Retrieved from Dictionary.apa.org: https://dictionary.apa.org/
divergent-thinking

9.25

Klien Ph.D., G. (2021, May 26). "Seeing What Others Don't." Psychologyto-
day.com. Retrieved from https://www.psychologytoday.com/us/blog/see-
ing-what-others-dont/201605/mindsets.

9.26

Merriam-Webster. (2021, July 14). Definition of Resilient. Retrieved from
https://www.merriam-webster.com/dictionary/resilient.

Guerrilla Marketing Case Study 5

Mintz, L. (2021, June 17). "From Investment Banking to World's First Cupcake Bakery: Interview with Candace Nelson Founder of Sprinkles."
Retrieved from Inc.com, https://www.inc.com/laurel-mintz/from-invest-
ment-banking-to-worlds-first-cupcake-bakery-interview-with-candace-nel-
son-founder-of-sprinkles.html.

Sprinkles.com. (2021, June 17). Our Story. Retrieved from https://sprinkles.
com/pages/our-story.

Guerrilla Marketing Case Study 6

BarnesAndNoble.com. (2021, June 18). About Barnes & Noble.com. Retrieved
from https://www.barnesandnoble.com/h/help/about/barnesandnoble.

BarnesAndNobleInc.com. (2021, June 18). Heritage. Retrieved from https://
www.barnesandnobleinc.com/about-bn/heritage/.

NPR.org. (2021, June 18). "Barnes & Noble Founder Retires, Leaving His
Imprint On Bookstore's History." Retrieved from https://www.npr.
org/2016/05/07/476931295/barnes-noble-founder-retires-leaving-his-im-
print-on-bookstores-history.

Olito, F. (2021, June 18). "Here are the oldest US retailers still in business today." Retrieved from BusinessInsider.com, https://www.businessinsider.com/oldest-us-retailers-still-in-business-today-2019-2.

Trachtenberg, J. A. (2021, June 18). "Barnes & Noble's New Boss Tries to Save the Chain—and Traditional Bookselling." Retrieved from WSJ.com, https://www.wsj.com/articles/barnes-nobles-new-boss-tries-to-save-the-chainand-traditional-bookselling-11607144485.

Guerrilla Marketing Case Study 7

AceHardware.com. (2021, June 18). About Us. Retrieved from https://www.acehardware.com/about-us.

MyAce.com. (2021, June 19). "Ace Hardware Reports Fourth Quarter and Full Year 2020 Results." Retrieved from https://myace.com/newsroom/ace-hardware-reports-fourth-quarter-and-full-year-2020-results/.

Newsroom.AceHardware.com. (2021, June 19). "Ace Hardware Ranks Highest In Customer Satisfaction by J.D. Power 2020." Retrieved from https://newsroom.acehardware.com/ace-hardware-ranks-highest-in-customer-satis-faction-by-jd-power-2020.

Guerrilla Marketing Case Study 8

BrooksBrothers.com. (2021, June 19). About Us. Retrieved from https://www.brooksbrothers.com/about-us/about-us,default,pg.html.

Definitions

Dictionary.apa.org. (2020, April 30). APA Dictionary of Psychology. Retrieved from Dictionary.apa.org: https://dictionary.apa.org/psychographics.

Dictionary.com. (2020, April 30). Demographics. Retrieved from Dictionary.com: https://www.dictionary.com/browse/demographics.

Falkner, C. (2020, April 04). "Linear vs. Advanced TV: The Current State of Television Advertising." Retrieved from www.cuebiq.com, https://www.cuebiq.com/resource-center/resources/linear-vs-advanced-tv/.

Forsey, C. (2021, July 7). "The Complete Guide to Firmographic Data." Retrieved from www.Blog.HubSpot.com, https://blog.hubspot.com/mar-keting/firmographics.

Levinson, J.C. (2007). *Guerrilla Marketing*, 4th Edition. In J.C. Levinson, *Guerrilla Marketing*, 4th Edition. Houghton Mifflin Harcourt.

Maguire, F. (2021, August 6). "Reaching Consumers With Video: The Interruptiblity Myth." Retrieved from adage.com, https://adage.com/article/sharethrough/reaching-consumers-video-interruptibility-myth/313945.

VWO.com. (2021, June 7). Push Notifications. Retrieved from https://vwo.com/push-notifications/.

Back Cover

James, Geoffrey. (2021, May 4). "Top 10 Influential Business Books of All Time." Retrieved from Inc.com: https://www.inc.com/geoffrey-james/top-10-influential-business-books-of-all-time.html

INDEX

CPSIA information can be obtained
at www.ICGtesting.com
Printed in the USA
JSHW041530180422
25052JS00001B/29